HOUSING AND THE NEW WELFARE STATE

Social Policy in Modern Asia

Series Editor
CATHERINE JONES FINER

In an age of globalization, this series is designed to help broaden the basis and the perspectives of international comparative social policy by introducing fresh countries and above all fresh perspectives on social policy into what has hitherto been very much a Western-dominated field. Topics to be covered include social care, welfare services, family structure, crime and punishment, pensions, housing, and healthcare in various countries including China, Taiwan, Malaysia, Indonesia and Thailand.

Also in this series

Social Policy Reform in China: Views from Home and Abroad
Catherine Jones Finer
ISBN 0 7546 3175 3

Ageing Matters: European Policy Lessons from the East
Edited by John Doling, Catherine Jones Finer and Tony Maltby
ISBN 0 7546 4237 2

Pathways to State Welfare in Korea: Interests, Ideas and Institutions
Gyu-Jin Hwang
ISBN 978-0-7546-4440-8

Housing and the New Welfare State
State
Perspectives from East Asia and Europe

Edited by

RICHARD GROVES
ALAN MURIE
CHRISTOPHER WATSON
University of Birmingham, UK

ASHGATE

Published by
Ashgate Publishing Limited
Gower House
Croft Road
Aldershot
Hampshire GU11 3HR
England

Ashgate Publishing Company
Suite 420
101 Cherry Street
Burlington, VT 05401-4405
USA

Ashgate website: http://www.ashgate.com

British Library Cataloguing in Publication Data
Housing and the new welfare state : perspectives from East
    Asia and Europe. - (Social policy in modern Asia)
    1. Housing policy - Asia 2. Welfare state - Asia
    I. Groves, Richard II. Murie, Alan III. Watson, Christopher
    363.5'095

Library of Congress Cataloging-in-Publication Data
Housing and the new welfare state : perspectives from East Asia and Europe / edited by Richard Groves, Alan Murie and Christopher Watson.
    p. cm. -- (Social policy in modern Asia)
    Includes bibliographical references and index.
    ISBN-13: 978-0-7546-4440-8 1. Housing policy--East Asia. 2. Housing policy--Europe. 3. Welfare state--East Asia. 4. Welfare state--Europe I. Groves, Rick II. Murie, Alan. III. Watson, C. J.

HD7366.5.A3H676 2007
363.5'565095--dc22

ISBN: 978-0-7546-4440-8

2006031597

Printed and bound in Great Britain by MPG Books Ltd, Bodmin, Cornwall.

Contents

List of Tables

List of Figures

List of Contributors

Richard Groves is Director of the Centre for Urban and Regional Studies in the School of Public Policy, University of Birmingham. His academic activities have been divided between the UK and developing countries. In the UK he has undertaken a wide range of research on issues of housing policy and urban renewal, whilst overseas his work has involved training, research collaboration and consultancy for government agencies in Malaysia, India, Hong Kong, China, and Korea. He has had experience, over many years, of the development of housing policy in several countries in south and east Asia.

Yosuke Hirayama is Professor of Housing and Urban Studies at the Faculty of Human Development, Kobe University, working extensively in the areas of housing and urban change, home-ownership and social inequalities, as well as comparative housing policy. His work has appeared in international journals such as *Housing Studies* and the *Journal of Housing and the Built Environment* and he is co-editor of a book on Housing and Social Transition in Japan (with Richard Ronald, Routledge, 2006). He has received academic prizes from the City Planning Institute of Japan, the Architectural Institute of Japan and Tokyo Institute of Municipal Research. He is a founding member of the Asia-Pacific Network for Housing Research and chaired its international conference on Housing and Globalization, held in Kobe in 2005.

Kwok-yu Lau is an Associate Professor of the Department of Public and Social Administration, City University of Hong Kong. He teaches on Housing Policy and Administration, Housing Policy and Management in mainland China, Social Policy and Policy Studies at undergraduate and post-graduate levels. His current research focuses on housing privatization, housing affordability, owners' involvement in property management, and urban housing reform in mainland China. Between 1996 and 2002 he served as a full Member of the Hong Kong Housing Authority. Dr Lau has been an Adviser to the Hong Kong People's Council on Public Housing Policy (now renamed Hong Kong People's Council on Housing Policy) since 1984. He is an advisor to the Federation of Hong Kong, Kowloon, and New Territories Public Housing Estates Resident and Shopowner Organizations. He also serves on the Review Committee and the Land, Rehousing and Compensation Committee of the Urban Renewal Authority. He is a Member of the Professional Practice Committee of the Hong Kong Institute of Housing. He has been a Member of the Panel of Experts in the Project on Social Development Index for Hong Kong of the Hong Kong Council of Social Service since 1999 and as a Member of the Guangdong Real Estate Research Association Experts Panel since 2002. He is a Member of the Sham Shui Po District Council Working Group on Private Premises Problems. He also served as a Member of the Housing Bureau (formerly known as the Housing Branch) Long Term Housing Strategy Review Steering Group between 1996 and 1998.

Alan Murie is Professor of Urban and Regional Studies at the Centre for Urban and Regional Studies in the School of Public Policy, University of Birmingham. He has been a long time contributor to research and publications related to housing and urban social change. He was the first editor of the journal *Housing Studies* and is the author of a number of books including most recently; *A Right to Buy* (with Colin Jones), Blackwell 2006; *Housing Policy in the United Kingdom* (with David Mullins), Palgrave Macmillan 2006; *Neighbourhoods of Poverty: Urban Social Exclusion and Integration in Europe* (edited by S. Musterd, A. Murie and C. Kesteloot), Palgrave Macmillan 2006.

Shin-Young Park is a specialist in housing studies and housing policy for low-income families. She is Senior Research Fellow of the Housing and Urban Research Institute, Korea National Housing Corporation and Professor at Seoul National University of Technology. Dr Park has done much research related to housing since 1991 when she received her PhD in public administration from Yonsei University. Her interests are in governments' intervention in the housing market and its consequences in different countries. She has published numerous papers on housing and land policy in Korea. She is co-author of *Housing* published by the Office of Statistics. Recently she has written on housing policy for the elderly. She is a member of the Presidential Committee on social inclusion and other government advisory committees.

Sock-Yong Phang is Associate Professor of Economics at the Singapore Management University. She obtained her PhD in economics from Harvard University in 1989. Her research interests are primarily in the areas of housing and transportation economics and policy. Her publications include the book *Housing Markets and Urban Transportation* (McGraw Hill), and articles on housing and transportation economics in journals such as the *Journal of Housing Economics*, *Journal of Transport Economics and Policy*, *Transport Policy*, *Transportation Research*, *Urban Studies*, *Housing Studies*, and *Transportation Journal*. She has served as a consultant to the World Bank as well as to a variety of Singapore public agencies. She also served as board member of Singapore's Land Transport Authority and Urban Redevelopment Authority and is currently a commission member of the Competition Commission of Singapore.

Pui Yee Connie Tang is a Postdoctoral Research Fellow in the Joint Centre for Scottish Housing Research (JCSHR) at the University of St Andrews. She is interested in comparative housing research between eastern and western developed countries, on which she has written 'Possibilities for change and system's inertia: Japanese housing system in the period of economic crisis,' in Lee, J.K.C. and Chan, K.W. *The Crisis of Asian Social Policy*. She is currently working on the differences in household composition between existing and new tenants in the housing association sector and the effect of rent restructuring on the changing profile of housing association households in England.

Ya Ping Wang is Reader in Urban Studies in the School of the Built Environment of Heriot-Watt University in Edinburgh. He is well-known as a researcher on contemporary Chinese urban studies. His research projects on Chinese housing and urban planning have been supported by the ESRC, DFID, British Academy and British Council. He has published widely in many international journals such as *Urban Studies, Housing Studies, International Journal of Urban and Regional Research, Urban Affairs Review* and *Urban Geography*. He is the co-author of *Housing Policy and Practice in China* (with Alan Murie, Macmillan, 1999), author of *Urban Poverty, Housing and Social Change in China* (Routledge, 2004), and a joint author of *Planning and Housing in Developing Countries* (with Paul Jenkins and Harry Smith, Routledge, 2006). He is a member of the Management Board for *Housing Studies* and is the journal's Reviews Editor.

Christopher Watson is Senior Fellow and Director of Graduate Research Studies in the Centre for Urban and Regional Studies, University of Birmingham. He was Director of CURS from 1987 to 1993 and Director of the University of Birmingham Japan Centre from 1993 to 2002. Christopher Watson's main interests are in housing and urban policy; and international urban development. He is a member of the European Network for Housing Research and the Asia-Pacific Network for Housing Research. He was Chairman of Mercian Housing Association, Birmingham from 1999 to 2005.

Preface

This book grows out of the long association of the Centre for Urban and Regional Studies at Birmingham University with the analysis of housing policy in East Asia. The Centre for Urban and Regional Studies was the first centre for housing and related research to be established in the United Kingdom. For more than 40 years, it has received students from many countries in Asia, and has had important programmes of research and teaching in Korea, Hong Kong, China and Japan.

The themes and content of this book draw specifically on two workshops, the first organised jointly by CURS and the Korea Housing Institute, held in Seoul in November 2000; the second organised by CURS and held in Stratford-upon-Avon in March 2005. The workshops focussed mainly on papers written by the authors of this book. The second workshop, in particular, identified common themes and approaches that have influenced the form of the country chapters (Chapters 2-7); while Chapters 1 and 8 and especially Chapter 9 reflect discussion at the workshop by all the contributors to this book.

The book draws also on the experience and understanding we have gained over many years through our work with a succession of doctoral and other graduate students; visiting academic staff; and staff from central and local government and other agencies within East Asia, some of whom have attended training programmes provided by the Centre. All these experiences have helped to shape our understanding of the development of policies in different countries and we are grateful to former students, visiting staff and the many people we have met whilst visiting their countries, both for the friendships that have been established and for the insights we have gained from working with them.

Through these activities, it is apparent that there is considerable merit in comparing and contrasting developments in housing and related policies in the countries of East Asia. In East Asia, there has been enormous interest in what has happened in the UK. Often seen as the model for enlightened town planning and effective housing policy, the progress of privatization and changes in policy over the last 30 years have been closely watched. At the same time, it has become clear that very strong alternative models for housing and welfare have been developing in East Asia. Some of these grew out of British experience and influence, for example in Hong Kong and Singapore. However as these economies and societies have developed along their own lines, the tendency has been neither to seek to copy the past policy associated with Britain or other European countries, nor to imitate the direction of change being adopted in Europe; rather it has been to develop a distinctive approach.

This book brings together material on six East Asian[1] systems: Singapore, Hong Kong, China, Korea, Japan and Taiwan, to discuss the distinctive approaches to housing that have developed. Comparisons are made with developments in the United Kingdom and to a limited extent, with other European countries. Through these comparisons, the intention is to highlight alternative models of welfare provision emerging in Asia. These 'new' emerging models are based on different principles and have grown from a different political and economic context than those of the 'old' welfare systems: the Beveridge welfare state in the UK, and those of a similar era elsewhere in Europe.

An underlying theme throughout the book is that rather than imitating or following the example of Europe, the East Asian countries have developed distinctive approaches of their own. In some respects, there are similarities between the six countries but there are also important differences. Moreover, there are signs that the British and European welfare states are beginning to follow what is happening in East Asia. This is evident in the greater concern in Europe that welfare systems should contribute to economic development, rather than be concerned solely with redistribution. It is evident also in the attention and prominence given to property ownership, asset based welfare and the view of housing as a store and source of wealth that offers opportunities for individual households to provide not only for their own shelter needs but also, through equity release, to finance other needs at different stages in the life cycle.

The role of housing within the welfare state and the emerging importance of asset based welfare is the central theme of this book. While we have sought to paint a broad background to the wider operation of the welfare state and to housing policy, the focus of the book is upon changes in housing policy and in the housing sector in recent years.

Richard Groves
Alan Murie
Christopher Watson

Centre for Urban and Regional Studies
University of Birmingham

August 2006

---

1   The region is referred to throughout as 'East Asia'. The country of Singapore and the Hong Kong Special Administrative Region of the People's Republic of China are sometimes referred to as 'city states'. The Republic of Korea, sometimes known as 'South Korea' is always referred to as Korea. The Republic of China is referred to as Taiwan. Sometimes, the six systems collectively are referred to as 'countries'. These conventions have been adopted for ease of writing and presentation.

Acknowledgements

We would like to acknowledge the support of the Centre for Urban and Regional Studies, University of Birmingham, the Korea Housing Institute which hosted the first workshop considering the issues discussed in this book; and the British Council, Korea which contributed to the funding for the initial workshop.

We also thank Carolyn Fox of the Centre for Urban and Regional Studies and Judy Tweddle for their help in preparing the text for publication.

Chapter 1

Four Worlds of Welfare and Housing

Richard Groves, Alan Murie and Christopher Watson

The focus of this book is upon housing and the changing nature and significance of housing provision within the context of welfare states. The book does not offer a new perspective on the welfare state itself but develops the debate about the significance of housing within the welfare state. It does not present an analysis of health, or education, or social security, or social welfare systems but the underlying contention is that existing debates about welfare state systems have neglected the importance of housing. To some extent, this neglect has weakened the analysis of traditional welfare state systems but more importantly, it presents an ethnocentric view of welfare state systems, it inadequately represents the types of welfare states that have developed in East Asia and it risks understating the significance of developments in housing provision for the changing nature of the welfare state.

The starting point for the book then, is a view that, rather than perceiving that there are three major welfare state types (Esping-Andersen, 1990), we should at least embrace a fourth – that associated with the East Asian economies and referred to by Jones (1990), Sherraden (1997) and others. There is a literature which adds a southern European, family centred welfare state model (Allen et al., 2004), and there are a number of discussions of hybrid welfare state systems; however it is our intention to focus upon the four worlds of welfare capitalism which emerge most strongly from the literature. Within that, the intention is to focus upon the fourth of these four worlds – the East Asian case. It is in that context that housing, rather than being a wobbly pillar of the welfare state, or a marginal element in the welfare state system, emerges as of much more central importance. The East Asian model puts property development and ownership in a much more significant position, but, as will be seen later from this book, rather different approaches have emerged in individual East Asian countries.

The intention then is to explore the nature of this distinctive and different model, and to move the understanding of the importance of housing within the developing welfare states of these economies beyond what is available elsewhere in the literature. However our intention moves beyond this. We are concerned also with the extent to which traditional welfare states, the other three worlds of welfare capitalism identified by Esping-Andersen and particularly the UK welfare state, have been evolving over a period of more than 50 years. Our aim is to draw attention to the significance of developments in housing policy in those older welfare states; and to suggest that the nature of the traditional welfare state is changing and in some respects is developing characteristics associated with the East Asian model. The property owning welfare state has a very different composition to the traditional welfare state. Its concern with expanding property ownership rather than citizenship rights marks a significant break in the approach to welfare provision and a move away from corporatist or egalitarian redistributive models towards a more individualized model in which the accidents of market-determined changes in the value of property affect the opportunities and life chances available to households to a much greater extent than in the past.

This chapter sets out some of the starting points for this discussion. It refers briefly to existing typologies of welfare states and of housing provision systems – starting with a brief discussion of the existing literature on welfare state regimes and referring principally to the important contribution by Esping-Andersen (1990). Against this background we then provide an overview of some of the considerations arising if more attention is placed on the experience from East Asia; and if we reflect upon the direction of change and especially the increasing role of individual property ownership in the new welfare model emerging through the East Asian experience, and in some of the more traditional welfare systems.

Welfare State Regimes

There is a strong and influential literature which categorizes different countries and groups them according to the nature of their welfare state systems. However this literature has limitations because it takes both too ethnocentric a view and too narrow a view of the nature and operation of the welfare state. The focus on cash benefits and social security arrangements fails to do justice to the nature of welfare state systems in which access to services in-kind – including housing services – is significant.

Perhaps the most influential contribution made to comparative studies of welfare states was by the Danish political scientist Gøsta Esping-Andersen (1990). His book *The Three Worlds of Welfare Capitalism* provided a sustained and detailed analysis of differences in the welfare regimes of different countries. He argued that simple comparisons of the levels of expenditure on welfare in different countries do not give an adequate picture of the different nature of their welfare systems. Countries with relatively high expenditure are not necessarily involved in major redistribution between income groups but could simply be confirming and rewarding existing patterns of inequality. To understand the differences between welfare state systems we need to move beyond these simple quantitative comparisons and assess the nature and operation of welfare states. At the same time Esping-Andersen argued that the development of welfare state regimes owes more to the specific historical and political development of different countries than it does to stages in economic development or global processes. The fact that countries all develop welfare states of some kind does not demonstrate that they develop because of some logic of industrialization or economic development. He rejected views that welfare states emerge as a result of universal physiological forces, technological determinism or as a consequence of industrialization. He also rejected the view that they are a necessary and inevitable consequence of political development and the growth of democracies. Esping-Andersen argued that welfare states are the product of local and national pressures rather than of reified social constructs or of global influences. Consequently welfare state systems will have different attributes and Esping-Andersen sought to make systematic comparisons between different welfare states and to understand the nature of these differences in terms of the different kinds of political processes which are common to similar regimes.

It is not the main intention of this book to provide a critique of this analysis. It is clear that it has been successful in stimulating debate but has very considerable weaknesses. Some of these were implicitly acknowledged by Esping-Andersen himself and have been discussed subsequently. Even in 1990 he acknowledged that certain countries were more difficult to fit into his typology and that the particular period in which he carried out his analysis may affect the results. If he had carried out the analysis at different points in time he would have produced different results. For this book our concern is the narrow basis on which he operationalized his approach to welfare states and the results that emerged.

Esping-Andersen emphasized the importance in the welfare state of rights and specifically of citizenship rights determining access to services. He associated this with a notion of decommodification and the extent to which people are entitled to services because of their citizenship status rather than because of their income. In this sense welfare states loosen the pure commodity status of products or services. Esping-Andersen (1990) stated: 'Decommodification occurs when a service is rendered as a matter of right and when a person can maintain a livelihood without reliance on the market' (p 22). He went on to operationalize this notion of decommodification and to establish the extent to which different systems enabled people to maintain their livelihood without reliance on the market. In doing this, his focus was purely upon income related benefits. He focused upon old age pensions, sickness benefits and unemployment insurance and was concerned to examine the eligibility rules, levels of income replacement and the range of entitlements offered in different countries. In effect he assessed how generous, universal and redistributive old age pensions, sickness and unemployment insurance systems were and how far different welfare states enabled people in older age, sickness or unemployment to maintain their livelihood. Esping-Andersen provided a decommodification score for each of the three areas identified, and the aspect of his work which emerged from this analysis and has commanded most attention was the combined decommodification score, reproduced as Table 1.1.

Table 1.1 Rank-order of welfare states – combined decommodification, 1980

	Decommodification Score
Australia	13.0
United States	13.8
New Zealand	17.1
Canada	22.0
Ireland	23.3
United Kingdom	23.4
Italy	24.1
Japan	27.1
France	27.5
Germany	27.7
Finland	29.2
Switzerland	29.8
Austria	31.1
Belgium	32.4
Netherlands	32.4
Denmark	38.1
Norway	38.3
Sweden	39.1

Source: Esping-Andersen 1990, p.52.

From this Esping-Andersen referred to three kinds of welfare state regimes. The lowest decommodification score related to liberal regimes that were minimalist in their approach and had the most limited income replacement and the most limited decommodification. It was argued that these welfare state regimes aimed to minimize the role of the state to that which was essential to maintain economic efficiency. The leading examples of this type of welfare state were in North America and Australasia.

He contrasted this liberal welfare state regime with a second group of corporatist welfare states which were more generous than the liberal regimes but were not concerned with redistribution. They were largely designed to support and preserve status differentials and key institutions including the Church and the family. The key examples of these kinds of corporatist welfare state systems were France, Germany and Italy.

Finally, Esping-Andersen identified welfare state regimes which he described as social democratic and in which decommodification was much greater; there was a universalist approach and redistribution and the promotion of equality were key aims of the welfare state. Denmark, Norway and Sweden were the principle examples in this group.

There is some literature that has added to Esping-Andersen's portrayal of the welfare state and this includes criticisms of the narrow range of welfare benefits that he referred to. While the framework for analysis and the focus on process and path dependency is a good one, the operationalization through a limited number of income benefits does not provide an adequate basis to typify different welfare state systems. There is a neglect of education, health, housing, transport and public utilities. There are other social security measures that are not included: child benefit and allowances, fiscal measures, and disability allowances. There are other measures of integration associated with minority groups and different types of households, including lone parents. Because social security measures are designed to complement and integrate with one another and with other related measures, a selected subset of measures may provide a distorted view. In addition to the concern that the particular time period selected influenced the results, the neglect of the role of other institutions such as the family, not-for-profit organizations and occupational welfare is referred to. As Table 1.1 indicates, the range of countries included in this is also limited. The analysis is based upon Northern and Western Europe, North America, Australasia and Japan. Only Japan is included from East Asia.

Eastern European regimes had distinctive welfare states at this stage because of the nature of their communist regimes. Nevertheless, there is a danger that Esping-Andersen has referred to countries which share some similarities in cultural, political and economic histories. How far does the approach hold up when looking beyond this range of countries?

Housing in the Welfare State

One of the areas of welfare state provision which is missing from Esping-Andersen's operationalization of decommodification is housing. The combined decommodification score in Table 1.1 is not affected by the extent of non-market housing provision, eligibility for that housing, and the extent to which people are able to continue to live in such housing even when they would not be able to afford the market price for it. It is also unaffected by the nature of health, education and other services: the discussion of welfare states is not comprehensive.

What happens if housing is included in the picture? One way of addressing this is simply to look at the size of the not-for-profit sector as an indicator of the extent of decommodified housing in different countries. When we do this the liberal welfare states referred to above tend to have very limited public and not-for-profit housing sectors and the redistributive regimes have larger not-for-profit and public sector housing provision. However, the fit is not a very good one – as Table 1.2 indicates. The data in Table 1.2 refer to European countries and come from a European Commission source. It is important to be cautious about the precision of these statistics: the original source presents statistics which divide the dwelling stock according to tenure (rented, owner occupied and other) and then divide the rented category between social, private or other. What is reproduced in Table 1.2 is a calculation based upon the stock identified as rented in the first place and, within the rental dwelling stock, as either social or social and other. The most obvious omission from this is co-operative housing, which would not be categorized as rented in the first place. To the extent that countries such as Sweden have substantial co-operative housing sectors, the decommodification of housing in this Table may be understated. In 1980, however, the statistics for Sweden indicated that 16 per cent of the overall dwelling stock was in the 'other' category, and this is the highest of any of the countries included. Consequently the extent to which decommodification is understated will be small and we believe these figures are a good indication of the relative levels of decommodification in different countries.

Table 1.2 Welfare states, decommodification and housing, 1980 and 1990

	Decommodification Score	Rented Housing: Social	Rented Housing: Social and Other	Rented Housing: Social	Rented Housing: Social and Other
	1980	1980	1980	1990	1990
Ireland	23.3	12.7	12.7	9.9	9.9
United Kingdom	23.4	31.9	31.9	25.6	25.6
Italy	24.1	6.8	10.1	5.8	7.5
France	27.5	13.5	14.4	14.4	15.6
Finland	29.2	11.3	11.3	14.0	14.0
Austria	31.1	17.2	21.1	19.7	22.9
Belgium	32.4	6.8	6.8	6.3	6.3
Netherlands	32.4	33.6	33.6	39.1	39.1
Denmark	38.1	14.4	18.5	16.8	23.5
Sweden	39.1	20.6	20.6	22.0	22.0

Source: estimates based on data in 'Housing Statistics in the European Union 1998', European Commission Brussels, 1998.

It is immediately apparent that, referring either to 1980 or to 1990, there is not a good fit between Esping-Andersen's decommodification scores and the levels of decommodified housing indicated by social rented housing or social and other rented housing in Table 1.2. If the expectation was that the highest levels of decommodified housing would be in those countries with the highest decommodification scores in Esping-Andersen's analysis, then this expectation is not realized. The most obvious exceptions are Belgium within the redistributive welfare state group (with only 7 per cent of rented housing in 1980), and Denmark (with 14 per cent), compared with the United Kingdom in the liberal welfare state group with 32 per cent of social rented housing in 1980. We know, however, that Australia, the USA, New Zealand and Canada all have low rates of social rented housing, so it may be that in the liberal welfare state group the United Kingdom is the exception, with Ireland to a lesser extent also an exception. These are both countries with a legacy of direct housing provision. They are also countries where housing finance and the way it interacts with taxation and benefit payments may mean that the high level of decommodification of housing is directly associated with the lower decommodification score in Esping-Andersen's analysis. For example, Britain is unusual in operating a housing benefit scheme which has provision to meet 100 per cent of rent costs. The benefit rates applying at the present time do not assume that any contribution is made from basic benefits towards rent. In other countries there is generally an assumption that some part of base benefits contributes to rent. This means that base benefits are set at a higher level elsewhere and in the UK are set at a lower level (see Kemp, 1997).

While it is clear that the fit between Esping-Andersen's decommodification and housing decommodification is not a good one, there are some other elements that can be noted from the data in Table 1.2. The corporatist welfare states do not show such a great variation in the level of decommodified housing. Taking social housing in 1980, the variation is from 6.8 to 11.3 compared with the variation amongst the redistributive welfare states, from 6.8 to 33.6 or amongst the liberal welfare regimes from 12.7 to 31.9. This would be consistent with the view that the corporatist welfare states tend to have had similar approaches to housing provision, with relatively lower levels of direct provision. In contrast, the liberal and redistributive regimes embrace very different approaches to housing provision in both cases.

There are also some significant differences between the data for 1980 and 1990. The corporatist welfare states show little change between these two dates. In two cases there seems to be a slight increase in decommodified housing, and in one case a decrease. The two liberal welfare states both show a marked decrease. Amongst the redistributive welfare states there was an increase in all cases except for Belgium. Again this highlights the extent to which the date chosen will impact upon the results of the analysis. If this analysis were to be taken forward ten years, the share of decommodified housing would have declined amongst some of the redistributive welfare states if not all of them.

From this initial perspective, it is worth exploring issues about decommodification of housing more fully. The United Kingdom in 1980 had a very large decommodified housing sector (one in three of all properties). Ireland in contrast had a very small decommodified housing sector. While this fits with the decommodification score in Esping-Andersen it neglects the fact that a very large part of Ireland's housing stock was built by the state and there has been a long history of privatization or subsidized sale. Consequently, the current housing structure obscures a much more substantial decommodified housing programme.

Most countries in Europe emerged from World War II with serious housing shortages, a damaged housing stock and in some cases a legacy of nineteenth century housing, much of which would subsequently be cleared or improved to more modern standards. In conditions of post-war shortage, there were strong political pressures for local and national governments to become deeply involved in housing, however small had been their pre-war role in this area of policy.

Britain was the first country in Western Europe to embark on a subsidized public sector housing programme. This began as early as 1919 and gathered pace throughout the 1920s and 1930s. In the years before and after 1919, however, there was a view of public housing as a temporary phenomenon that would not be needed when conditions returned to 'normal' and housing was much less a feature of the consensus that built up around policies for health, education and social security that were the foundations of the post-World War II welfare state.

This was true also in other Western European countries, as shown in work by the United Nations Economic Commission for Europe (1966) that put forward a classification of housing policy regimes in the member countries of the Economic Commission for Europe;[1] and which became well known through the publication in 1967 of Donnison's book *The Government of Housing*. Looking at the countries of western and southern Europe, a classification was proposed of:

1. countries with 'embryonic' housing policies such as Greece, Turkey and Portugal, reflecting the relative lack of development in those countries at the time;
2. countries with 'social' housing policies where 'government's principal housing role is to come to the aid of selected groups in the population and help those who cannot secure housing for themselves in the "open market" ... Thus government is not assumed to be responsible for the housing conditions of the whole population' (Donnison 1967, 93). These countries included Switzerland, the UK, Belgium, Ireland and the USA;
3. countries moving 'towards a comprehensive commitment' where governments 'shape and control the market to such an extent that their housing responsibilities have assumed a national or comprehensive form' (p 97). As a generalization, these were countries that had experienced or still faced in the 1960s a 'sense of crisis' about their housing problems and 'a determination to solve them': they included Sweden, Denmark, Norway, France, West Germany and the Netherlands.

A further classification was put forward by McGuire (1981) based on an analysis of trends in twelve, mostly western, countries but including some in Central and Eastern Europe, as well as Japan and Brazil. McGuire's 'housing policy cycle' (pp 11–13) begins with a first phase which occurs 'in the face of an acute housing

---

1   The countries of Western, Central and Eastern Europe (including the USSR), the USA and Canada.

shortage' that is 'now the case in less-developed countries and was the case in the advanced countries at the turn of the twentieth century and again following World War II' (p 12).

The next stage is characterized by an emphasis on providing larger housing units to achieve more space; then there is a stage where a higher level of quality or amenity is required; and finally the point is reached at which basic needs are met. This stage 'manifests itself as a conscious attempt by the state to reduce the enormous financial burden it has had to assume for housing' (p 12) and is addressed in two ways, first by eliminating indiscriminate subsidies (from 'bricks and mortar' to personal subsidies) and second, by encouraging home-ownership, including sales to sitting tenants. This privatizes both the affected housing stock and the future responsibility for its repair and maintenance.

A similar but more refined formulation was proposed by Boelhouwer and van der Heijden (1992), based on a study of five countries in Western Europe. This assessed in particular the level of high government involvement in housing policy, especially to alleviate housing shortages; the shift in focus from a concern with housing quantity to the promotion of better housing quality; and the growing pressures, in some countries, arising from worries about the level of public expenditure on housing.

To a considerable extent, these classifications by Donnison, McGuire, and Boelhouwer and van der Heijden conform to Esping-Andersen's distribution. Doling (1997, 213; 1999, 230) argues that other contributions by Kemeny (1981) and Barlow and Duncan (1994) further extend the Esping-Andersen typology to housing policy and focus inwards on understanding housing policy differences in terms of the particular course and nature of economic and political developments which have characterized older industrial countries.

We are left with a rather unsatisfactory situation in which the analysis of welfare states does not adequately incorporate discussion of housing. At the same time comparative analyses of housing are often limited in the range of countries they consider and are unduly influenced by the welfare state regime literature; or are considerably out of date.

Introducing the East Asian Experience

The relative neglect of East Asian countries in analyses of welfare states has been recognized previously. Catherine Jones (1990), referring to Hong Kong, Singapore, Korea and Taiwan, argued that the success of these 'economic tigers' was 'contrived' rather than a matter of chance. All were 'war-torn' economies where economic growth was not an option but a pre-requisite for post-war reconstruction. At the same time a cultural homogeneity (Chinese) was important and at the heart of this was 'Confucianism' emphasizing the role of the family as the nucleus of society and the values of 'harmony, solidarity, pride and loyalty'. The good society was seen as resting not on individualism, responsibility and citizenship but on 'interlocking groups' and 'ascending orders of duty and obligation'.

In this context, the role of the state was viewed very differently than in the west. There was no concept of government as the property of the people, nor of the existence of 'rights'; nor of the concept of reform founded on the basis of 'struggle' – at least not class struggle! Families were seen as 'subjects' rather than having electoral rights and the state was driven by duty rather than electoral pledges. The pursuit of economic development was the primary goal and designed to ensure that government was beneficial. Within that, state housing provision and the release of land were both particularly important in Singapore and Hong Kong – and seen as economic drivers rather than social necessity.

The culture of politics was also very different. 'The proper place for politics is behind the scenes, out of sight, absorbed into the administration'. There was, as a consequence, not much respect for professional politicians and none of these countries was characterized by the ideals of Western European, liberal, social democracies. In terms of governance – despite the very different histories of these countries (including one former and one soon-to-be former British colonies, an ex-military dictatorship and the 'democratic' Republic of China) – Jones argued that there was some common ground. Governance was by an 'establishment' – a ruling elite, seeking consensus in the interests of the whole of society.

Jones argued that the initial aim of these countries after the Second World War was to build 'communities' – communities characterized by 'order, discipline, loyalty, stability, and collective self-help' because 'without order there could be no sustained economic growth; without economic growth there could be no future'. This meant supporting the family as a 'bulwark of society' and 'rendering the neighbourhood the functional equivalent of the traditional village'. She cited examples of top down 'community' initiatives. Similarly the provision of services was characterized for the 'mainstream' rather than a system of selective benefits for the poor or the less well off. The pursuit of economic development was the primary goal.

There is also some commonality in the way that state housing services were provided by large, state-run enterprises: the Housing and Development Board in Singapore, the Hong Kong Housing Authority and the Korea National Housing Corporation. These were generally responsible for the direct development of estates, or the supervision of construction under contract. The residential developments, moreover, often had their own unique characteristics, i.e. collectivized forms of construction in high-rise apartments, which were individually owned but 'managed' by state agencies.

Jones concluded that the welfare states of the eastern 'tigers' were not characterized by participatory democracy, the promotion of citizens' rights, social obligations or assistance for the poor – indeed they were characterized by the reverse. These East Asian societies rewarded those who helped themselves – according to Jones, a 'welfare capitalism that works'.

An important later paper by Sherraden (1997) suggested that western scholars worked with too ethnocentric a view of the welfare state and assumed that countries that did not have significant and generous transfer payment and social security systems had underdeveloped welfare states. However, in his paper Sherraden suggested that the welfare state model developed in Singapore was an important alternative. The welfare state which places asset ownership and the appreciating value of property assets at the core of welfare provision should not be regarded in any way as less effective or less viable. Compulsory savings which encourage people to invest in property and which directly and indirectly provide resources in older age and in periods of low income are a significant alternative which should not be dismissed simply because it does not follow the western model.

It is in this context that housing becomes more significant. In the East Asian economic welfare states the housing sector is of considerable importance. This is recognized elsewhere. Doling (1999) discussed material related to Hong Kong, Singapore, Korea and Taiwan but his approach focused upon the market mix and the different contributions of market and state in development, construction and consumption. Looking more widely at eight countries in east and south-east Asia, Doling (2002, 184) distinguished between 'strong state providers and developers' (Singapore and Hong Kong) and 'state supported self helpers' (Indonesia, Thailand and Malaysia); with Japan, Korea and Taiwan occupying 'intermediate positions' where selective support has been used to help low income groups meet their housing needs within a market framework. In other contributions Taiwan, Japan and Korea are regarded as developmental states (Johnson, 1982, 1987; Weiss, 2000). The literature on comparative social policy refers elsewhere to an 'East Asian' welfare state model (Kwon 1997; Gough 2001), in contrast to the 'western' models of Esping-Andersen. Others have referred to East Asian countries with prominent 'developmental welfare systems' (White and Goodman, 1998) or 'tiger welfare regimes' (La Grange and Yung, 2001) with an emphasis on economic rather than social development. Holliday (2000) proposes that East Asia comprises a fourth welfare regime of 'productivist welfare capitalism', in which social policy is subordinated to economic policy. There is a general agreement that East Asian countries have approaches to welfare that are distinctive from the older welfare states of the West because of their focus on economic growth.

Changing Regimes

What is set out above is an agenda which relates to the welfare state and to the provision of housing within the welfare state. But the relevance of this debate is increased by patterns of economic and welfare change. Both welfare state arrangements and housing provision systems have been going through major changes especially since the mid-1970s. Fiscal pressures have added to ideological and electoral support to roll back the traditional western welfare state; and the privatization of state housing has been significant in some of the countries with the most substantial decommodified housing systems.

Looking at the United Kingdom, or at a number of other systems, the more recent history of decommodified housing provision has been one of commodification. It has involved the privatization of housing and the movement of public and not-for-profit housing systems towards market systems. In Britain the Right to Buy, movements in rents and changes in subsidy have reduced the extent of decommodification. There is a smaller public sector and it is less universally subsidized with a switch from object subsidies towards means tested subject subsidies.

Different patterns apply in other countries with large decommodified housing systems such as the Netherlands but the same process is apparent with rents moving towards market levels and the distinctions between state and not-for-profit housing and other parts of the housing system being reduced. From a view that sees housing as a fundamental component of the welfare state, then this process of privatization must mean a weakening of the welfare state.

To what extent is there also a weakening of the welfare state through similar processes in East Asia? Privatization has been a major element in housing programmes in China and until recently, in Hong Kong. To what extent has this represented a dismantling of the welfare state, or merely a reorganization and re-labelling of the system? In Singapore the role of the private sector as such remains relatively small and although it is being expanded, it will remain very small in international comparative terms. However the state system has labels that are market labels. Again, is there a process of privatization taking place that changes the nature of the welfare state or is there no fundamental change but rather a change in the appearance and the re-badging of different policies?

Conclusions

This book develops the debates introduced in this chapter. It examines the approaches to housing provision and the nature of the welfare state in different countries. It focuses on the new welfare states of East Asia and considers the alternative approaches they have adopted to the 'traditional' western welfare model. In doing so, the book considers whether there is a common 'East Asian' approach or a variety of approaches. It also considers how far the adjustments to the traditional western welfare state have involved some adoption of the approach exemplified in East Asia. Rather than the western model being the dominant one, is there a convergence on a more eastern model?

To answer these questions requires a better understanding of the East Asian model of welfare. How important is state and not-for-profit housing in the systems of welfare provision? How far does an understanding of these systems enable us to rethink some of the basic assumptions which underlie the existing literature about housing and welfare state systems? And how far are processes of privatization the same in each of these countries? Can a better understanding of privatization give us an improved understanding of change within each of these systems and in the older industrial countries, such as the United Kingdom?

The issue in understanding housing systems is the same as the one in understanding welfare states. Where these arrangements change significantly over time, the point at which the analysis is carried out may be very important in the conclusions that are presented. The welfare state in the United Kingdom in the late 1940s was very different to that in the early 21st century and the stages between the two are likely to be typified in different ways.

The next six chapters refer to six separate East Asian welfare systems and focus on the recent development of housing policy. The chapters examine Singapore, Hong Kong, Korea, Japan, China and Taiwan. Following this, Chapter 8 explores changes in older welfare systems and particularly in the UK system, to identify continuities and differences. Finally, Chapter 9 reflects upon the body of material presented and its implications for debates about housing within evolving welfare state systems. An important aim is to explore how the older welfare states of Europe, exemplified by the United Kingdom, are beginning to adopt features of the East Asian approach, in their shift towards an asset-based welfare system.

Chapter 2

The Singapore Model of Housing and the Welfare State

Sock-Yong Phang

Introduction

While Singapore is not generally regarded as a welfare state, the provision of housing welfare on a large scale has been a defining feature of its welfare system. The extensive housing system has played a useful role in raising savings and home-ownership rates as well as contributing to sustained economic growth in general and development of the housing sector in particular. Few would dispute the description of Singapore's housing policies as 'phenomenally successful' (Ramesh 2003). Singapore's economic growth record in the past four decades has brought it from third world to first world status (Lee, K.Y. 2000), with home-ownership widespread at more than 90 per cent for the resident population.

Singapore is a densely populated high-income city-state with 4.2 million people and a land area of only 697 square kilometers. Of the 4.2 million people in 2004, 3.5 million were residents (citizens and permanent residents) and 0.7 million were foreigners.[1] Its Gross Domestic Product in 2004 was S$181 billion or US$109 billion.[2] The World Development Report 2004 estimated Singapore's 2002 GNI per capita at US$29,610 (using purchasing power parity GNI and exchange rates), ranking it 19th highest in its PPP GNI per capita list.

A British colony from 1819, Singapore attained self-government in 1959, joined the Federation of Malaysia in 1963 and became an independent city-state in 1965. The People's Action Party, which was elected in 1959, has been returned to power at every election since. During the politically traumatic 1960s, the government concentrated on issues of employment creation and housing provision, adopting a strategy of export oriented growth through attracting foreign investment. Today, there are more than 5,000 foreign companies located in Singapore and many multinational corporations have established regional operating and manufacturing bases on the island.

---

1   In the 1990s, the growth rate for foreigners was 9.3 per cent compared to 1.8 per cent for local residents. Department of Statistics, *Census of Population 2000*.

2   Ministry of Trade and Industry, *Economic Survey of Singapore 2004*. The nominal exchange rate in February 2005 approximates S$1.65 to US$1.

Table 2.1 shows the Gross Domestic Product for 1970, 1980, 1990 and 2000
– real GDP more than doubled in each decade. Singapore's economic growth
record and ability to attract foreign investments stem from effective public sector
planning and management of its economy and society. A network of competent and
reliable institutions and government-linked companies provides rich public sector
capacity. The Singapore government plays an extensive and multi-dimensional
developmental role in the economy. The state owns 90 per cent of the land and
determines the deployment of substantial domestic savings. The scope of public
enterprises in Singapore encompasses manufacturing, trading, financial, transport
and other services. This reliance on the public sector as the catalyst for change, with
private initiative to fill the gaps, is most visible in the areas of urban housing and
infrastructure development.

Despite the very visible presence of the state and government-linked companies,
provision of welfare as is generally understood in Europe has not been a feature of
the economic system. For much of its history since independence, Singapore has
enjoyed high economic growth rates accompanied by full employment, with a tight
labour market necessitating the importation of foreign workers (see Figure 2.1). In
the period after independence and prior to the 1997 Asian financial crisis, 1985 stood
out as the only year when the city-state experienced negative GDP growth; pre-
Asian financial crisis unemployment rates were generally frictional in nature and
below four per cent. Economic growth rates since 1997 have however been more
volatile with growing concern over structural unemployment (above five per cent for
2002–04) associated with the restructuring of the economy.

Given the long record of full employment (until recently), the absence of
unemployment safety nets is not surprising. Government policy has focused instead
on managing income inequality through spreading the benefits of growth through ad
hoc measures that would not reduce incentives to work and save. The government's
budget has been described as biased towards large and persistent structural surpluses
(Asher 2004). Special transfers announced in the Minister for Finance's annual
budget speech since 1994 have included utility and rental rebates, top-ups to Central
Provident Fund accounts, New Singapore Shares, Economic Restructuring Shares,
as well as grants, scholarships and bursaries made through an Edusave Scheme to the
accounts of each student. Needy Singaporeans, including those who are unemployed,
are helped through a slew of financial assistance schemes offered by a range of
government and non-government organizations, aimed at providing short-term relief
and retraining without creating a dependency culture (Yap 2002).

Table 2.1 Key indicators of Singapore's housing sector

	1970	1980	1990	2000
Total Population (millions)	2.075	2.414	3.047	4.017
Resident population (millions)	2.014	2.282	2.736	3.263
Non-resident population (000s)	61	132	311	755
Resident home-ownership rate	29%	59%	88%	92%
Resident population in HDB dwellings	36%	73%	87%	86%
Macro-economic Data				
GDP (S$m, 1995 market prices)	$16,207	$37,959	$77,299	$162,162
GNP per capita (S$ current)	$2,825	$9,941	$22,645	$42,212
Unemployment rate	6%	3.5%	1.4%	3.5%
Exchange rate (S$/US$)	S$3.09	S$2.14	S$1.81	S$1.73
Gross National Saving/GNP	19.3%	34.2%	43.9%	51.5%
Gross Capital Formation/GNP	32.2%	42.2%	31.6%	27.6%
Residential Construction/GNP	6.2%	5.9%	5.2%	6.18%
Housing Loans				
Total Housing Loans (S$m)	$215	$2,421	$19,151	$101,384
Housing Loans/GDP	4%	10%	29%	64%
HDB Mortgage Loans/Housing Loans	58%	60%	54%	59%
Banks' Housing loans*/Housing Loans	42%	40%	46%	41%
Central Provident Fund				
Balance Due Members (S$m current)	$777	$9,551	$40,646	$90,298
Employee Contribution Rate	8.0%	18.0%	23.0%	20.0%
Employer Contribution Rate	8.0%	20.5%	16.5%	12.0%
Prices				
CPI (Nov 1997–Oct 1998=100)	36.5	68.2	85.2	101.1
Private House Price Index (1998=100)	-	27.3	57.7	130.3
HDB Resale Price Index (1998=100)	-	-	34.1	104.9
Price of new 4 room HDB flat in new town location (≈ 100 sq m in S$)	$12,500	$24,200	$76,100	$98,000
Housing Price Affordability (4-rm HDB flat price to GNP per capita)	4.42	2.43	3.36	2.32
Housing Stock (HS)	305,833	467,142	690,561	1,039,677
Public sector built	120,138	337,198	574,443	846,649
Private sector built	185,695	129,944	116,118	193,028
4 room and larger HDB flats/HS (%)	1%	13%	40%	51%
Persons per dwelling unit	6.7	5.1	4.4	4.2

Note: * includes Finance Houses and Credit POSB.
Sources: Various Singapore government publications and websites.

The government relies almost exclusively on the Central Provident Fund (CPF) scheme, a mandatory savings scheme, to finance a range of different welfare services: housing, healthcare, insurance, tertiary education and retirement (Asher 2004). On the supply side, the government is also directly involved in the provision of subsidized education and healthcare; the Housing and Development Board (HDB) has been the largest housing developer for the past three decades. That more than 85 per cent of the resident population live in HDB housing has been described by Pugh (1985) as a 'symbol of pride, of nationhood, of the political achievement of the People's Action Party, and of government benevolence towards the public interest'.

Prime Minister Lee Hsien Loong's 2005 budget speech provides a precise description of the government's approach toward welfare:

> We must not breed a culture of entitlement, encouraging Singaporeans to seek Government support as a matter of right, whether or not they need it ... The better-off must help the poor and the disadvantaged – the sick, the elderly, the disabled and the unemployed. In many developed countries, the state takes on this responsibility, but this is invariably financed by high taxes and levies on businesses and those who are working. Our social compact is rather different. It is based on personal responsibility, with the family and community playing key roles in supporting people through difficulties. The state will provide a safety net, but it should be a last resort, not a first resort, and should focus on the minority who need help the most. We thus avoid state welfare, which will erode our incentive to achieve and sap our will to strive. Our social compact enables us to keep taxes low, and lets people keep the fruits of their labour and businesses the rewards of their enterprise. And when we do well and have budget surpluses, we can distribute some of them back to Singaporeans (*The Straits Times*, 19 February 2005).

The 2005 budget reduced the top marginal personal income tax rate from 22 to 20 per cent, introduced incentives to develop Singapore further as a financial, logistics and tourism centre, and provided resources for worker re-training and skills upgrading through a S$500 million transfer to the Lifelong Learning Fund. Targeted special transfers to individuals included utility rebates that varied from S$60 (five room HDB flats) to S$200 (one and two room HDB flats); Medisave account top-ups ranging from S$50 (ages 21–39) to S$350 (60 years and above); and CPF top-ups of S$100 for those aged 50 and above. Special transfers to funds that provide the social safety nets for the poor included S$100 million for the Medifund and S$250 million for the recently announced Com-Care Fund to support needy Singaporeans, including children from disadvantaged backgrounds.

The next section describes the phases of housing policy in the post-war period. This is followed by a brief description of housing tenure forms in Singapore. We then evaluate the socio-economic benefits from such comprehensive attention to housing sector development. Inevitably, the long-term bias of directing credit and resources to the housing sector has resulted in other economic problems, which are also analyzed. We conclude with a discussion of policy lessons from Singapore in the approach to the welfare state, and evaluate the transferability of the Singapore experience.

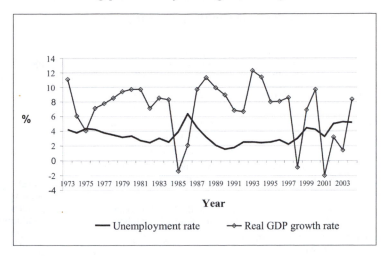

Figure 2.1 Real GDP growth and unemployment rate, 1973–2004

Phases of Housing Policy in the Post-war Period

Housing policy in Singapore has gone through a number of distinct phases as summarized in Table 2.2.

Phase I: Building shortages

The immediate postwar period in Singapore was characterized by chronic housing shortages. In 1947, the British colonial government implemented rent control to protect tenants – premises built on or after 7 September 1947 had rents pegged to rates that existed on 1 August 1939. The Singapore Improvement Trust (SIT), the then town planning authority, stepped up public housing construction, building an estimated 20,907 units between 1947–59. At the time of self-government in 1959, deplorable housing conditions and housing shortages exacerbated by rapid post-war population growth prevailed. The then newly elected People's Action Party government made housing a priority area of policy concern. Housing institutions and policies were developed systematically and comprehensively to advance social development and economic growth. There exists a vast literature on various aspects of the housing sector in Singapore (see for example books by Castells et al. 1990 for comparison with Hong Kong; Chua 1997; Low and Aw 1997; Phang 1992; Wong and Yeh 1985; and the sample of articles referenced here). Here we provide a brief overview of the institutions and policies that have shaped the housing sector: the Housing and Development Board and the Central Provident Fund.

Table 2.2 Phases of housing policy in the post-war period

Year	Housing developments		Phase
	What happened?	**Why?**	
1947	Rent control at 1939 rents	To protect tenants at a time of severe housing shortages	
1955	Central Provident Fund (CPF)	To provide social security for the working population	
1959		Self governing colony	
1960	Housing & Development Board (HDB)	To provide housing for all those who needed them	I. Developing housing
1963	Merger with Malaysia		policies and
1964	HDB's Home Ownership Scheme (HOS)	To enable the lower income group to own their own homes	institutions to cope with
1965	Independence: Separation from Malaysia		building shortages
1966	Land Acquisition Act	To facilitate land acquisition by the state	
1968	CPF Approved Housing Scheme	To allow CPF savings to be used to support the HDB's HOS	
1971	Resale market for HOS	To allow owners of HOS flats to exit the sector	
1979	Easing of restrictions on resale of HOS flats	To facilitate upgrading to a second new HDB flat as well as residential mobility within the sector	
1981	CPF Approved Residential Properties Scheme	To allow CPF savings to be used for private housing mortgage payments	
1985	First economic recession since independence		II. Deregulation as shortages
1988	Phasing out of rent control	To facilitate private sector participation in the conservation of historical areas	eased
1989	Citizenship requirement and income ceilings for resale flats lifted	To allow permanent residents access to resale HOS flats. To facilitate residential mobility	
1993	More housing loans for HDB resale flats	To bring HDB housing loans policy for resale flats closer to market practices	
1994	CPF housing grants	To facilitate demand side housing subsidies for resale HOS flats	
1995	Executive Condominiums	To provide private housing at affordable prices to the upper-middle income group	III. Financial liberalization and housing price inflation
1996	Anti-speculation measures	To curb speculative activities and rapid rise in housing prices	
1997	Asian financial crisis		
2002	Caps on CPF withdrawals for housing	To reduce risk of over concentration of household assets in housing	IV. Excess housing stock
2003	HDB downsizes	In view of fall in demand for new flats and 17,500 unsold HDB flats in 2002	

The Housing and Development Board The Housing and Development Board (HDB) was set up as a statutory board in 1960, replacing the SIT, to provide 'decent homes equipped with modern amenities for all those who needed them'. A target of 110,000 dwelling units was set for 1960–70. From 1964, the HDB began offering housing units for sale at below market prices, on a 99 year leasehold basis, under its Home Ownership Scheme (HOS). The HDB was able to price its units below market prices mainly because HDB flats are built on state owned land, much of which had been compulsorily acquired from private landowners at below market prices (Phang 1996). This was made possible by the Land Acquisition Act, enacted in 1966, which abolished *eminent domain* provisions.

The political and economic motivations for the HOS are perhaps best understood in the words of the then Prime Minister, Mr Lee Kuan Yew:

> My primary preoccupation was to give every citizen a stake in the country and its future. I wanted a home-owning society. I had seen the contrast between the blocks of low-cost rental flats, badly misused and poorly maintained, and those of house-proud owners, and was convinced that if every family owned its home, the country would be more stable (page 116) … I had seen how voters in capital cities always tended to vote against the government of the day and was determined that our householders should become home-owners, otherwise we would not have political stability. My other important motive was to give all parents whose sons would have to do national service a stake in the Singapore their sons had to defend. If the soldier's family did not own their home, he would soon conclude he would be fighting to protect the properties of the wealthy. I believed this sense of ownership was vital for our new society, which had no deep roots in a common historical experience (Lee, K.Y. 2000, 117).

Policies were introduced to achieve the goal of a home-owning society. Table 2.1 shows the rapid increase in the HDB housing stock: from 120,138 units in 1970 to 846,649 units in 2000. The home-ownership rate for the resident population increased from 29 per cent in 1970 to 92 per cent by 2000. Singapore's large public housing sector is therefore in ownership terms, a largely privatized sector. However, ownership tenure of a HDB dwelling differs in many aspects from ownership of a private dwelling. Ownership rights are limited by numerous regulations concerning eligibility conditions for purchase, resale, subletting and housing loans.

The Central Provident Fund While HDB and related construction finance and land policy brought about a transformation of the housing supply side, demand for home-ownership was 'created' by directing savings in the Central Provident Fund (CPF) towards housing. The CPF had been in existence before the HDB, having been established as a pension plan in 1955 by the colonial government to provide social security for the working population in Singapore. The scheme required contributions by both employers and employees, respectively, of a certain percentage of the individual employee's monthly salary toward the employee's personal and portable account in the fund. All employers are required to contribute monthly to the fund. The bulk of contributions can only be withdrawn for specific purposes (of which housing dominates), on retirement at age 55, or on the permanent incapacitation of the contributor concerned. The interest rate on CPF Ordinary account savings is based on a weighted average of one-year fixed deposit and month-end savings rates of the local banks, subject to a minimum of 2.5 per cent. Savings in the Special and Medisave accounts earn additional interest of 1.5 percentage points above the normal CPF interest rate.

The CPF became an important institution for financing housing purchases from September 1968 when legislation was enacted to allow withdrawals from the fund to finance the purchase of housing sold by the HDB and subsequently sold by other public sector agencies as well. The contribution rates at the inception of the CPF in 1955 were five per cent of the monthly salary for employees and five per cent for employers. From 1968, the rates were adjusted upward and peaked at 25 per cent of wages for both employers and employees from 1984–86. Contribution rates are currently 20 per cent of wages for employees and 13 per cent of wages for employers, up to a salary ceiling of S$5,000. Contribution rates are lower for workers above 55 years of age, and the proportion of contributions allocated for investments, retirement, and healthcare (in the Ordinary, Special and Medisave accounts) also varies with age (Asher 2004). Rates have varied depending on economic conditions, and changes to contribution rates have been used as a macro-economic stabilization instrument to limit inflation or to reduce wage cost.

The HDB provides mortgage loans and mortgage insurance to purchasers of its leasehold flats (both new and used). The typical loan quantum is 80 per cent of the price of the new flat and the maximum repayment period is 25 years. The mortgage interest rate charged by the HDB is pegged at 0.1 percentage points above the CPF Ordinary account savings interest rate, which in turn is based on savings rates offered by the commercial banks, subject to a minimum of 2.5 per cent. The HDB is a recipient of government loans to finance its mortgage lending, interest on which is pegged to the prevailing CPF savings rate. The mortgage lending rate charged by the HDB to home-owners is 0.1 percentage point higher than the rate that it borrows from the government, thus ensuring the sustainability of the financing arrangement. Housing loans for private housing are provided by commercial banks and finance houses. A schematic view of how housing is financed in Singapore is shown in Figure 2.2.

Phase II (1979 – early 1990s): Deregulation and creation of resale market as shortages eased

The desirability of any asset is determined to a large extent by its liquidity. Ease of trade determines the efficiency of a market. The promotion of ownership of subsidized new HDB dwellings therefore had to be accompanied by policies concerning the secondary market for that housing. However, from the perspective of public policy, there was early concern that given the then general housing shortage, HDB dwellings should not become a vehicle for speculation by allowing the price subsidies to be capitalized on a secondary market. Resale regulations were therefore extremely onerous in the early days of the housing programme. These regulations were eased as the housing stock increased over time and the housing market became more mature (Phang 1992, 92–4).

Prior to 1971, there was no resale market for owner-occupied HDB dwellings. HDB required that owners who wished to sell their flats had to return them to the HDB at the original purchase price plus the depreciated cost of improvements. In 1971, a resale market was created when the HDB allowed owners who had resided in their flats for a minimum of three years to sell their flats at market prices to buyers of their choice who satisfied the HDB eligibility requirements for home-ownership. However, these households were debarred from applying for public housing for a year. The debarment period was increased to two and a half years in 1975. The minimum occupancy period before resale was increased to five years in 1973 and has remained in place since.

The debarment period, a great deterrent for any household considering sale of its dwelling, was abolished in 1979 thereby greatly facilitating exchanges within the public housing sector. This was replaced by a five per cent levy on the transacted price of the dwelling to 'reduce windfall profits'. A system of graded resale levy based on flat type was introduced in 1982, and rules regarding circumstances under which levies could be waived were fine-tuned in the 1980s (Phang 1992, 93). The resale levy system ensures that the subsidy on the second new flat purchased by the household from the HDB is smaller than that for the first flat.

Between 1968–81, CPF savings could be withdrawn only for purposes of down payment, stamp duties, mortgage, and interest payments incurred for the purchase of public-sector-built housing.[3] In 1981, the scheme was extended to allow for withdrawals for mortgage payments for the purchase of private housing. From 1984, rules governing the use of CPF savings have been gradually liberalized to allow for withdrawals for medical and education expenses, insurance, and investments in various financial assets (Asher 2004).

Only citizens, non-owners of any other residential property, households with a minimum size of two persons with household incomes below the income ceiling set by the HDB were eligible to purchase new or resale HDB flats prior to 1989. In 1989, residential mobility was enhanced when the income ceiling restriction was removed for HDB resale flats; the resale market was opened to permanent residents as well as private property owners who had to owner-occupy their HDB flat. HDB flat-owners who could not own any other residential property before, could also invest in private sector built dwellings. From 1991, single citizens above the age of 35 have been allowed to purchase HDB resale flats for owner-occupancy.

---

3   A relatively minor scheme introduced in 1978 allowed withdrawals to be made for the purchase of shares in Singapore Bus Services, the then monopoly provider of public bus services.

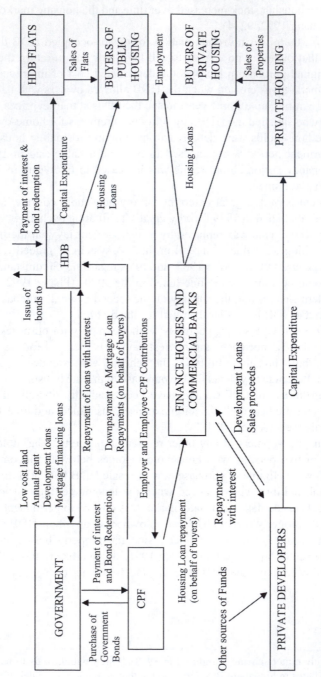

Figure 2.2 A schematic view of the housing finance market in Singapore

Phase III (early 1990s–1997): Financial liberalization and housing price inflation

The HDB also provides loans to buyers of resale HDB flats. Loan financing prior to 1993 was based on 80 per cent of 1984 HDB new flat (posted) prices. As both new and resale prices rose (see Figure 2.3), households purchasing resale flats had to pay an increasingly larger proportion of the price in cash. In 1993 HDB moved its mortgage financing terms closer to market practice by granting loan financing of up to 80 per cent of current valuation or the declared resale price of the flat, whichever was lower. In 1993, the CPF Board also began to allow withdrawals of CPF savings to be used to meet interest payments on mortgage loans for resale HDB and private housing purchases. Before this, CPF members were only allowed to withdraw 100 per cent of the value of these properties at the time of purchase.

Deregulation of the HDB resale market has been accompanied by an increase in the number of transactions. The transaction volume of resale HDB flats increased from fewer than 800 units in 1979, to 13,000 units in 1987, 60,000 units in 1999, and 31,000 in 2004 (HDB Annual Reports). Resale transactions as a proportion of total (new and resale) owner-occupied public housing transactions, were three per cent, 37 per cent, 64 per cent and 68 per cent in 1979, 1987, 1999, and 2004 respectively. The increase in the demand for resale flats in the latter half of the 1990s is in part due to the introduction of demand side housing grants.

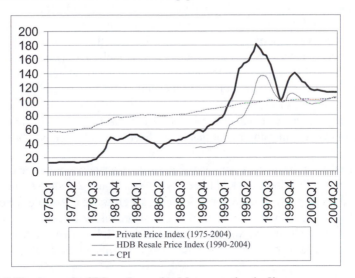

Figure 2.3 Singapore's CPI and nominal house price indices

Notes: CPI, 1975–2004 (November 1997 – October 1998 = 100); Private house price index, 1975–2004 (1998 Q4=100); HDB resale price index, 1990–2004 (1998 Q4 = 100).
Sources: Singapore Ministry of Trade and Industry, Economic Survey of Singapore; Singapore Urban Redevelopment Authority, Real Estate Information System; Singapore Housing and Development Board website.

In 1994, demand-side subsidies in the form of CPF housing grants for the purchase of resale HDB flats were introduced. This represents a shift from total reliance on subsidies tied to new flats to a system of partial reliance on subsidies tied to resale flats. The subsidy is deposited into the CPF account of the eligible household when it applies to purchase a resale HDB flat. Under the scheme, the government provides the first-time applicant household with a grant of $30,000 to purchase a HDB resale flat close to either parents' or a married child's residence. In 1995, the grant was increased to S$50,000. The government also introduced a more general grant of S$40,000 for eligible households that purchase a resale flat which does not need to satisfy the criterion of being close to parents/married child's residence.

The shift towards constrained housing grants for the purchase of housing on the secondary market was necessary for the following reasons. In the first three decades of the HDB's existence, annual supply of new public housing added substantially to the housing stock particularly in the early 1980s. It was a rapid rate that was consistent with high income and population growth combined with a situation of grave housing shortage. The supply policies of the HDB that were suitable under the above circumstances had to be reviewed as population growth stabilized and as basic housing needs were generally met.

In cities of developed countries, new construction of housing is a small percentage of existing stock and comprises mostly high quality housing. Even as the construction of the basic one to three room HDB flats has been phased out, the construction of four room HDB flats may eventually meet with the same fate. The housing board's ongoing modernization of older estates and its selective en-bloc redevelopment scheme (under which old apartment blocks are repurchased, demolished, and new estates built) will be even more important then. Owner-occupier subsidies (which almost all new households and a large proportion of existing households have come to expect as a right of citizenship[4]) will, as a matter of economic efficiency if not political efficacy, have to be increasingly in the form of housing grants for the purchase of existing housing rather than subsidized prices for the purchase of a new unit.

Financial liberalization as well as the positive macro-economic factors resulted in rapidly rising housing prices in the early 1990s. Figure 2.3 shows the trends for private and resale public housing price indices as well as the Consumer Price Index.[5] In response to the growing concern over the affordability of private housing, the government introduced the Executive Condominium (EC) scheme, a hybrid public-private house type in 1995. The EC scheme also facilitated the HDB's withdrawal

---

4   The HDB has been described as 'a ticket to an easier life for the average Singaporean' and 'a cash cow for the milking of housing subsidies' (*The Straits Times*, 19 April 1997).

5   The price indices are compiled by the Urban Redevelopment Authority and the Housing and Development Board and are not quality-controlled. While it would be more appropriate to use hedonic price indices for housing, these are not available. It is likely that the quality of housing transacted (both in the public and private sectors) has been improving over time.

from the upper-middle-income housing market, allowing it to close the queue for its Executive Flats. Its similarity with 99 year leasehold private condominiums provides the government with another instrument on the supply side to impact on private housing prices. The government auctions land for the development of EC units to housing developers (private as well as government-linked companies) who are responsible for the design, construction, pricing and arrangements for financing and estate management. Applicant households have to satisfy eligibility conditions and abide by resale and other regulations governing these units.

Despite an increase in HDB supply of new housing and the introduction of the EC scheme as well as an increase in government land sales for private housing development, house prices continued to soar (with the private housing price index more than tripling between 1990–96). On 15 May 1996, the government introduced a package of anti-speculation measures to curb real estate speculation. These included capital gains taxes on the sale of any property within three years of purchase, stamp duty on every sale and sub-sale of property, limitation of housing loans to 80 per cent of property value, as well as limiting foreigners to non S$ denominated housing loans. The immediate effect of these measures was to cool the property market, which however entered a slump with the onset of the Asian economic crisis in 1997 (see Figure 2.3).

Phase IV (1998–present): Excess housing stock

In response to the fall in demand for housing during the Asian financial crisis, which was particularly pronounced in 1998, the government halted land sales and also ended its long standing policy of not providing housing subsidies for singles by introducing a S$15,000 CPF housing grant for eligible single persons to purchase resale three room or smaller flats. As housing prices declined further, the CPF housing grants were reduced in stages over ten months from January to October 1999 – S$500 per month for the Single Citizen housing grant, and $1,000 per month for the other housing grants. (In FY 2003/04, 7,260 households purchased a resale flat under the CPF housing grant scheme.)

Both the private and public housing sectors were faced with a situation of declining prices and unsold units. A study in 2001 estimated unsold housing stock of about 19,800 units for the private sector (Monetary Authority of Singapore, 2001). With more than 17,500 unsold new flats in early 2002, the HDB suspended its Registration for Flat or queuing system, diverting remaining and new applicants to its Built-To-Order programme under which flats are built only when there is sufficient demand for them. In July 2003, in a major restructuring exercise, the HDB's 3000 strong Building and Development Division[6] was re-organized and the

---

6   At the time of restructuring HDB's staff strength was 8,000, including 3,000 in the Building and Development Division. The new HDB Corp took in about 800 to 1,000 staff. (Ministry of National Development, Housing and Development Board Press Release, 26 February 2003.)

HDB Corporation Private Limited (HDB Corp) set up as a fully-owned subsidiary of HDB. In November 2004, HDB divested its 100 per cent shareholding in HDB Corp to the government's investment holding company, Temasek Holdings. HDB Corp was assigned responsibility for the design and development of all HDB projects until June 2006. The subsidiaries of HDB Corp now include the Surbana group of companies, which have also ventured into housing development projects overseas.

The HDB provides loans to purchasers of both new and resale flats, with the CPF having first claim on a property if a borrower defaults on his loan, thus protecting the CPF savings of the purchaser. Interest rate is at the CPF savings rate plus 0.1 percentage point. The recent low interest rate environment has however given rise to the anomaly where interest rates for commercial bank housing loans have been lower than HDB's 'subsidised' loans (as there is a 2.5 per cent floor on the CPF ordinary account savings rate). From September 2002, commercial banks have been given the go-ahead to compete for a slice of the S$63 billion HDB loans market pie. However, as is the case for private housing, banks instead of the CPF would be given first claim for such housing loans.

Housing Tenure Forms in Singapore

Given the large number of foreigners living, working or studying in Singapore, population and housing statistics in Singapore make a distinction between resident and non-resident population (see Table 2.1). Resident population comprises Singapore citizens and permanent residents. Non-resident population comprised 19 per cent of the total population in 2000. However, official government statistics, including census data on housing and households often refers only to characteristics of the resident population. The housing market however caters to both groups and there is often confusion when statistics on the resident population are misinterpreted as referring to the total population or housing stock (see Table 2.3). Housing tenure forms in Singapore are also incredibly complex, with public-private hybrids defined by ownership or rental as well as HDB or private. Land ownership is also further defined by freehold, state-owned leasehold (and number of years of remaining leasehold), fully owned or part owned (strata-title) status. This section serves to clarify some of these issues as well as explain housing tenure forms in Singapore.

We infer from census data (see Table 2.3) that 40,813 or 4.2 per cent of households in 2000 were non-resident households. While 88 per cent of 923,325 resident households reside in HDB flats, 79 per cent of the 964,138 occupied dwellings were HDB flats, with 21 per cent of occupied dwellings being private sector housing. The total housing stock in 2000 was 1,039,677 units, of which 81 per cent was HDB housing (see Table 2.1). The housing vacancy rate in 2000 (occupied dwellings to housing stock) was about 7 per cent. Within the private housing sector, 15,367 of the 40,813 foreign households were owner-occupiers in 2000 (data from URA REALIS) – a home-ownership rate of 38 per cent. As such, the home-ownership rate based on occupied dwellings rather than resident households would have been 90 per cent.

With regard to the housing stock, 83 per cent were owner-occupied, 10 per cent were tenanted, and 7 per cent were vacant units. The private housing and rental sectors are therefore larger than reference to statistics on the resident population alone would suggest.

Table 2.3 Occupied houses and resident households, 2000

	Occupied houses by type of dwelling	Resident household distribution by type of dwelling	Resident home-ownership rate by dwelling type
Total	964,138	923,325	
Total %	100.0%	100.0%	92.3%
HDB flats	79.1%	88.0%	93.2%
1 & 2 room	4.8%	5.0%	19.2%
3 room	22.9%	25.7%	96.4%
4 room	29.5%	33.2%	98.3%
5 room &	21.4%	23.7%	98.7%
Executive			
Others	0.5%	0.4%	60.4%
Condominiums			
& Private Flats	7.9%	6.0%	82.8%
Private houses	6.3%	5.1%	90.3%
Others	6.7%	0.9%	83.8%

Source: Singapore Department of Statistics 2001, Singapore Population.

Owner-occupied public housing sector

As can be seen from the data, the dominant housing sector is the HDB owner-occupied sector. New flats are sold by the HDB at what were considered subsidized prices in the past as there were long waiting lists of up to 140,000 households in the mid 1990s. Demand is regulated by eligibility rules such as household income (income ceiling of S$3,000 for those purchasing three room flats and S$8,000 for those purchasing four room or larger HDB flats), non-ownership of private properties at the time of application and citizenship status. The owners of a new HDB flat purchase a 99 year leasehold title on the flat. The government retains ownership of the land and common areas within the estate. Subletting of rooms within a flat (but not renting out the entire unit) is permissible. The sector may be considered a publicly managed private sector as home-owners usually finance their purchase with an HDB mortgage loan, and administration and maintenance of the estate is the responsibility of the town council which is chaired by the Member of Parliament for the constituency. As such, the state remains very involved even after the HDB flats are sold, albeit not in a direct controlling way.

A mature resale (secondary) market for these flats allow transactions at prices determined by market forces (see Figure 2.3 for the HDB resale price index), although the HDB continues to regulate eligibility and credit conditions. Various rules such as a minimum occupation period of five years before resale on the market are in place to curb speculative activity. There is significant mobility within the housing sector, with 58 per cent of households in 2000 having changed residences during 1991–2000 (Singapore Census of Population, 2000).

Since 1994, CPF Housing Grants (of up to S$50,000 per flat) have been introduced for the purchase of resale flats provided the household meets eligibility conditions. In recent years, a combination of factors – economic recession, overbuilding, demand side subsidies and administered prices that were not adjusted downwards have led to a situation of excess supply of new HDB flats (17,500 in early 2002).

Prices for new HDB flats are administered prices and are relatively more stable than resale prices. Prices for three and four room flats are pegged to average household income levels to ensure that at least 90 per cent of all households can afford a three room repurchased flat[7] and 70 per cent a new four room flat (HDB Annual Report 1996–97, 17). The ratio of the average price of a five room flat to per capita GNP has been below 6.5. This is comparable to the range of housing price affordability ratios for the OECD countries.[8] In the first quarter of 2005, the price range for four room flats purchased directly from the HDB was between S$85,000 and S$297,000, while the range for five room flats was between S$161,000 and S$450,000, with prices varying with location and design.

Rental public housing

The public housing rental sector represents the social housing sector in Singapore, especially since rent control in the private housing sector has been phased out. It is completely regulated by the HDB and provides minimum standard housing (one or two room flats) for families whose household income must not exceed S$1,500 per month at the time of application. Households in the income ceiling range of between S$801 to S$1,500 pay monthly rentals pegged at 30 per cent of the market rent. For households with incomes not exceeding S$800, the monthly rentals are around ten per cent of the market rate. A proportion of rental units also caters to 'transitional' families waiting for their Home Ownership flats as well as to foreign workers in Singapore.

7　The HDB purchases three-room flats in the resale market and sells them to eligible households at a price discount.

8　Miles (1994, p. 98) presents estimates of the average price of a new house as proportion of per capita GDP in 1990: UK (6.6), US (5.4), France (5.3), Germany (10.6), Netherlands (4.8), Sweden (4.1), Japan (9.2), Italy (5.7) and Canada (5.9).

Private home-ownership sector

The private housing sector caters largely to the upper echelons of Singapore society, expatriates, and foreign investors. Over time, dwindling private land supply (freehold and 999 year leaseholds) has increased the importance of government land sales (99 year leaseholds) for residential development in determining the level of new supply. On the supply side, planning regulations on density, land use and redevelopment of private properties affect the responsiveness of private supply to market conditions. Government regulations affect the sector in other important ways. Foreigners are prohibited from owning private landed properties and private flats in buildings of less than six storeys without government approval. Foreign demand for housing assets in Singapore is thus effectively confined to the private flats and condominiums.

Hybrid regulated private housing

Executive Condominiums are classified as private housing, but purchasers face many of the restrictions that apply to HDB home-owners. As mentioned earlier, the government auctions state land on a 99 year leasehold basis for the development of EC units to housing developers (private as well as government-linked companies) who are responsible for design, construction, pricing, arrangements for financing and estate management. Applicant households have to satisfy eligibility conditions and abide by resale and other regulations governing these units (household income below S$10,000 per month). The units can be sold only after five years to Singaporeans and permanent residents, and can be sold after ten years to foreigners. Buyers of EC cannot buy an HDB flat directly from the government again, although first-time home-owners are eligible for the CPF housing grant which can be used toward the down payment.

Rental private housing

Rent control has been completely phased out and rents in the non-controlled private housing sector are market determined, with the sector catering mainly to the expatriate population in Singapore.

The Socio-Economic Benefits of Singapore's Housing Welfare Model

Improvements in the urban environment and the standards of housing in Singapore over the past three decades provide very tangible and visible evidence of the success of the economic development and housing strategy adopted by the Singapore government. This overwhelming success has been well documented in the existing literature (see references in previous section). Table 2.1 provides an overview of the macro-economic and housing sector indicators for 1970, 1980, 1990 and 2000.

As described in the previous section, Singapore's housing sector is a rather unique hybrid of public-private elements that has worked for the city-state. Faced with a largely immigrant population, a grave housing shortage as well as insufficient private sector resources and capacity to provide an adequate solution, the government took upon itself the task of building a home-owning society. That a large public housing programme could deliver satisfactory housing for the majority in a relatively affluent city testifies to the production efficiency and responsiveness to changes of the Singapore government. This public provision of a private good on a large scale was accompanied by numerous regulations on eligibility, resale and financing, which in the earlier decades resulted in some consumption inefficiencies (Phang 1992). The public-private hybrid has however allowed the government to regulate, deregulate and re-regulate the sector with changes in socio-economic as well as market conditions. This section highlights the following favorable socio-economic effects of the housing welfare approach:

Increase in savings rate

At the inception of the CPF home-ownership scheme in 1968, the Gross National Saving to GNP ratio was less than 20 per cent (see Table 2.1) and insufficient to fund the country's investment needs (32 per cent of GNP). The increase in CPF mandatory contribution rates to a peak of 25 per cent of wages for employees and 25 per cent for employers by the mid 1980s contributed to a significant leap in the savings rate to more than 50 per cent of GNP by 2000 – certainly the highest savings rate in the world and more than sufficient to meet the country's investment needs.

Increase in quantity and quality of housing stock

The housing welfare approach enabled Singapore to mobilize long term resources on the demand side to finance the rapid supply of housing by the public sector with minimal involvement of government expenditure. Krugman (1994) has critically described the overall process as 'a mobilization of resources that would have done Stalin proud'. Within three decades of its existence, the HDB had solved the housing shortage problem and had progressed to providing larger and better quality flats for upper-middle income households (comparable in quality to and competing with private sector built apartments), redevelopment of older estates, and retrofitting existing flats. By 2004, the HDB had 876,000 flats under its management, 94 per cent of which were owner-occupied, and 68 per cent of which were four room or larger units (see Table 2.1 for comparison with earlier years). Upgrading within the HDB sector has been facilitated by the development of an active secondary market and a system that allows an eligible household to apply for a second (usually larger) subsidized flat after a minimum occupation period.

Increase in home-ownership rate

The development of well functioning mortgage markets, though desirable in itself, is often viewed as a means to achieving a higher home-ownership rate. Home-ownership is considered a merit good deserving of policy attention by most societies and various policies and institutional arrangements exist to provide incentives for home-ownership by reducing its costs relative to renting. In addition to government provision of affordable subsidized HDB housing and HDB mortgage loans, the policy of allowing high mandatory savings to be used for home purchase and not rental made home-ownership the dominant option for almost all Singaporean households. Not surprisingly, and given sustained income increases and low unemployment rates, the home-ownership rate for the resident population increased from 29 per cent in 1970 to 88 per cent by 1990 (see Table 2. 1), and was 93 per cent for 2004.

Development of mortgage market

Housing policy has contributed in a major way to the development of the mortgage sector in Singapore. In 1970, shortly after the implementation of the CPF Approved Housing Scheme, outstanding housing loans were a mere S$215 million (see Table 2.1). This constituted only four per cent of GNP, a figure within the range presently prevailing in Central Europe and Russia (Renaud, 2004). Even at that early stage, HDB loans had already exceeded banks and finance houses loans, comprising 58 per cent of the total. With increases in home-ownership rates and housing prices (see Figure 2.3), housing loans grew rapidly from S$215 million in 1970 to S$113,081 million by 2003. The 2003 ratio of outstanding housing loans to GDP at 71 per cent is certainly the highest in Asia (compare Hong Kong at 39 per cent, Japan 35 per cent, Taiwan 26 per cent, Malaysia 22 per cent, Thailand 16 per cent, Korea 14 per cent, Philippines 12 per cent and China eight per cent).[9]

Despite the increase in the population residing in HDB flats over time and hence increases in HDB mortgage loans, commercial banks[10] have maintained their share of the housing loans market (at more than 40 per cent). Since January 2003, the HDB has stopped providing market rate loans to buyers who are not eligible for its concessionary rate loans. This constituted a deliberate policy to increase the market share for commercial banks. Within the year, bank origination of HDB mortgage loans and refinancing of existing HDB loans grew to S$3.5 billion by the end of 2003 (Monetary Authority of Singapore, 2003/2004). This has increased commercial banks' share of housing loans from 41 per cent in 2000 to 47 per cent in 2003, with the proportion set to increase further in the future.

---

9   Figures for other Asian countries are from Renaud (2004) and are for 2001-2002.

10 Commercial banks here include Credit POSB and finance houses. See Phang (2001) for details of financial institutions involved in housing loans origination in Singapore.

Social policy

The large public-built-private-owned housing sector plays an extremely important role in the shaping of Singapore society. The physical plans of HDB new towns have been designed to integrate the various income and racial groups within the public housing programme, and this has prevented the development of low-income or ethnic ghettos. Singapore is a multi-racial society[11] where racial issues are considered potentially explosive and therefore carefully managed. The colonial administration had in its early days of town planning, followed a policy of racial segregation. Together with the communist threat, the management of racial tensions (there were race riots on a number of occasions) was a major political challenge in the 1960s. Beginning in the 1970s, the HDB allocated new flats in a manner that would give a 'good distribution of races' to different new towns. The public housing programme provided the government with a potent tool to break up ghettos and through such dispersion to contribute to social integration and nation-building. However, by 1988, a trend of ethnic regrouping through the resale market was highlighted as a housing problem, which would lead to the re-emergence of ethnic enclaves. In 1989, the HDB implemented an Ethnic Integration Policy under which racial limits were set for HDB neighbourhoods. When the set racial limits for a neighbourhood is reached, those wishing to sell their HDB flats in the particular neighbourhood had to sell it to another household of the same ethnic group. The government had emphasised that 'our multiracial policies must continue if we are to develop a more cohesive, better integrated society. Singapore's racial harmony, long term stability, and even viability as a nation depend on it' (Ooi et al. 1993, 14).

Housing policy has also been tailored to support the family institution, and to discourage individuals whether young or old, from living on their own. Singles, until today, remain ineligible to apply directly to the HDB for subsidized housing, although they have, since 1991, been allowed to purchase resale flats. Unmarried mothers are also similarly disqualified from applying directly to the HDB for subsidized housing. To promote closer family relations, a variety of housing priority schemes allowed applicants residing with or close to their parents/children a shorter waiting period before being allocated flats. Households applying for the CPF Housing Grant also enjoy an additional premium if the resale flat purchased is within the same town/estate or within two km for adjacent town of parents'/married child's residence.

In 1987, as part of a bevy of measures to encourage couples to have more children, a Third Child Priority Scheme allowed families with at least three children priority in obtaining larger HDB flats. The lower income group were however to be discouraged from having large families. Under the Small Families Improvement Scheme introduced in 1994, the poor were encouraged to limit their family size to no more than two children. In return, the children enjoy education bursaries, and a

---

11 The resident population is 76.8 per cent Chinese, 13.9 per cent Malay, 7.9 per cent Indian, and 1.4 per cent others (Census 2000).

housing grant of $16,000 is paid to the CPF account of the mother, which can be used to buy a three or four room HDB flat.

The HDB is also empowered to fine errant residents, cancel applications, and evict families for various offences such as late payment of bills, illegal renting out of entire flats, breaking immigration laws by harboring illegal immigrants, or being convicted for a 'killer-litter' offence. Motorists who do not pay their parking fines are also not given the keys to their flats until they pay their fines.

Impact on economic distribution

The vast majority of households in Singapore have benefited from access to ownership of affordable public housing. The active resale market allows for mobility within and out of the market and for the benefits of price discounts to be capitalized after a minimum occupancy period. Each household is allowed to apply twice for a 'housing subsidy' (a price discounted flat or a CPF grant) that has been described as 'a ticket to an easier life for the HDB heartlander' (*The Straits Times*, 19 April 1997). A study of housing wealth by Phang (2001) indicates that the 86 per cent of households residing in HDB flats owned at least 48 per cent of the gross housing wealth (HDB households are also allowed to own other private residential properties provided they satisfy various requirements). Housing policy and housing asset inflation have over time increased both gross and net housing wealth significantly. This has however contributed to a situation where housing price appreciation and depreciation (see Figure 2.3), with their attendant wealth and distributive consequences, have become politicized issues.

Another related measure has been the retrofitting (upgrading) of older public housing estates at considerable public expense since 1989. This multi-billion dollar exercise is part of the government's 'Asset Enhancement' programme and represents yet another round of subsidies for households that benefit from the substantial improvements made to their homes and housing estates. House type as a proxy for household wealth has also become a means of facilitating redistribution via the budget. The regressivity of the Goods and Services Tax implemented in 1994 was offset by annual rebates (announced as part of the fiscal budget and *varying with flat type*) to households residing in public housing in the form of waivers on rents and service and conservancy charges (S&CC). In 2001, S&CC rebates were implemented to help lower income Singaporeans cope with the recession. In the 2002 budget, rent and S&CC rebates for HDB flats were extended to 2008. Since 2000, transfers to individuals in the form of CPF Top Ups, New Singapore Shares and Economic Restructuring Shares used house type and/or house value as one of the factors in determining allotment.

Contributions to macro-economic growth and stabilization

Sandilands (1992) describes the construction sector as a leading sector, as its growth rates were above the rate of growth of overall GDP, and because its fluctuations were a leading indicator of fluctuations (down as well as up) in GDP. Between 1965–98, the real growth rate of the construction sector averaged 9.4 per cent per annum while average real GDP growth was 8.8 per cent. Despite the various inefficiencies associated with the regulated nature of the housing sector, the priority accorded to housing has not had an adverse effect on overall economic growth.

The impact of housing policy on macro-economic stability in the short term is less clear. For the earlier period when a serious housing shortage existed, Wong and Wong (1975) estimated an impact multiplier for HDB construction activity at 1.277 for 1960–69. Low and Aw (1995, 42) mention the use of public housing activities as a macro-economic stabilizer to create income and employment whenever a recession loomed during the 1960s and early 1970s. However with increases in income and a tight labour market since the mid 1970s, the construction industry has become highly dependent on non-resident workers and has long ceased to be regarded as a venue through which domestic employment can be generated.

Krause et al. (1987) have suggested that public sector construction (especially by the HDB) has been used as a pump-priming device in times of economic slowdown in 1975–76 and 1982–83. The acceleration in public housing construction in 1982–83 was considered by Krause to have been excessive in that it contributed towards 'over-heating' of the economy and the property slump and recession which followed in 1985–87 (Krause, 161). 189,000 HDB flats were constructed during the Fifth Five-Year Building Programme when the original target set in 1980 was for the construction of 85,000 to 100,000 flats. It was hypothesized by Krause et al., that the acceleration in public housing construction served other than a growth objective – 1984 being an election year as well as a year for celebrating 25 years of achievement as an independent nation. As acknowledged by the then Prime Minister Lee, 'We made one of our more grievous mistakes in 1982–84 by more than doubling the number of flats we had previously built.' (Lee, K.Y. 2000, 120). The subsequent deceleration in public sector construction, although necessary, was also ill timed from a macro-economic stabilization perspective as it coincided with a decline in private sector construction as well as a slow down in general economic activity.

Besides HDB construction activity, government policy impacts on housing asset prices in other important ways. A study by Phang and Wong (1997) shows that policies on the availability of HDB and CPF finance for housing had the most significant impacts on housing prices. These policies include extending the use of CPF savings for private housing in 1981, liberalizing the terms of HDB mortgage loans for resale flats in 1993, and the introduction of CPF grants for purchasing HDB resale flats in 1994. Such 'shocks' on the demand side needed to be offset by government policies to generate the requisite supply, although these have not always been well synchronized. Citing the Minister Mentor Lee:

> I should have known that it does not pay to yield to popular pressure beyond our capacity to deliver. Yet I was party to a similar mistake in the early 1990s. As property prices rose, everybody wanted to make a profit on the sale of their old flat and then upgrade to a new one, the biggest they could afford. Instead of choking off demand by charging a levy to

reduce their windfall profits, I agreed that we accommodate the voters by increasing the number of flats built. That aggravated the real estate bubble and made it more painful when the currency crisis struck in 1997. Had we choked off the demand earlier, in 1995, we would have been immensely better off (Lee, K.Y. 2000, 121).

The asset bubble that developed in the early half of the 1990s was choked off when anti-speculation measures, in the form of capital gains taxation, were implemented in May 1996 (ahead of the 1997 Asian economic crisis). The HDB also tightened various regulations: in April 1997, HDB flat buyers were limited to two subsidized loans, where there had been no limit before. In May 1997, the HDB implemented various measures to curb housing demand of upgraders (households applying for a second new subsidized flat from the HDB). These measures include lengthening the time period before flat lessees are eligible to purchase a second new flat from the HDB from five to ten years, and revising the graded resale levy system.

The increasing integration of the private and public housing markets as evidenced by their increased substitutability and correlation in price trends (see Figure 2.3), provided policymakers with more housing market instruments to affect the housing market in other defined ways. First, the Executive Condominium scheme represents a private-public hybrid development that has allowed HDB to 'privatize' the construction and financing of its Executive flats. These flats are close substitutes for 99 year leasehold private condominiums that are open to foreign investors and therefore have seen the highest price volatility in the past. The supply of ECs thus provides the government with a direct instrument to affect prices in the sector and to ensure that housing for the upper middle group remains affordable.

Secondly, the government has also developed the capacity of government-linked companies (such as CapitaLand and Keppel Land) to compete in the housing developers market, thus reducing the oligopolistic power of a few large private developers in the small private housing market.

Thirdly, HDB pricing policy together with the CPF housing grant, introduced in 1994, has served a useful function of supporting prices in the HDB resale market amidst the recent economic downturn. Prices for HDB new flats have declined only marginally and these prices effectively set the floor for the housing market. With the recent decline in HDB resale flat prices, an increasing number of applicants on the queue for new flats opted out of waiting for their flat to purchase one on the resale market with the CPF grant. The rate of application for the CPF Housing Grant increased from 500 per month in 1997 to 2,200 per month by the end of 1998. In 1999, the HDB adjusted the S$40,000 grant downwards by S$10,000. The variability of the grant with market conditions provides the government with yet another policy to affect housing demand.

Finally, the extreme openness of the Singapore economy has meant that economic growth has been largely foreign investment and export driven, both of which are affected significantly by external factors. Pump-priming, in the traditional Keynesian sense of increased government expenditure, has limited effectiveness due to high leakages – an estimated 54 cents of every dollar spent leaks abroad through imports (Lee, H.L. 1999) so that the multiplier effect of government spending is small. In both the 1985 and 1998 recessions, the Singapore government utilized a cut in the employer's mandatory CPF contribution rate as a means of reducing wage costs and restoring competitiveness (from 25 to 10 per cent in 1986 and 20 to 10 per cent in 1999). In the absence of other measures, and given the prevalence of the use of the CPF contributions for housing mortgage payments, the CPF cuts would have increased the mortgage default rate and possibly affected the stability of lending institutions.[12] However, adjustments were concurrently made by the CPF to allow automatic withdrawal of funds from a member's CPF Special Account (meant for old age) to service mortgage payments, should there be a shortfall. The CPF Board also made bridging loans available for those who had depleted savings in both their Ordinary and Special Accounts.

The HDB as the largest player in the housing loans market made available various help schemes for those affected by the recession and/or CPF cut. These included a five-year reduction in monthly mortgage payments (payments to be reassessed from the sixth year), payment of mortgage loan arrears by instalments over six months to a year, deferment of payment, extension of loan repayment periods, and including more family members as joint owners. Such measures undoubtedly reduced the default rate on mortgage loans, thus contributing to the overall stability of the financial sector in the midst of the Asian crisis.

The extreme openness of the Singapore economy limits the macro-economic tools available to the government for short run stabilization purposes to the exchange rate and measures that directly affect business costs. The structure of the housing market has allowed the CPF contribution rate to be more effectively used as a discretionary instrument to affect labour cost. The integral comprehensiveness of economic, housing, and housing finance policies thus also serves the useful purpose of providing policy makers with the flexibility to steer housing policy to achieve desired (short as well as longer term) economic objectives.

Problems Associated with Singapore's Housing Welfare Model

The housing approach adopted in Singapore has undoubtedly increased the savings and home-ownership rates, mobilized resources for the housing sector and contributed to an increase in housing loans and the development of the primary mortgage market. However, the approach is not without its detractors. Singapore's

---

12 Low and Aw (1997) provide a description of how an increase in the CPF contribution rate is used as an anti-inflationary tool in mopping up excess liquidity and spending during times of rapid wage growth. However Low and Aw suggest (before the 1998 recession) that the CPF as a macro-economic stabilization tool has probably reached its limits as 'it would be too disruptive economically and politically to change the rules with so many people committed to large housing mortgages and repayments. This lock-in effect of many CPF schemes must also be noted as they effectively reduce the degree of flexibility the next time CPF adjustments are considered in any macro-economic stabilization exercise' (page 101).

housing strategy is inherently policy driven and centrally controlled, with major decisions on savings rate, savings allocation, land use, housing production and housing prices being largely determined by the government. It is, in other words, a neo-classical economist's nightmare. Pugh (1985), in the context of providing a set of operating guidelines for a good housing system, and advocating Singapore's strategy as a good model, writes:

> … do not be too perturbed if some orthodox (neo-classical) economists argue that housing is over-allocated by subsidy. Show them that 'subsidy' is a concept which cannot be fitted easily to housing, and produce counter arguments, which are respectable in economics, and which are readily available.

However, two decades and 35 years later, it may no longer be 'respectable' to continue to argue for the continuation of a system that has outlived certain aspects of its usefulness. While the CPF-HDB housing scheme had its merits in the past; the objectives that the scheme set out to achieve have been surpassed and the policy problem has become one of how to reduce its dominance with minimal upsets to asset values, household wealth and lenders' balance sheets. This section reviews a number of problems that have become associated with the large-scale directed credit to the housing sector, and may serve as guidance for other countries with, or contemplating, the adoption of similar schemes.

Crowding out

Singapore's housing strategy has been criticized for over-allocation of resources to housing, resulting in crowding out of consumption, as well as human capital and corporate investments. Despite widespread home-ownership and rapid increase in housing wealth, Phang (2004) found no evidence that house price increases have produced wealth or collateral enhancement effects on aggregate consumption. Instead, due to the mandatory nature of the CPF as well as households' inability to withdraw housing equity to finance consumption, households in Singapore face strong liquidity constraints. In addition to the welfare loss from consumption denied, Bhaskaran (2003) is of the view that the low percentage of disposable income spent has hurt the development of the retail sector in Singapore.

The CPF has also been blamed for a weak domestic corporate sector (since potential entrepreneurs are unable to access their savings for start-ups), and the crowding out of domestic private sector investments. The corporate sector in Singapore is dominated by MNCs and government-linked companies – the study by Bhaskaran (2003) confirms that indigenous firms earn lower returns than foreign-owned firms within Singapore, and lower returns as compared to listed companies in Hong Kong, Japan, Korea, Taiwan and the US. Krugman (1994) and Young (1992; 1995), for example, have questioned the basis and sustainability of Singapore's economic growth in a series of studies as far back as the early 1990s. Pointing to the low contribution of total factor productivity (TFP) growth, Krugman referred to the Singapore miracle as having been based on 'perspiration rather than inspiration'

– 'All of Singapore's growth can be explained by increases in measured inputs. There is no sign of increased efficiency.'

Housing sector impacts

Given the nature of the real estate industry, the tilt of resources to the housing sector is not easily matched by corresponding increases in supply. *Ceteris paribus*, one can infer that housing and land price levels in Singapore are higher with the CPF housing scheme than without. In the first decade (1968–81) when the CPF savings was directed only toward public housing, administered prices, stringent eligibility criteria, and long waiting lists were used to allocate the HDB's supply of new flats. Moreover, in the absence of a secondary market for HDB flats during that period, the inflationary impacts on a tightly regulated housing sector were not immediately apparent.

However, such mechanisms could not be used when savings were similarly directed to private housing beginning in 1981. The 1981 liberalization as well as the 1993 liberalization of HDB and CPF regulations for HDB resale flat housing loans had significant impacts on housing prices, contributing to the development of speculative bubbles that subsequently burst (Phang and Wong 1997).

When the CPF contribution rates were used for macro-economic stabilization, increased to mitigate inflationary pressures from higher wages (1978–84) or cut to reduce wage costs and preserve jobs (1985–98), the effect was to exacerbate the housing price boom and bust (see Figure 2.3 for housing price index) by channelling resources into real estate during an inflationary period and reducing resources to the sector during a recession.

Consumption inefficiencies

Singapore's mandatory savings and housing policies have very substantial impacts on households' consumption and investment patterns. Savers' and consumers' rights in decision-making are constrained by numerous CPF and HDB restrictions and regulations. Consumption inefficiencies arise when households value the in-kind transfers/subsidies at less than the costs of providing them, or alternatively, at less than an equivalent cost but unrestricted cash grant. Moreover, numerous regulations to prevent profiteering and speculation as well as restrictions in housing location choice resulted in inefficient location and commute patterns for households (Phang 1992).

Over the years, both the CPF and HDB have found it necessary to become more saver/consumer responsive and have liberalized regulations in order to reduce distortions and provide more investment as well as housing options. There is now a wider range of investment and merit good related consumption (education and health) options for CPF members. The shift toward demand-side subsidies in the form of CPF housing grants to subsidize the purchase of resale HDB housing since

1994 has been very well received. This has improved households' ability to optimize with regard to their housing options.

Retirement financing

The typical household in Singapore has the bulk of its wealth invested in housing (Phang 2001). Despite the high savings rate, overinvestment in housing and over exposure to the risk of a decline in housing price affecting the retirement (and healthcare) financing of an ageing population have become issues of policy concern, especially since the bursting of the real estate bubble in 1997 (see Figure 2.3). Lim (2001) projects that 60–70 per cent of the 50–55 years age group will not have sufficient funds in their account to meet the government stipulated minimum sum needed for retirement of S$80,000 in 2003.[13] Analyzing CPF data for 2000, Asher (2004) finds the average balance for active CPF contributors was S$53,000, equivalent to 1.27 times the per capita GNP – inadequate to finance retirement of more than 20 years duration on the average.

McCarthy et al. (2002) through simulations, show that the average worker in Singapore is likely to be 'asset-rich and cash-poor' upon retirement with 75 per cent of his retirement wealth in housing asset, provided housing values continue to rise in real terms. In contrast, an American elderly household would have only 20 per cent of their retirement wealth in housing asset. If the housing market were to take a downturn and remain depressed for years (as in Japan), this could reduce retirement asset accumulation for the Singapore worker substantially. This raises the problematic issue of over concentration of household assets in housing resulting in a risky under-diversified portfolio at retirement.

A report by the government appointed Economic Review Committee in 2002 arrived at a similar conclusion that CPF members were 'asset rich and cash-poor', and made recommendations to limit CPF withdrawals for housing, and for the government to explore ways for home-owners to monetize their property.[14] However, the committee was also cognizant of the need to implement changes gradually, in order not to further destabilize the fragile post Asian-crisis real estate sector. Agreeing with the committee's recommendations, the government moved to cap CPF withdrawals for housing at 150 per cent of the value of the property, with the

---

13 At age 55, a CPF member may withdraw his CPF savings, but is required to leave a minimum sum in the CPF of S$80,000, of which at least half must be in cash and the other S$40,000 may be in property. The cash amount is released in instalments from the age of 62 years until it is exhausted. The member may also choose to buy a life annuity with an insurance company or deposit it in a bank.

14 Economic Review Committee: Sub-committee on policies related to taxation, the CPF system, wages and land (2002). 'Refocusing the CPF system for enhanced security in retirement and economic flexibility.' Reverse mortgages in Singapore are available only for owners of fully-paid up private properties aged 55 or above. Between 1997–2004, only 215 home-owners have taken up loans worth S$100 million (channelnewsasia.com). Asher (2004) views the reverse mortgage as suffering from severe technical problems and high transactions costs.

cap moving down gradually to 120 per cent over five years for new private housing loans.

Lack of unemployment insurance

With recent changes in the macro-economic environment, unemployment rates above five per cent for 2002–04, and greater volatility in economic growth, there is growing concern over structural unemployment associated with the restructuring of the economy. Various programmes exist to help the unemployed find jobs, upgrade their skills or retrain for employment, so that they can become economically independent again. These programmes may be considered *short-term* unemployment benefits under a different name. However, the lack of unemployment insurance and limited public social assistance available when structural unemployment is expected to be long term has led some to question the viability of the current welfare system. Yap (2002) has proposed that an employment insurance scheme be introduced as another component of the CPF. Asher (2004) makes a strong case for the introduction of tax financed schemes to address the needs of the *lifetime* poor, and social risk pooling to address longevity and inflation risks. According to him:

> This case has become stronger due to the unilateral alteration of the implicit social contract by the government. This contract provided for acceptance of government's socio-economic engineering and political control in return for job security and full employment. The government is not able to fulfill the latter element, but still wants to continue to undertake socio-engineering and maintain political control. This is a disequilibrium situation, which will need to be resolved.

However, Asher acknowledges that the prospects for the required mind-set change by policymakers are not encouraging.

Financial sector development

As required by the CPF Act, the CPF channels members' deposits to the purchase of government bonds. The government through the Government of Singapore Investment Corporation invests the bulk of the funds directly abroad, thus bypassing Singapore's financial markets. Bhaskaran (2003) contrasts the 'remarkably poorly developed' status of Singapore's savings industry against its high savings rate. 'Financial planners, unit trusts, stock brokers, pension funds, pension advisors, wealth management associated with middle-class households, financial journals, etc are all under-represented in Singapore compared to say Hong Kong.' It has also been observed that the debt market in Singapore has remained relatively unsophisticated and illiquid due primarily to the cash rich public sector and the dominance of MNCs that typically do not depend on domestic sources of capital (Committee on Singapore's Competitiveness, 1998).

A similar observation can be made with regard to the mortgage sector. While the housing loans to GDP ratio has exceeded 70 per cent, more than half of outstanding housing loans are originated by the HDB, which in turn obtains mortgage-funding loans from the government. The HDB is not a financial institution while the CPF is described as a non-bank financial institution. The size of the mortgage *market* as such is smaller than one would expect, given the high loan to GDP ratio. The mortgage sector's linkages with capital markets are weak and mortgage instruments relatively unsophisticated – there is no secondary mortgage market.

In recent years, efforts to improve the mortgage sector's linkages with capital markets have taken a number of forms: (a) though the government traditionally runs a budget surplus each year and has no need to borrow, the issue of bonds by the government and statutory boards to create a bond market has been undertaken with the objective of establishing a S$ yield curve for the debt market. In line with the objective, the HDB has started issuing bonds from 1999 to fund its building programmes; (b) from 2002, instead of the CPF having first claim on a property if a borrower defaults on his housing loans (which protects his retirement savings), banks have been given first claim for private housing loans, thus paving the way for standardizing mortgages for securitization; (c) from 2003, banks have also been allowed to make loans to those buying HDB flats with unsubsidized housing loans and to offer refinancing for these loans; banks would also enjoy first charge over the CPF for these HDB properties (Phang 2003). These efforts to enlarge the role of commercial banks in the mortgage market will help to improve the integration of the mortgage sector with the rest of the financial sector.

Governance issues

Pension fund governance issues relating to the responsibilities of trustees, accountability, and transparency are important areas of concern for all stakeholders. In the US for example, the principles and procedures required of pension fund fiduciaries are legislated under the Employee Retirement Income Security Act. In the Singapore context, the CPF balances due to members at S$110 billion (in September 2004) are considerable. Their ultimate investment by the Government Investment Corporation of Singapore has however been described by Asher (2002) as 'by law non-transparent and non-accountable, leading to a highly regressive large tax on provident fund wealth and to low replacement rates'. These concerns as well as that of ensuring the core administrative tasks are performed satisfactorily are major challenges for any mandatory pension scheme.

Transferability of Singapore's Housing Welfare Experience

The success of the Singapore's housing welfare model demonstrates what can be achieved with strategic planning to mobilize resources and guide key investments. Complemented by close attention to the supply part of the equation as well as policies which created markets over time and accommodated private initiatives to fill the gaps, the process has helped Singapore to avoid the worst outcomes of the extremes of central planning and unplanned growth. Numerous city governments in former socialist countries and in Asia are also major landowners, yet the absence of markets often makes these cities inefficient. Those cities can learn much from Singapore's planning process and its active role in creating markets.

However, while similar approaches have been adopted by governments elsewhere, it is, in this day and age, difficult to find strong advocates for government-centered housing welfare systems. The transferability of Singapore's experience needs to be juxtaposed with the local political and social context, in particular, the city-state's ability to control the entry of migrants who can impose a strain on the housing service sector. Moreover, the tactics on which Singapore relies – compulsory savings, state land ownership, and state provision of housing, complemented by an extensive public sector – could easily have spawned widespread inefficiency and corruption.

Singapore's effective implementation of such planning and regulation is attributable to a network of competent and reliable organizations that together provide rich public sector capacity. The quality of public administration in Singapore is a result of recruitment based on merit, competitive pay benchmarked against private sector salaries, extensive computerization and a civil service culture of zero tolerance for corruption (Phang 2000). Where governments and public sector leadership are weak and/or corrupt, such extensive intervention and government control over resource allocation can be potentially abused and may carry a higher cost than inaction. The need for strong legislation and a proper fund governance structure to ensure that the interests of provident fund members are adequately protected cannot be overemphasized.

The housing welfare strategy is itself a legacy of the post-World War II years, when 'only governments could marshal the resources necessary to rebuild devastated and dislocated nations' (Yergin and Stanislaw 2002). In the last two decades, the focus of attention has shifted from market failure to government failure – with privatization and deregulation as the preferred strategy generally, as well as in the development the housing sector. The present concerns faced by Singaporeans, in particular the lack of unemployment safety nets and the possible inadequacy of personal resources for retirement and healthcare in the future, serve to highlight the risks of overemphasizing housing in the welfare system for too long. Policymakers now have to grapple with tradeoffs and difficult decisions in trying to reduce the dominance of housing welfare without adversely affecting housing asset markets.

Chapter 3

The State-managed Housing System in Hong Kong

K Y Lau

Introduction

In Hong Kong out of a total land area of 1,097 square kilometres, 83 per cent is non-built up land and only 5.3 per cent is residential built up area. 6.7 million people are housed in a high-density residential environment. The 2001 Census shows that out of 2.24 million available units in total there are 2.05 million households living in 2.01 million domestic units. The state has played a major role in the development of the housing market in Hong Kong. This chapter sets out the longer term development of what is best described as a state-managed housing system and goes on to refer in more detail to changes since 1987.

The State-managed Housing System

The Hong Kong housing system is described in this chapter as a state-managed system. The principle of state intervention in housing has been to enable the provision of social housing while at the same time encouraging private developers to provide a commercial and lively housing market. This has involved other objectives than simply providing assistance for the needy to solve their housing problems. The earliest estates were built to ease clearance of squatter areas, and release land useful for economic development. The active promotion of a state supported home-ownership policy was also driven by economic considerations – to recoup cash proceeds from sales, (to pay for capital expenses arising from new public sector housing programmes), and to provide a cheaper subsidy to help those in housing need into home-ownership and to cross-subsidise the Housing Authority's deficit accounts in social rented housing.

The economic considerations of the Ten Year Housing Programme were stated clearly by Donald Liao, former Chairman of the Hong Kong Housing Authority (HKHA):

[The Governor, Sir Murray MacLehose] thought that the economic growth of the 1960s had enabled citizens to basically solve the problems of food and clothing. But the problem of shelter was still outstanding. Hong Kong did not have sufficient land to build on, and the cost of gaining land by levelling or reclamation was high. Naturally, land and property prices were high and unaffordable for the average citizen. If the government could actively participate in providing low-cost housing for needy citizens, society would not only gain stability, the construction of housing estates would increase employment opportunities and stimulate consumption, and so bring further economic growth. (Leung 1999, 142–3)

Hence state invention in housing is considered important and necessary for the survival of a capitalist society such as that in Hong Kong. Castells (1977) regards housing as an integral part of the process of 'collective consumption' in cities. Castells and his colleagues (Castells et al. 1988), argue that the government of Hong Kong has played a decisive role in the Territory's economic growth and that Hong Kong is also a case of state-led economic development. Housing is important where economic policy is state driven as in Hong Kong. Public housing serves as a comprehensive social wage system, which in turn fosters and sustains economic development (Castells et al. 1990, 5) and the government also recognizes the social functions of housing intervention. As capital concentrates and centralizes, the labour reproduction process becomes more interdependent and reliant upon a range of consumption needs that cannot be met efficiently or profitably by private capital. A public housing authority (such as HKHA), is needed to provide necessary housing assistance to counter the undesirable effects of a market economy.

When the Hong Kong government first became involved in social housing provision in 1954, only basic shelter of minimal standards was provided for families affected by squatter clearance projects, or by fire and natural disasters. About ten years later, housing standards improved for new social housing, as self-contained housing units were built to house the needy. In 1973, when the Ten Year Housing Programme began, more public rental housing units were built in the New Towns and a large-scale redevelopment of non-self-contained resettlement estates was rolled out (Table 3.1). About 25 years after the government's first involvement in social housing, it expanded its involvement by building or encouraging private sector developers to build subsidized flats for sale to target recipients (the well off public tenants in social housing and the low- to middle-income private tenant households aspiring to become home-owners).

Table 3.1 Key developments in housing policy in Hong Kong

Period/ Year	Housing Development		Main Features
	What happened?	**Policy issues**	
Before 1954	No provision of public housing	Housing shortages, poor housing conditions	Non-intervention
1954–64	Provision of basic shelter to meet needs of some low-income households in squatter areas and in old tenement blocks	Response to Christmas fire 1953 and thousands of homeless families; illegally occupied land cleared for economic development; low rent housing provision as social wage to reduce labour costs	Housing shortage
1965–72	All public rental housing flats built to meet self-contained social housing standards	Non-self-contained resettlement housing blocks built in the past seen as not meeting basic needs	Meeting minimum housing standards
1973	Housing organizations merged and reconstituted to form a new Hong Kong Housing Authority. Expansion of social housing/New Town programme and redevelopment of substandard public rental estates	Announcement of Ten Year Housing Programme as one of the four pillars; redevelopment of 240 non-self-contained resettlement housing blocks affecting 84,450 households, inducing people to move to less densely populated New Towns	Improvement of housing quality
1977	HKHA Home Ownership Scheme and Private Sector Participation Scheme	Subsidized built-for-sale flats become exit points for better off public tenants and an entry point for low- to middle-income private tenants aspiring to become home owners	Promotion of home-ownership with in-kind subsidized housing
1987	Housing Subsidy Policy	Policy devised to make better off tenants pay additional rents	Reduction of housing subsidy to less deserving tenants

Period/Year	Housing Development		Main Features
	What happened?	Policy issues	
1987	Long Term Housing Strategy announced - to include Comprehensive Redevelopment Programme	Extension of redevelopment programme to include resettlement blocks built between 1965 and 1972	Housing quality upgrading
1988	Home Purchase Loan Scheme (interest free help with down-payment on private sector purchase)	Private Sector developers helped in meeting home-owning needs of low- to middle-income families	Consumer housing subsidy begun
1993	Sandwich Class Housing Loan Scheme followed by Sandwich Class Housing Scheme	Government responses to demand from all parties to help group finding private sector housing increasingly unaffordable	Meeting needs of middle-income households' home purchase
1996	Safeguarding Rational Allocation of Public Housing Resource Policy (SRA) introduced	Policy set to require well-off tenants to declare their assets, after paying double rent for two years. Households with net assets above the prescribed limits were required to pay market rent	Removal of housing subsidy to tenants deemed not to need state assistance
1997	Hong Kong Special Administrative Region (SAR) Chief Executive announced his three housing pledges after 1 July 1997 handover	Three targets: 85,000 annual housing production; 70 % home-ownership rate by 2007; average waiting time for public rental housing applicants be cut to three years by 2005	Further promotion of home-ownership through enhanced schemes and meeting poor families' need quickly
1997	Economic downturn and property prices drop due to Asian financial crisis	Land/house price fall	House shortage ended

Period/ Year	Housing Development		Main Features
	What happened?	Policy issues	
1998	Tenants' Purchase Scheme Phase 1 (a total of six phases involving about 250,000 tenant households)	Tenants of selected public rental estates given opportunity to buy rental units at deeply discounted price	Privatization of public sector housing
1998	Promulgation of Housing White Paper. Home Starter Loan Scheme introduced	Low-interest loan scheme introduced to help first-time home buyers	Induced demand for private housing
1998	Comprehensive Means Test (CMT). This test includes income and asset tests	Occupants affected by clearance projects on or after 11 September 1998 required to pass CMT	More controls on entry into public rental housing
1999	Termination of Sandwich Housing Scheme	Private sector housing prices continued to fall	State-managed housing system takes shape
2000	85,000 housing production target dropped by Chief Executive of H K SAR mid 2000. Sales under HOS/PSPS suspended for six months	Further fall in house prices	State-managed housing system developed further
2001	Another moratorium on the sale of HOS/ PSPS flats until mid 2003. Between mid 2003 and March 2005, annual sales of HOS/PSPS flats restricted to 9,000 units.	House prices continued to drop	State-managed housing system further developed

Period/ Year	Housing Development		Main Features
	What happened?	Policy issues	
2002	Government decision June to reduce annual build of HOS/PSPS flats to 2,000 units from 2006/07. In November 2002, Government issued Statement on Housing Policy that HOS/PSPS sale and production would cease indefinitely from 2003; Tenants' Purchase Scheme to halt after sale of Phases 6A and 6B; land sale suspended until end 2003.	Property prices continued to fall	A clear reflection of a strong state-managed housing system
2003	Home Purchase Loan Scheme and Home Starter Loan Scheme merged to form Home Assistance Loan Scheme (interest free).	Quota of Home Assistance Loan Scheme maintained at 10,000 to encourage the affordable to raise demand for private sector housing	Use of housing subsidy to improve market housing demand
2004	In mid–2004 the Government decided to terminate the Home Assistance Loan Scheme.	A reflection of government's repositioned policy of complete withdrawal from the private residential market	Social housing seen as safety net: state to cease promotion of home-ownership activities.

Policy Developments Since 1987

The state has played a major role in shaping housing tenure changes since 1987 (Table 3.2) by providing housing assistance through two public organizations: the Hong Kong Housing Authority (HKHA) and Hong Kong Housing Society (HKHS). Housing subsidy in Hong Kong has taken different forms: 'bricks and mortar' subsidy (in-kind subsidized housing) is the major form of housing assistance in Hong Kong.

Public Rental Housing (PRH) and built-for-sale subsidized housing schemes are typical of in-kind subsidized housing provision. Built-for-sale subsidized schemes include the Home Ownership Scheme (HOS), Private Sector Participation Scheme (PSPS), and Sandwich Class Housing Scheme, (SCHS). Over one million subsidized flats have been built in the past two decades.

Subsidies to induce households to purchase owner-occupied dwellings, as interest free/low interest loans or as rent allowance to help meet part of rental charges in private sector rented dwellings, have been adopted as alternatives. This latter approach is normally known as consumer subsidy.

A consumer subsidy was introduced in 1988 as a non-interest bearing loan (the Home Purchase Loan Scheme, HPLS[1]) to encourage eligible applicants to purchase private sector flats. By September 2003, HKHA had granted 56,700 and 3,300 loans/ subsidies under the Home Purchase Loan Scheme (HPLS) or the Home Assistance Loan Scheme (HALS) for the purchase of flats. On top of the HPLS/HALS, there were below-market interest-bearing loan schemes:

- the Sandwich Class Housing Loan Scheme: between 1993–97, benefiting 5,700 families.
- the Home Starter Loan Scheme: later merged with the HPLS to form the Home Assistance Loan Scheme (HALS) in 2003. Applications were closed on 31 March 2002. Altogether 23,735 families and 9,699 single people have benefited (Hong Kong Housing Society website 18 February 2005).

The pilot rent allowance scheme for elderly public rental housing allocation applicants was first introduced in July 2001. By early 2005 only 623 households had taken it up. Due to the low response[2] and the ample supply of PRH units the scheme was terminated in September 2003.

In early 2005, the Housing Authority decided also not to pursue rent allowances in helping families in need of assistance. After a four year feasibility study, a detailed subsidy comparison of rent allowances and public rental housing units (PRH) was considered by the HKHA. This showed that in terms of pure monetary costs, rent allowance was more than twice the cost of PRH.[3]

Altogether, fewer than 100,000 households were granted a loan or rent allowance. This is less than 10 per cent of the total number of households living in PRH/HOS/ PSPS flats. Table 3.2 shows the proportion of people housed in different forms of housing.

---

1   Successful applicants to the Home Purchase Loan Scheme could opt for a non-repayable monthly subsidy for 48 months after late 1991 in lieu of the lump-sum interest free loan.

2   17,000 letters were issued to eligible elderly persons to fill the 1,100 quota. Only 623 elderly households accepted the allowance for renting accommodation in the market.

3   HKHA (2005) Press Release 14 January 2005. This rent allowance cost does not include the foregone land value.

Table 3.2 Key demographic, housing and economic statistics for Hong Kong, 1986, 1991, 1996 and 2001 (thousands)

	1986	1991	1996	2001
Population at mid year*	5,525	5,752	6,435	6,725
Number of households*	1,473	1,602	1,864	2,078
Tenure				
Owner-occupied	514	690	855	1,084
Subsidised sale flats	58	117	195	364
Private (including subsidized sale flats that can be traded in open market)**	456	573	660	720
Public rented	533	597	667	636
Private rented (included rent free)**	308	240	292	329
Temporary housing	119	74	49	29
Total GDP at constant (2000) market prices (HK$ thousand Million)	646	879	1,134	1,294
Change over the preceding year (%)	+11.2	+5.3	+4.6	+0.5
Per Capita GDP ($ thousand)	117	153	175	192
Unemployment (Number)	76	50	89	175
%	2.8	1.8	2.8	5.1
Underemployment (Number)	46	45	53	85
%	1.7	1.6	1.7	2.5

Notes: *Census and Statistics Department *Statistics on Domestic Households* http://www.info.gov.hk/censtatd/eng/hkstat/fas/pop/by_sex.xls>
* Census and Statistics Department *Statistics on Domestic Households.* <http://www.info.gov.hk/censtatd/eng/hkstat/fas/pop/domestic_hh.htm>
** Figures are calculated according the data extracted from *Hong Kong Annual Digest of Statistics* 2001 & 2002 eds. and *Hong Kong Social and Economic Trends 1997, 1999 eds.*

Sources: 1986 figures are extracted from Hong Kong Census and Statistics Department, *Hong Kong Annual Digest of Statistics* 1996 edition, pp. 8, 14 and *Hong Kong Social and Economic Trends* 1997 ed. 119, 121.
1991 figures are extracted from Hong Kong Census and Statistics Department, *Hong Kong Annual Digest of Statistics* 2001 edition, xiii, 5, 12, 13, 21, 22.
1996 figures are extracted from Hong Kong Census and Statistics Department, *Hong Kong Annual Digest of Statistics* 2001 edition, xiii, 5, 12, 13, 21, 22.
2001 figures are extracted from Hong Kong Census and Statistics Department, *Hong Kong Annual Digest of Statistics* 2002 edition, xiii, 12, 13, 21, 22.

Social Housing as a Safety Net

Social rental housing has provided a safety net for the poor in Hong Kong. It combines this with clearance of illegal squatter huts occupying valuable sites suitable for economic and social development. Since 1987 the Hong Kong Housing Authority has become more aware of the need to conserve public rental housing resources. Policies were devised to encourage better off public tenants to leave the sector and to restrict the entry of better off private households (affected by clearance projects). After the late 1980s, the role of the state in managing scarce public rental housing resources has been subject to change. The state managed housing system has been further enhanced as government delimited its role in housing provision after the Asian financial crisis in 1997.

Allocation of public rental housing resources

There are two sets of policies targeted at existing and prospective public tenant households. The first set deals with well off public tenants already accommodated. This comprises the Housing Subsidy Policy (HSP), introduced in 1987 and revised in 1993, and the Safeguarding the Rational Allocation of Public Housing Resources Policy (SRA) implemented in 1997 and revised in 1999. The second set is called Comprehensive Means Test Policy (CMT), which deals with all prospective tenants of public rental housing. Applicants subject to CMT policy include those already on the waiting list, those affected by clearance projects, and those seeking to inherit a grant of new tenancy following a death. All of them need to pass tests of income and assets. Various policies developed and implemented in the past two decades have rectified the shortcomings of the non-discriminatory nature of former policies. Those policies targeted at the needy in public estates have broadened in scope and were developed incrementally. The Housing Subsidy Policy introduced in 1987 was the first policy to ensure the effective and rational allocation of housing resources. Under this policy, tenants who had been living in public housing for ten years or more[4] were required to declare their income every alternate year to determine their continued eligibility for housing subsidy. Those whose declared household income exceeded the Subsidy Limit (which was twice the Waiting List Income Limit) and those who failed to declare, had to pay double net rent plus rates. In April 1994, the Housing Subsidy Policy was subsequently revised and implemented. Under this revised policy, tenants with a household income between two to three times the Waiting List Income Limits are required to pay 1.5 times net rent plus rates. Those with an income above three times the Waiting List Income Limits are now required to pay double net rent plus rates. By April 1992, 34 per cent (or 63,058 households)

---

4 Before 1 June 1996, tenants affected by involuntary transfers (Comprehensive Redevelopment Programmes and major improvement programmes) were not subject to HSP after ten years' residence in PRH. After that date they were not granted a ten-year exemption from HSP upon rehousing.

of 187,232 households who had been living in PRH for ten years were paying double net rent plus rates. This represented 11 per cent of the HKHA's total number of tenant households (570,557 in April 1992). After the modifications to the Subsidy Income Limits, the total number of households paying extra rent recorded a drop of 23 per cent from its height at 63,058 in April 1992 to 48,880 in April 1994. Out of 48,880 households, 34,979 paid double net rent plus rates and 13,901 paid one and a half net rent plus rates. They represented 8.3 per cent of all households in the HKHA's rental units. In subsequent years the number of double-rent paying households dropped further. As at 1 April 2003, only 3,346 households were paying double rent – less than 6 per cent of the number in April 1993. The number of households paying 1.5 times the net rent has become more stable since April 1998 – around 16,000 households in April of each financial year.

The principle underlying the changes to the Subsidy Income Limits in the existing HSP policy is a clear reflection of the authority's understanding and consideration of the financial position of tenant households at different stages of their life cycle.

> The household income of PRH tenants will increase as their children grow up but will drop when their children move out subsequently. By allowing tenants an option to stay in their PRH units by paying higher rents when they are in good financial position and to revert to normal rents when their income drops, will do them far more good than evicting them. (HKHA 1993)

The relaxation of the Housing Subsidy Limit (in terms of monthly household income) has allowed many better off tenants to stay in PRH and hence resulted in a mixed income community.

The Housing Authority endorsed in April 1996 the implementation of the Policy on Safeguarding Rational Allocation of Public Housing Resources (SRA) whereby household income and net asset value were adopted as the two criteria for determining whether public rental housing (PRH) tenants could continue to receive public housing subsidy.

Under this policy, tenants paying double rent were required to declare their net assets at two-yearly intervals. For the first batch of double rent paying tenants declaring their net assets in mid 1996, if their household net assets exceeded 110 times the Waiting List Income Limits (these limits are generally known as Net Asset Limits, NAL) they were required to pay market rent. However, the following categories of households were exempted from income and asset declarations: (a) households on shared tenancies; (b) households receiving Comprehensive Social Security Assistance; and (c) households with all members aged 60 or over. Households choosing not to make a declaration of net assets had to pay market rents.

The Net Asset Limits were determined at a level that enabled a household to acquire alternative accommodation of a standard comparable to a Home Ownership Scheme flat. The limits were reviewed annually with regard to prevailing Home Ownership Scheme prices and set with reference to the prices of three-bedroom Home Ownership Scheme (HOS) flats in the urban area with variations allowed for household sizes. The 2002/03 asset limits were set at about 84 times the 2002/2003

Waiting List Income Limits (WLIL). These limits were subject to review annually having regard to the price of prevailing HOS flats.

To encourage better off tenants to vacate public rental flats for reallocation among more needy families, double-rent and market-rent paying tenants not in possession of private domestic properties were given second priority in the purchase of public Home Ownership Scheme flats, without quota restriction (HKHA 1995).

In order to ensure the recovery of flats for reuse, on 4 February 1999 the Housing Authority Rental Housing Committee endorsed a new policy that Market Rent paying households should be asked to quit. To allow reasonable time for these households to seek alternative accommodation, they will be served a Notice to Quit (NTQ) but will be allowed subsequently to stay put on an application basis for a temporary period of not more than 12 months. During this temporary stay, a licence fee will be charged equivalent to the market rent of the flat occupied. Moreover households required to quit under the revised SRA policy and not in possession of domestic properties are accorded first priority in HOS/PSPS flat selection.

It is evident that there has been a significant drop in the number of market rent paying households (from 3,606 in April 1997 to 149 in April 2003). Between April 1988 and March 2003, 19,421 households paying additional rent (including those paying 1.5 times the net rent, double rent and market rent) purchased HOS or PSPS flats and moved out. In the same period, 3,557 households paying additional rent made use of the interest-free loan or monthly subsidy provisions under the Home Purchase Loan Scheme (HPLS) and left the PRH sector. In addition, 8,155 households paying additional rent voluntarily surrendered their PRH flats for reallocation. In other words, a total of 31,133 PRH flats have been recovered from the well off tenants for reallocation to the needy. Consequently the number of well off tenants has decreased.

The implementation of the Comprehensive Means Test (CMT) policy has finally put the Housing Authority back on track in ensuring that applicants admitted to the PRH sector are those in genuine need. Whilst the number of cases screened out is small, the principle of allocating PRH to those in genuine need of housing has become firmly anchored.

The impact of the measures inducing better off tenants to leave public rental sector housing has meant that the proportion of public tenant households in the top income decile group has dropped from 4 per cent in 1981 to 1 per cent in 2001.[5]

From Home-ownership Promotion to Withdrawal of Home Assistance Subsidies

The Hong Kong Government first engaged in promoting home ownership through the Home Ownership Scheme (HOS). This scheme was introduced in the mid 1970s, and the supplementary Private Sector Participation Scheme (PSPS), introduced in

---

5   Census data retrieved by City University of Hong Kong housing researchers.

1978, aimed to provide adequate flats for sale at prices well below market value to low-income or middle-income families. These families were not eligible to apply for Public Rental Housing (PRH) as their income exceeded the PRH Waiting List Income Limit but they were seen as not able to afford the increased cost of flats in the private market. On the other hand, the scheme also aimed to release the pressure on demand for PRH by selling the HOS flats to those public housing tenants not subject to any income limit.

Between 1979/80 and 2003/04, 325,556 HOS & PSPS flats were completed. These included 223,180 HOS flats (68.6 per cent) and 100,136 PSPS flats (31.4 per cent). On average, about 13,022 HOS & PSPS flats were produced annually in this 25 year period (8,927 HOS flats and 4,005 PSPS flats). The production peak was in 2000/01.

In 1979/80, the first HOS project was completed with 2,439 HOS flats – a number exceeded in each of the next 25 years. Apart from the first phase, the lowest annual production of HOS and PSPS flats was in 1994/95.

From 1979/80–1998/99, HOS & PSPS flats accounted for an increasing proportion of overall production of HKHA public housing flats. At the end of 1998/99, 63 per cent of the HKHA public housing flats were HOS & PSPS flats. However, the proportion dropped to 16 per cent in 2001/02 as policies on reducing HOS & PSPS production were implemented. Table 3.3 shows the production of HOS & PSPS flats and other HKHA public housing flats in the 25 year period.

Production in 2001/02 was low as the government changed the housing policy. In November 2002, the government decided to cease the production and sales of HOS & PSPS flats. It put an end to the project and only flats under construction were produced in 2002/03 and 2003/04.

Forrest and Murie (1995) suggest that privatization of public housing involves disposals of public rental flats at non-market prices favourable to purchasers. In the author's view, the disposal of newly completed public built-for-sale flats should also be classified under housing privatization. Such a process has been managed and promoted by the state with the objective of achieving a change in ownership rather than to create market exchange. Through time, changes are beginning to occur as these former state-owned dwellings and build-for-sale flats now privatized are exchanged in the private market and 'it is at this point of resale that a more profound transformation occurs – when privatization becomes commodification' (Forrest and Murie 1995).

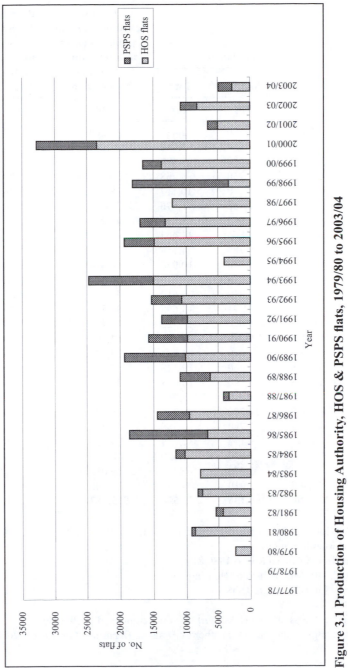

Figure 3.1 Production of Housing Authority, HOS & PSPS flats, 1979/80 to 2003/04

Source: Information provided to the author by Housing Department on 19 July 2004.

Table 3.3 HOS, PSPS and other public housing flats built, 1979/80–2003/04

| Year | Production of | | | Overall production of all public housing flats (excluding Housing Society flats) | Percentage of HOS& PSPS flats to overall production of all HA public housing flats |
| | HOS flats | PSPS flats | Total | | |
	(a)	**(b)**	**(c)**	**(d)**	**(c) / (d)**
1979/80	2,439	0	2,439	32,204	7.6
1980/81	8,674	#506	9,180	35,949	25.5
1981/82	4,399	#1,000	5,399	36,745	14.7
1982/83	7,508	760	8,268	36,147	22.9
1983/84	7,877	0	##10,117	38,681	26.2
1984/85	10,168	1,408	11,576	37,930	30.5
1985/86	6,688	11,902	18,590	47,976	38.7
1986/87	9,538	4,866	14,404	41,477	34.7
1987/88	3,370	784	4,154	24,145	17.2
1988/89	6,300	4,646	10,946	50,464	21.7
1989/90	10,048	9,298	19,346	53,256	36.3
1990/91	9,802	5,810	15,612	48,231	32.4
1991/92	9,804	3,894	13,698	34,888	39.3
1992/93	10,652	4,670	15,322	37,470	40.9
1993/94	14,973	9,770	24,743	44,591	55.5
1994/95	4,004	0	4,004	28,444	14.1
1995/96	14,868	4,460	19,328	33,887	57.0
1996/97	13,188	3,690	16,878	31,824	53.0
1997/98	12,040	0	12,040	30,101	40.0
1998/99	3,320	14,700	18,020	28,499	63.2
1999/00	13,778	2,780	16,558	48,484	34.2
2000/01	23,542	9,172	32,714	89,002	36.8
2001/02	5,080	1,540	6,620	40,249	16.4
2002/03	*8,272	**2,470	10,742	29,032	37.0
2003/04	*2,848	**2,010	4,858	20,006	24.3
Total:	**223,180**	**100,136**	**325,556**	**979,682**	**33.2**

Note: Public Housing Development Programme (PHDP) (1980–2003, March Editions) and PHDP (2004 March Edition)

Based on HKHA Annual Report 1980/81

Including 2,240 'Middle Income Housing' flats

* Surplus HOS not-for-sale as HOS

** Surplus PSPS

NA: Not Applicable as the first HOS court was only completed in 1979/80.

Source: Information provided to the author by Housing Department on 19 July 2004.

There have been resale restrictions in all public housing sales programmes. Home Ownership Scheme flats were subject to resale restrictions. Conditions of resale were introduced to minimize the chance of speculative sales. Before 1997 owners of Home Ownership Scheme dwellings could (a) in the five years from first assignment, resell to the Housing Authority only at the original price; (b) in the sixth to tenth years resell to the Housing Authority at prevailing Home Ownership Scheme prices; (c) after ten years, they were free to sell on the open market subject to payment of a proportionate premium.

In order to create an active second hand market within the Home Ownership Scheme sector, restrictions on resale were relaxed in late 1990s. HOS and PSPS owners were then free to sell the properties on the open market after five years on condition that the original portion of discount was paid to the HKHA. Owners could sell the properties to the Housing Authority within the first two years at the original price. This buy-back arrangement has in effect provided the purchasers of HOS/PSPS flats with a sense of security. The Housing Authority (HA) formally established the HOS Secondary Market Scheme (HOSSMS) in June 1997. It enables public housing tenants and Green Form Certificate holders to purchase flats sold under Home Ownership Scheme (HOS)/Private Sector Participation Scheme (PSPS)/ Tenants Purchase Scheme (TPS) with the date of first assignment from the third year onwards. Transactions in the HOS Secondary Market are similar to that in the open market. The purchaser and the seller may negotiate the price freely and conclude the deal either directly or through an estate agent. Purchasers of flats in the HOS Secondary Market will assume the liability to pay the premium if they sell their flats at the open market in the future. At the end of July 2000, out of 177,272 HAHOS and PSPS flats reaching the expiry of the resale restriction period, 20,326 flat owners (or about 12 per cent) had paid the premium. Between January 2001 and December 2004 a total of 16,690 HOS/PSPS flats were sold in the open market.[6]

Among the 225,415 HOS and PSPS flats, which have become eligible for resale on the secondary market, 7,431 transactions (or about 3.3 per cent) were recorded by mid September 2000.[7] Overall, about 12.3 per cent of HOS and PSPS flat owners who were qualified for reselling their flats either on the open market or on the secondary market have chosen to resell their flats. The majority (87.7 per cent) still continue to live in the HAHOS/PSPS flats. Hence the proportion of resale HOS is limited.

The Sandwich Class Housing Loan Scheme

'Choice' has been the catchword for the introduction of many home purchase loan schemes in Hong Kong since April 1988. There are a number of interest-free or low-

6   Figures for 2004 (5,840 flats sold) are provisional. In 2001: 3,560; 2002: 3,500 and 2003: 3,790 HOS/PSPS flats were sold in the open market (HKHA 25 February 2005).

7   Figures on the number of premiums paid by HAHOS/PSPS flat owners and transactions in the secondary HAHOS/PSPS market provided to the author by HKHA 19 September 2000.

interest loan schemes to help lower and middle-income households (the Sandwich Class) and first-time home purchasers to buy flats in the private sector. On top of the interest-free Home Purchase Loan Scheme operated by the Hong Kong Housing Authority, the government earmarked HK$2,000 million in 1993 to set up a Sandwich Class Housing Loan Scheme to assist 4,000 families in purchasing private sector dwellings over the following three years. A new home-starter loan was introduced in 1998 to assist first time buyers to buy their own home in the private sector. The Hong Kong Housing Society has been appointed management agent of these last two schemes.

The first subsidized loan scheme was called Home Purchase Loan Scheme (HPLS) introduced in 1988. It was financed and administered by the Housing Authority. According to the Hong Kong Housing Authority, HPLS provides the lowest amount of subsidy among various government housing schemes (public rental housing, HOS/ PSPS, and HPLS). Based on the average figures for the ten year period 1992–2001, the total subsidy[8] spent on each PRH unit was HK$1.03 million, the subsidy on each HOS unit was HK$0.65 million and the subsidy on each loan under the HPLS was HK$0.21 million. As the land premium, property prices and rental charges were all reduced in later years the respective subsidies based on the average figures for the three year period 1999–2001 were as follows: for each PRH unit HK$0.73 million; for each HOS unit HK$0.4 million; and for each HPLS loan HK$0.19 million.[9]

Eligible applicants are offered an interest free loan, repayable over the same period as the bank mortgage, up to a maximum of 20 years. Alternatively, they may opt for a monthly non-repayable subsidy for 48 months. In May 1995, to increase the popularity of the scheme, the loan and monthly subsidy were increased to HK$400,000 and HK$3,400 respectively. Tenant households in the private housing sector were eligible to apply if their total monthly income did not exceed HK$30,000 (as during the period April 1997 to March 1998). In June 1995, to encourage more sitting tenants to purchase property and give up their rental flats for reallocation, the loan and the monthly subsidy available to public tenants was further increased to HK$600,000 and HK$5,100. In mid 1998, this loan amount was increased again to HK$800,000 if tenants agreed to repay it in 13 years. Such a loan was available to purchase HOS flats sold in the secondary market. By the end of March 1996, 12,137 loans and 651 monthly subsidies had been granted, and 7,121 public housing units had been recovered for reallocation (HKHA 1995/96, 74). The increase in the loan amount in mid 1998 attracted more applicants to use the HPLS loan. By the end of 2002 56,761 HPLS loans and monthly subsidies had been granted.

Another scheme, called the Sandwich Class Housing Loan Scheme (SCHLS), was administered by the Hong Kong Housing Society which was commissioned to

---

8   Total subsidy amount includes direct expenses (e.g. site formation and construction costs) and opportunity cost (revenue foregone by government as land is given to HKHA for public housing). See Lau, K Y (2002).

9   Since October 1983, the Hong Kong dollar has been linked to the US dollar at the fixed rate of HK$7.8 to US$1.

build 50,000 dwellings for sale to sandwich class households by the end of 2006 (Government of the Hong Kong SAR 1997, 17). The Sandwich Class Housing Loan Scheme was first introduced in 1993 to help families with monthly incomes of between HK$25,001 and HK$50,000 to buy their own home in the private housing market. These income limits were revised to HK$30,001 to HK$60,000 in 1997 when private sector property prices increased sharply. The loan scheme, with a government grant of HK$3.38 billion from public funds, was designed to assist 6,000 families to purchase private flats. Additional grants were given to the Housing Society subsequently to increase the loan quota. Successful applicants could borrow up to 25 per cent of the flat price or HK$550,000, whichever was less, to purchase a property that was not older than 20 years and worth not more than HK$3.3 million. The loan was repaid, in 120 equal instalments starting from the fourth year after the loan was made. Interest per annum was charged at 2 per cent, which was much lower than the market interest rate (at 10 per cent in 1997). By June 2000, some 5,700 loans had been granted (HKHS website accessed June 2000). This loan scheme has since been terminated.

Since mid–1997 various new measures have been introduced to help enhance the rate of home-ownership. These were to help achieve the target of 70 per cent home-ownership rate by 2007 as pledged by the then Chief Executive of the Hong Kong Special Administrative Region, Tung Chee-hwa. It was an extremely ambitious target as the home-ownership rate in 1997 was only 50 per cent. The introduction of the Home Starter Loan Scheme (HSLS) in the Chief Executive's policy address in October 1997 was one of these new measures.

Under the HSLS, low-interest loans were to be granted to citizens who aspired to become first-time homeowners. A total sum of HK$18 billion was provided for the Scheme for allocation to 30,000 eligible families in the coming years. Each successful family was entitled to a maximum loan amount of HK$600,000. Interest was to be charged at the rate of 2 per cent per annum for those families with a total monthly income of not more than HK$31,000. For those families with a total monthly income of between HK$31,001 and HK$60,000, a 3.5 per cent interest rate per annum was charged. Such interest was calculated from the date of advance of the loan. Applications for the loan under the HSLS were closed on 31 March 2002. A total of 23,735 families and 9,699 single people benefited (HKHS website accessed February 2004).

In 2003 government merged the Home Purchase Loan Scheme with the Home Starter Loan Scheme to form the Home Assistance Loan Scheme (HALS, quota: 10,000) and the take-up rate between 2 January 2003 and 31 March 2004 for HALS was 76 per cent (3,801 loans and 3,787 subsidies were granted during this period). As government decided to withdraw its assistance to all homeowners the HALS was also terminated in mid 2004.

All these subsidized loans were considered additional choices for eligible applicants of HOS and Sandwich Class Housing Scheme flats. They were there to encourage families to purchase mainly private sector flats.

Disposal of Public Rented Flats

In 1997, the most significant housing privatization policy implemented was the Tenants Purchase Scheme (TPS). This policy offered the opportunity for at least 250,000 selected tenant households to purchase their public rental dwellings at huge discounts over the coming decade (1998–2007). This was an important measure to promote home-ownership among existing public housing tenants and enable them to buy their existing flats. It was packaged as an additional choice on top of the provision of the Home Ownership Scheme flats. The TPS was rolled out in phases and in the first four phases about 25,000 flats per annum were to be available for sitting tenants to purchase. Disposing of public rented flats in phases was intended to avoid the undesirable impact of a new supply of cheap public sector flats on the prices of private property.

The pricing arrangement for Phase 1 TPS estates sold in 1998 can be used as an illustration of its attractiveness. The arrangements for the sale price were that a market price assessment was made for individual dwellings and the price was set at 30 per cent of this market value. On average the age of the selected dwellings for sale was five to 12 years old and the discount of 70 per cent took the age into consideration. To induce tenants to buy early and to encourage quick sales, a further inducement discount of 60 per cent and 30 per cent was given to first-year and second-year buyers respectively. In other words if tenants decided to purchase in the first year of the offer, the price would only be 12 per cent of the assessed market value of the dwelling. The price would go up to 21 per cent of the assessed market value if tenants opted to buy in the second year of the offer. In the third year and thereafter, the price would be 30 per cent of the assessed market value. Tenant purchasers would be free to pay for another 20 per cent of the assessed market value of the properties (to increase the price paid up to 50 per cent of the assessed market value) if they chose to.

As the Housing Authority provided a full guarantee against mortgage defaults of the public rental purchasers, most banks were prepared to provide loans at lower than normal home mortgage interest rates. The loan amount could go up to 95 per cent of the sale price (normally purchasers of private properties were provided with mortgage loans of no more than 70 per cent of the assessed sale value). This also made the purchase easier among public housing tenants. To ease purchasers' worry on the future costs of maintenance, the Authority agreed to make a one-off contribution, equivalent to HK$14,000 per household, to the pooled maintenance fund. Furthermore, management responsibilities of these TPS blocks were to be taken up by the Owners' Corporations (which then would appoint a private management agency to do the day–to–day management) within the first two years after the sale programme of each TPS estate.

In the six Phase 1 TPS estates, 74 per cent of tenants purchased their flats to benefit from the deep discount[10] in the first year (1998). Two-thirds of tenants in Phase 2 TPS estates did the same within the first year (1999). About 70 per cent of tenants in Phase 3 TPS estates also joined the owner-occupiers sector in 2000. Sixty one per cent of Phase 4 and 62 per cent of Phase 5 TPS tenants purchased with full credit in 2001 and 2002 respectively.[11] Better off tenants have chosen to purchase within the first year of offer, as they would maximize the benefits of high discounted sale prices. Tenants with financial hardship more generally remained as tenants paying normal rents or receiving rent assistance, either from the Housing Authority (in form of half rent reduction) or from the Social Welfare Department (in form of cash assistance for paying of rent given to social security recipients).

Between 1998 and March 2004, five phases involving 30 public housing estates (133,713 rental units) were endorsed for sale at substantial discounts and with special credit arrangements. The biggest discount was given to Phase I applicants in TPS flats. If tenants of Phase I estates bought within the first year of offer, they would only need to pay 12 per cent of the assessed market price of the rental units. If they bought in the second year, they would pay 21 per cent of the assessed market value; if they bought in year three or subsequently they would pay 30 per cent of the assessed market price. For Phase IV and V TPS estates, the discount and credit were slightly smaller than for Phase I TPS tenants. The above three figures were 20.25 per cent, 32.625 per cent and 45 per cent of the assessed market prices respectively. By 31 March 2004, 68 per cent of TPS rental units offered for sale were sold to tenants.

According to the government, 'the scheme opens up a window of opportunity for PRH tenants, who would otherwise not be able to afford private housing, to become home-owners. It also helps reduce the Housing Authority's operating costs' (Secretary for Housing, Planning and Lands 2002). Based on the information of TPS Phase 5 (available for sale from early 2002), for every PRH unit sold, HKHA and the government would receive HK$177,178 as the sale income, but would need to pay HK$132,585 for construction charges, site formation charge, operating charges and appropriation into the TPS estate maintenance fund. The net surplus for each sale unit would be HK$44,593. Because of sales, the HKHA would lose rental income of HK$16,535 per annum. At the same time it would save HK$3,220 required each year to subsidize the deficit in the rental housing operating account arising because rental income was insufficient to cover operating costs (HKHA 2001).

---

10 Purchasers who paid 12 per cent (within the first year of the launch of the Scheme) were deemed to have paid 30 per cent of the market value of the TPS dwellings. After five years, if the TPS flat owners sold their flats in the open market, they then are liable to pay 70 per cent of the prevailing sale price to the Housing Authority.

11 *Housing Authority Quarterly Statistical Report (March 2004)*, Table 2.3.

Mortgage Subsidy Scheme

In September 1998 the Hong Kong Housing Authority introduced a pilot Mortgage Subsidy Scheme (MSS). The main objective of this MSS was to give prospective tenants affected by the Public Housing Comprehensive Redevelopment Programme and Cottage Area Clearance Programmes a choice of either rental or home-ownership tenure. Under this scheme, affected tenants could buy transfer block flats or HOS flats with a monthly mortgage subsidy amounting to a total of HK$162,000 over a six year period. Up to the end of 1999, about 3,600 households became home-owners through this initiative. The Mortgage Subsidy Scheme was subsequently terminated because of the low response to it.

Buy or Rent Option

In March 1999, The Hong Kong Housing Authority introduced a Buy or Rent Option (BRO) to enable prospective applicants on the public rental housing Waiting List and residents affected by the Comprehensive Redevelopment Programme/cottage or squatter areas clearance operations, as well as junior civil servants, to choose to buy rental flats from the outset as a form of rehousing. Eligible BRO applicants were to receive a monthly mortgage subsidy up to a maximum of HK$162,000 over six years. A total of 2,700 flats were designated for sale in Phase 1 of the BRO scheme in June 1999. The response was lukewarm as only 1,800 applicants joined this scheme and only two-thirds of the flats on offer were taken up.

The requirement to convert completed public rental housing blocks into public sale blocks, when the need arises, has become a major consideration for upgrading the design and standards of public rental housing. The further upgrading of security facilities and services (for example, installation of main entrance gate, door phone systems, closed circuit television in lifts and at main entrance, 24–hour service of security guard posted on main entrance of every rental housing block) has made public rental blocks very similar to public sale blocks in many aspects.

In the state-managed housing system in Hong Kong, policy makers are keen to create ample opportunities for eligible applicants to become homeowners. Measures such as the TPS, MSS and BRO plus the expanded quota of Home Purchase Loan Scheme were introduced to create a combined effect to open the opportunity of eventual ownership to many more families entering public housing. In the words of Tony Miller, Director of HKHA:

> ... the aim of these reforms should be to ensure that there is a range of types, sizes, ages and prices of flats available to our clients and a range of financing options so that families move around and trade up within the system one rung at a time, or more if they are able. What we will be offering them is a way through subsidized public rental housing and into ownership in an increasingly private market which for many simply is not there at this time (Miller 1997).

Without governmental assistance it is true to say that many low-income households would not have got such a chance to become home-owners.

In this state-managed housing system, tenants in the public rental housing sector are induced to become home owners while better off tenants are given lower subsidies or no subsidy at all. The state has also intervened in the state-managed housing system by regulating the supply of land and subsidized housing. When the market prices of housing dropped, land and subsidized housing supply were also adjusted (a downward adjustment or suspension).

Reduction of Built-for-Sale Public Flats

The government originally planned an annual production of over 29,000 public built-for-sale flats between 2000 and 2004 (HKHA 2000). However this plan was dropped in mid 2000, as there was no sign that the slackening property market would recover soon. On top of the announcement of the termination of the Sandwich Class Housing Scheme in 1999, the Financial Secretary of the Hong Kong Special Administrative Region stated that no more than 20,000 public built-for-sale flats would be provided. His announcement was made only three weeks after the Housing Authority's Home Ownership Committee had endorsed its Business Plan of supplying 27,000 Home Ownership Scheme flats for sale in the financial year 2000/01. Evidently HKHA was very worried about the impact of the falling property market on the economy of Hong Kong and therefore wished to exercise control (a state-managed move) over the supply of public sector flats. The total number of HOS/PSPS flats actually completed in the four-year period (2000/01 to 2003/04) was 59,000 (or less than 15,000 units per annum). These 59,000 units include 16,000 surplus HOS/PSPS flats (produced in 2002/03 and 2003/04) and not available for sale.

Impacts of the State-managed Housing System on Social Housing

The social rented housing stock has been reasonably maintained since it was built. The replacement of the older non-self-contained public rental dwellings with the modern standard self-contained dwellings under the Comprehensive Redevelopment Programme upgraded the housing conditions of 200,000 households during 1985–2000. The redeveloped social rented dwellings constituted about one-third of all social rented stock. The low rental charges for public tenants is a praiseworthy policy which allows families of public housing estates a strong sense of tenure security and a higher disposable income after meeting their housing costs. Critics have argued that the government has become the victim of its own success with the public rental housing programme because most tenants prefer to stay in the social rented sector as long as they are allowed. Adult children 'inherited' the public tenancy upon the death of their parents prior to 1999, as there was no restriction against this. Some of them were well off families who might not have needed subsidised housing. Such criticism is understandable in view of the fact that the number of low-income households on the waiting list for social rented housing has been high (150,000 in most years during the period 1990–95 and 113,000 at the end of 1999). On average, families on the waiting list had to wait for over 6.5 years in the second half of the 1990s before allocation (HKHA 2004). The various incentives to induce better off public tenants to purchase Home Ownership Scheme flats and the deep-discount provision to sitting tenants to purchase social rented dwellings under the Tenants Purchase Scheme were important housing privatization measures to change the tenure mix within the public housing sector. Within the permanent public housing, home-ownership rates increased from 5 per cent in 1983 to 13 per cent in 1988, to 24 per cent in 1995/96 and to 35 per cent in 2003/2004 (see Table 3.4).

The success of the Home Ownership Scheme and PSPS is reflected in a number of ways. It is estimated that 80 per cent or some 141,000 public tenants, upon purchase of HOS/PSPS flats, returned their original rented flats to HKHA for reallocation among the needy families.

As the HOS/PSPS flats were sold at affordable prices and with buy-back provision, purchasers were less likely to encounter the same problems as those of the private sector home purchasers. 2001 Census statistics showed that the median monthly mortgage payment in subsidized housing was HK$5,900 and the Median Mortgage to Income Ratio: 23.4 per cent. These were much lower than those of the private housing sector (median monthly mortgage payment was HK$11,000 and Median Mortgage to Income Ratio: 30.7 per cent).

Table 3.4 Home-ownership in Hong Kong, 1993/94–2003/04

Year	Owner Occupied units within:		
	Public Housing	**Private Housing**	**All Hong Kong**
	%	%	%
1993/94	23	75	50
1994/95	23	74	50
1995/96	24	72	50
1996/97	25	72	50
1997/98	26	72	50
1998/99	30	71	51
1999/00	33	72	53
2000/01	36	74	55
2001/02	36	75	56
2002/03	37	74	56
2003/04	35	75	57

Note: Home-ownership rates here refer to the proportion of owner-occupied living quarters in permanent housing to the total number of occupied permanent housing units. From 2001/02 onwards, HOS flats that can be traded in the open market (i.e. flats sold prior to HOS Phase 3B or flats having paid off premium) are classified as private permanent flats and are excluded from subsidized sale flats. Figures refer to the end of each financial year.
Source: Hong Kong Housing Authority (2004) Housing Authority Performance Indicators March 2004 Edition. Hong Kong: Hong Kong Housing Authority.

HOS/PSPS made an important financial contribution to the Housing Authority. The relationship between the sale proceeds and the total costs of development ranged from 1.9:1 in Phase 13A (April l991) to 3:1 (August 1993). The average ratio was about 2.5:1. Each HOS flat sold generated proceeds sufficient to build 2.5 flats in the next building cycle. This success enabled the Housing Authority to become financially self-supporting after 1992. In 1995/96, revenue from HOS sales amounted to 56 per cent of the income of the Housing Authority. The financial contribution of HOS/PSPS was an essential element in the Housing Authority's ability to maintain services and fund continuing public housing production.

For many years, the Housing Authority was committed to building a massive number of new flats. This public housing production (including the comprehensive redevelopment programme), maintenance programmes and the cheap sale of public rented dwellings to sitting tenants was only possible because the Hong Kong Housing Authority was cash-rich before 2000. As the government decided to scale down the building and sale programme of HOS/PSPS, this situation changed – especially after 2003 when the government stopped HOS/PSPS sales. The consolidated operating surplus of HKHA was as high as HK$15,361 million in 1998/99. In 2001/02 to 2003/04 the net surplus dropped substantially, and in 2003/04, it turned into a deficit for the first time in seven years.[12] It was forecast to drop to HK$129 Million in 2004/05.

The public housing disposal programme under the Tenants Purchase Scheme made an important contribution in terms of providing affordable access to low price home-ownership of a reasonably good standard. Between 1998 and March 2004, 90,668 tenant households (68 per cent of TPS flats endorsed for sale) became owners through this scheme (HKHA 2004, 53).

The relaxation of restrictions on the resale of public sale flats aimed at promoting greater mobility within and between the rungs of the home-owning housing ladder. With this greater mobility, it was expected that the housing market would be active and housing developers' interest in property development would be maintained and enhanced. As the property market had an important bearing on the overall economy of Hong Kong, its maintenance and enhancement was a significant part of the macro-economic policy of the Hong Kong Government.

On the other hand the Tenants Purchase Scheme generated great expectations from sitting and prospective tenants as they all expected to enjoy deep-discount purchase. This reduced the demand from public tenants to leave the social rented sector to purchase Home Ownership Scheme flats. Coupled with the dampened economy, the number of HOS applicants amongst social rented tenants dropped substantially from 45,000 in June 1997 to 11,000 in March 1999. After the reports of uneven piling in some Home Ownership Scheme high-rise dwelling blocks, the number of HOS applicants from the social rented tenants dropped further to only 5,000 in Phase 22A in 2000 (HK Government Housing Department 1999).

---

12 http://www.legco.gov.hk/yr04-05/english/sec/library/0405in14e.pdf

The Asian Financial Crisis – Housing Challenges in Hong Kong

The Long Term Housing Strategy promulgated in 1987 was a 'Private Sector Priority Strategy'. Government aimed to maximise the contribution of private housing developers to meet the identified housing demand. The public sector was expected to complement the private sector and not to compete with it.

The impact of the 1997 Asian financial crisis on the Hong Kong economy was far-reaching. In 1998, the Gross Domestic Product (at constant 2000 market prices) recorded negative growth (minus 5.0 per cent)[13] Since then unemployment and under-employment figures rose and reached their peak in 2003 (Census and Statistics Department 2005), (with 7.9 per cent unemployment and 3.5 per cent under-employment respectively). Property prices recorded a 66 per cent increase between the fourth quarter of 1995 and the third quarter of 1997, and then dropped drastically by mid 2000 to around 50 per cent of peak prices in October 1997.[14] According to a Hang Seng Bank research report (1998), falling property values damaged the economy and government coffers. The drop in property values led to a contraction in bank credit, which in turn contributed to a reduction in bank deposits. This resulted in higher interest rates and a tight liquidity situation. Falling property prices also reduced consumer spending and exerted a deflationary impact. Falling property values also impacted adversely on public finances because revenue from land/property-related transactions had accounted for an average of 21 per cent of total government revenue over the previous ten years – the majority arising from land premium.

In June 2000, a pro-business Liberal party estimated that there were 170,000 property owners suffering from negative equity (Hong Kong Economic Journal 2000). The percentage of defaults on property loans increased from 0.29 per cent in June 1998 to 1.19 per cent in May 2000 (Cheung 2000). The number of Home Ownership Scheme (HOS) applicants dropped from its peak of 112,000 (in August 1994) to 29,000 (in mid 2000) and 5,117 in July 2002 (HKHA 2003). Though all HOS flats put up for sale between 1978–99 were sold, the demand has dropped as the economy has failed to recover. Moreover, the building quality scandal in some HOS estates hurt the confidence of prospective purchasers. In the financial year 1999–2000, about 25 per cent of HOS flats put up for sale could not find purchasers. The vacancy rate in private dwellings also rose to the highest figures in two decades – rising from 3.9 per cent in 1997, to 5.9 per cent in 1999, and to 6.8 per cent in 2003 (HK Government Rating and Valuation Department, various).

In this adverse economic climate, the housing pledges of the Chief Executive of the Hong Kong Special Administrative Region in his 1997 Policy Address (to increase the home-ownership rate from 50 per cent in 1997 to 70 per cent in 2007,

---

13 Figures obtained from Census and Statistics Department Website: http://www.info. gov.hk/censtatd/eng/hkstat/fas/nat_account/gdp/gdp1_index.html

14 Rating and Valuation Department website: http://www.info.gov.hk/rvd/property/ index.htm

to provide land to build 50,000 public dwellings and 35,000 private dwellings per annum) came under serious scrutiny from mid-1998. Private developers and owners suffering from negative equity criticized the Chief Executive for over-intervening in the market with an over-supply of public sales flats and over-provision of land for private dwellings. Days before the Hong Kong SAR celebrated its third anniversary, the Chief Executive admitted in public that the housing production target of 85,000 dwellings per annum had been shelved since October 1998 (Wen Hui Pao and Ming Pao, *Daily News* 2000). He further added that the new housing policy comprised three basic points:

- flexible adjustment of the Home Ownership Scheme production targets and increased use of loans to encourage home purchase in private sector;
- stabilization of property prices (to ensure adequate supply of land for public and private housing developers); and
- provision of affordable public housing to all those who could not afford private sector housing. Average waiting time for public rented housing applicants should be cut short to three years from 2003 onwards.

A housing delimitation strategy was used to control the supply of flats for public sale. In adverse economic circumstances (including the fear among many middle-income households of losing their jobs), it was doubtful whether the reduction in the numbers of public flats being sold and the provision of more zero or low-interest loans would result in a higher demand for private home purchase and would stabilise property prices. Property prices are more sensitive to changes in the economy than to changes in government housing policy.

The shorter waiting time for social rented applicants as reflected in the third point mentioned above by the Chief Executive is only a by-product of a policy which turned 16,000 HOS flats into social rented flats for allocation during the four year period (2000/01 to 2003/04). It is evident that the government did not turn HOS flats into social rented flats because demand for social rented housing was high. The number of applicants on the waiting list was as high as 150,000 in each year between 1994–98. Subsequent demand was much lower (there were only 91,000 households applying for social rented housing in March 2004). Despite it being denied, it is clear that the adjustment of the HOS supply was a direct response to the private developers' call for reducing or stopping the supply of HOS flats.

Despite the government's good intentions in using housing policy to stabilize the property market, it is doubtful whether the measures proposed in the state-managed housing system could redeem a situation determined by underlying economic problems (high interest rates coupled with deflation). The fear among public and private sector employees of losing their jobs has also contributed to the low take-up of offers promoting home purchase. It is also unrealistic for the Chief Executive to have insisted on reinforcing policy measures for a home-ownership target of 70 per cent by 2007. After three years of effort, the overall home-ownership rate stood at only 53 per cent in 2000. It is difficult to believe that households in Hong Kong in the future will crave home purchase as many people did before 1997 and be unaffected by the trauma of a drastic drop of property prices coupled with actual or potential job losses or a reduction of income in the subsequent period.

Under a market economy the degree of housing commodification relates to the proportion of privately owned dwellings and the number of transactions involving privately owned dwellings. Exchange value is emphasized in a highly commodified housing market. Price fluctuations are inevitable. One way of addressing price instability in a market economy is to turn housing into a de-commodified service. In theory, in a de-commodified housing market, government would emphasize the use value of housing and the consumption of housing will be immune from market forces as government would provide affordable housing to all. Experience of socialist economies however, suggests that de-commodified housing markets have problems, including the inequitable allocation and corrupt practices identified in former socialist countries in Central and Eastern Europe (Turner, Hegedus, and Tosics 1992) as well as in mainland China (Wang and Murie 1999a). As one is not building the housing system from the beginning however, it is necessary to strike a balance between the interests of existing home-owners (56 per cent of resident households in Hong Kong in 2001) and those of prospective housing consumers when developing a new housing strategy for Hong Kong.

The State-managed Housing System Reconsidered

Hong Kong is described in this chapter as a state-managed housing system because of its interventionist approach. The Hong Kong housing system is not a state-controlled system like that of Singapore in which the government has dominated the housing provision (over 80 per cent of Singaporeans are housed in dwellings administered by the public sector) leaving a small role for the private sector. In Hong Kong, the government has been conscious of its housing delimitation role. Housing delimitation strategy is used with a two-pronged approach: to contain the supply of public sector housing and to induce demand for private sector housing. More stringent entrance criteria were introduced to restrict the growth of eligible public rental housing applicants. New policies were executed in parallel with more incentives for home purchasers (Table 3.5).

The master plan, though denied by government officials, was to provide subsidized public dwellings for no more than half of Hong Kong's population. A delicate balance of 1:1 public to private housing was maintained throughout recent decades and was intended for the future. This meant that real estate developers were more certain that their housing investment would be attractive. Sufficient demand for private housing could be expected as government would not expand the public housing programme either to compete with or damage the interests of property developers. An interventionist approach was adopted in mid-1998 and reinforced in 2003 to stop land sales in order to stabilize the property market and save property prices from falling. The scaling down of supply and the subsequent termination of the sale of public flats under the Home Ownership Scheme was another feature of the state-managed housing system.

Table 3.5 Housing delimitation strategies in Hong Kong

Objective	Strategy/ Approach
Contain supply of and demand for public sector housing	• Delimit public housing and land supply • Apply more stringent eligibility criteria to reduce the number of eligible applicants
Induce demand for private sector housing	• Introduce new policies to require well off families to leave public rental housing • Provide interest free or low-interest loans to induce people to become home-owners • Introduce Mortgage Interest Tax Allowance for all home-owners • Control private land supply; suspend land supply (July 1998) for nine months and for over one year (2003) when property prices have experienced a sharp drop.

All land within the Hong Kong Special Administrative Region is state property. The government is responsible for the management, use and development of the land and for its lease or grant to individuals or organizations for use or development (Howlett 1998). The controlled supply of housing land is an important part of the state-managed housing system. In 1999 the government changed its way of granting land and put some residential sites on a reserve list (the Application List system). It would not auction them unless a sufficient number of developers had indicated their interest in acquiring them. Since 2004, the Application List system has always been adopted before land was put up for auction.

Despite all these examples of state-management in the housing system, the Hong Kong government has not made any attempt to over-provide public housing itself. It would be impossible for the government to do this as real estate developers have had a strong influence over housing strategy. As property prices continued to fall in the period 1998–2003 (Figure 3.2), the state responded quickly to this falling demand and strong pressure from the developers to cut HOS supply.

A state-managed housing system has its limitations. Despite repeated efforts (the suspension of land sales, termination of the Sandwich Class Housing Scheme, reductions and eventual termination of HOS flat sales) property prices continued to fall until mid-2003. The impact of the Asian financial crisis was reflected in rising unemployment and under-employment rates (Table 3.2).

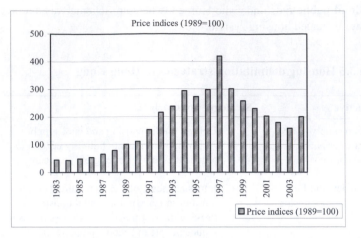

Figure 3.2 Price indices of private domestic properties, 1983–2004

It is time to consider whether the state-managed housing system could have a greater impact on housing conditions, rents and affordability in public sector housing than it does on private sector housing. Yet its impact on the urban and new town development pattern is definite and positive.

Concluding Remarks

Housing policy has always been used as an important part of macro-economic policy involving the reduction/termination of public built for sale flat supply when demand slackens in the private property market.

The impact of a state-managed housing system on public sector housing is positive and impressive. Its impact on private sector housing and the general economy has to be further tested in times of economic downturn. After five and a half years of falling property prices, the complete withdrawal of government's assistance to potential home buyers (through sale of HOS/PSPS subsidized built for sale flats and interest free loans) appears timely. The number of Residential Mortgage Loans (RMLs) in negative equity has declined by more than 80 per cent from the peak of about 106,000 cases (22 per cent of total RMLs) in June 2003 to 19,215 cases (4 per cent of total RMLs in December 2004). At one time, it was estimated that in mid-2000 there were as many as 170,000 property owners experiencing negative equity. The fall in property prices hit hardest on those entering the property market in the late 1990s. Forrest and Lee (2004) explore aspects of wealth accumulation in the home-ownership sector and the impact of policy change and house price trajectories on different cohorts of households entering the home-ownership sector in different periods. The post-2000 housing policy changes targeted those losing wealth in the falling property market. The property sector was seen as a major pillar of Hong

Kong's economy and as closely interwoven with every aspect of people's daily lives. Together with the construction industry, it accounted for an average of 14 per cent of the Gross Domestic Product over the five year period of 1998–2002 (Secretary for Housing, Planning and Lands 2002).

It seems there is a limit on the use of a housing delimitation strategy to stabilize the private property market. A revival of a healthy property market is dependent on purchasers' confidence about their future incomes and this is directly related to the performance of the economy. Policy makers in the state-managed housing system have to reconsider appropriate housing policies to meet the challenges at times of economic prosperity as well as economic downturn.

HKHA echoed the government's call for stopping the sale of HOS/PSPS with effect from late 2002 and stopped building flats for sale in the future. This revealed a need to find new ways of funding the public housing construction programme. Divestment of HKHA commercial properties and car parks could generate an estimated fund of about HK$23 billion (Legislative Council Secretariat 2004). This would meet its funding requirement for only two to three years. What would happen after that? There is a need for the government to renew its financial commitment to social rental housing through allocation from its own general funds.

There have been broader achievements in terms of community building, territorial development and urban renewal. In the view of Miller:

> public housing estates provide the essential infrastructure for new communities to gather, communicate and grow. The well-managed, self-contained and estate-based communities have provided a strong social centre of gravity for local residents, which have helped foster a sense of belonging and coherence as development has extended across the territory. This has contributed positively to Hong Kong's stability amidst the various economic and social turmoils of the past five decades (Miller 2000).

Public rents have been set with reference to the affordability of the tenants and have stayed low for years. Public tenants enjoy a long period of stable rent, and are therefore able to save money for expenses, such as sponsoring children for university education locally or overseas, or paying home mortgages for improving housing conditions.

If public housing estates had not been built in new towns, private sector development would not have existed there. Public housing estates were regarded as a major component of the new towns and became a catalyst for the private development that followed. Miller (2000) remarks that governmental efforts in new town development in the 1970s and thereafter have turned many remote and suburban areas into modern and strategic growth areas. Many estates in the new towns are now the focus of transportation, commercial and recreational facilities that preceded and now support the private development nearby in new towns. In 2000, about 2.9 million people or 43 per cent of the total population were living in these new towns. In some new towns, for example, in Tseung Kwan O and in Tin Shui Wai, 82 per cent and 74 per cent of people respectively lived in public sector housing (2001 Census data).

Without the active involvement of the Hong Kong Housing Authority (HKHA) in the redevelopment process of older public rental housing estates, the improvement in housing conditions, landscape and spatial distribution of modern housing estates would have been impossible. The HKHA may be considered a pioneer in driving forward the rejuvenation of older urban areas through the massive redevelopment programme. The first programme started in 1973, involving 12 of the oldest public rental estates, 240 housing blocks, 84,450 households, 526,000 residents, 6,446 shops and 3,668 hawkers (Crosby 1986). The redevelopment programme was further extended in 1988, and renamed the Comprehensive Redevelopment Programme, involving other types of old public housing estates. Statistics show that between April 1988 and March 2000, about 10,000 old rental flats were demolished per annum. In the four year period (April 2000 to March 2004), 57,000 public rental flats were redeveloped (HKHA 2004). These old and crowded estates were demolished and replaced by high-rise modern buildings. Through redevelopment, new town standards (better housing design, open space and community facilities) are being introduced into the older urban areas. This has not only improved living standards for residents in these estates and people living nearby (the externality effect), but has also helped to optimize land use and induced social rejuvenation in the community by attracting and encouraging more young families to move into these areas (Miller 2000).

The Hong Kong government has played a significant role in housing. It has provided a safe and affordable home for half of Hong Kong's population. The living standards of many have been improved. New towns have been developed. With the aim of striking a right balance (in terms of public and private housing provision), the government's various intervention strategies are expected in the future to contribute to the building of a healthy property market and a socially mixed public housing community.

The sustainability of a continued public housing programme is at stake, however, following the government's decision to stop providing 'built for sale' flats (the cash proceeds generator of the Hong Kong Housing Authority). There is now a need for the government to commit its resources to building future public rental housing to meet the future housing needs of deprived groups who will be unable to afford private rental housing.

Chapter 4

The State and Housing Policy in Korea

Shin-Young Park

Introduction

Since 1998, when Korea was seriously affected by the Asian economic crisis, the Korean government has put special emphasis on the social safety net because of a great increase in poverty and unemployment. In 1999, the Government and the National Assembly introduced the National Basic Livelihood Security Act, under which the government calculates the minimum monthly cost of living[1] according to the size of household to serve as the basis for determining wage levels and eligibility for the Basic Livelihood Guarantee. Since 2000, the Korean government has provided living expenses to those who earn less than a specified minimum, regardless of their age and ability to work. The public assistance in the National Basic Livelihood Guarantee consists of the livelihood allowance, educational aid, medical aid, maternity aid, funeral aid and self-support aid for low-income people who are on job training.

In housing policy in 2002, the Korean government, for the first time, established the Construction Plan for One Million National Rental Housing Units from 2003–12. The aim is to ensure a supply of good quality affordable rented housing for low-income families. This was considered necessary even though Korea's housing stock has increased dramatically and housing conditions have significantly improved since the early 1990s. Additionally, in 2004, the Korean government established the Korea Housing Finance Corporation to promote home-ownership for low- and middle-income families by providing long term mortgages. The long-term aim of the Korean government proclaims that all households should be able to obtain a decent home at a price within their means, echoing the policy of the United Kingdom government in the 1970s.

This chapter, however, shows that Korea has its own system of housing policy and provision, reflecting the needs and progress of Korean society. The first section reviews the information available on the housing situation in Korea. The second section discusses the government's strategies in responding to its housing problems. The third section examines the relationship between policy objectives and results. The chapter concludes by outlining some characteristics of Korean housing policy in their socio-economic contexts.

---

1   The calculation for the minimum cost of living is reviewed every five years.

The Housing Situation in Korea

Housing supply and demand

Korea's population in the year 2000 was 46 million: about 84 per cent larger than it was 40 years previously. The number of households increased by 3.27 times from 4.4 million in 1960 to 14.3 million in 2000. The rate of household formation far exceeded the rate of population growth. These trends were due to the diffusion of the nuclear family system and in particular, to the increase in the number of single person households. In response to the rapidly growing number of households, the housing stock has also grown rapidly from 3.5 million in 1960 to 11.4 million in 2000. But the rate of housing growth, while faster than that of population growth, has been somewhat slower than the growth in the number of households.

Table 4.1 shows that the number of both 'households' and 'ordinary households'[2] increased rapidly from 1960–2000. For this reason, the housing supply ratio, namely the ratio of housing stock to the number of ordinary households, declined from 83.8 per cent in 1960 to 72.4 per cent in 1990. However, owing to the Two Million Housing Construction Plan including five New Town Development Projects from 1989–93, the housing supply ratio began to increase. In 2000, the housing supply ratio nationally was 96.2 per cent and it reached 100 per cent in 2002.

Table 4.1 Population, households and housing stock, 1960–2000

	1960	1970	1980	1990	2000
Population ('000)	24,989	31,435	37,407	43,390	46,125
Households ('000)	4,378	5,576	7,969	11,355	14,391
Ordinary households ('000) (A)	4,135	5,197	7,470	10,223	11,928
Housing stock ('000) (B)	3,464	4,359	5,318	7,374	11,472
Housing supply ratio (B/A)	83.8 %	78.2 %	71.2 %	72.4 %	96.2 %

Source: National Statistical Office, Five yearly Population and Housing Census.

There have been specific problems of shortage in particular locations or affecting certain income groups. For example, there was housing shortage in Seoul Metropolitan Area (SMA).[3] Many low-income families live in poor and unsatisfactory housing that

---

2 An 'ordinary household' excludes non-family related households and one-person households.

3 Seoul Metropolitan Area, which includes Seoul, Inchon, and Gyeonggi Province, occupies 11.8 per cent of Korea's total land area [just under 100,000 sq km]. In 1960, 20.8 per

is not equipped with modern facilities such as a kitchen and inside w.c. In addition, it is said that in some cases, three or four households live together in one housing unit and among them 1,120,000 have the use of only one room, with shared facilities in many cases.

Tenure

Trends in housing tenure[4] are shown in Table 4.2. The proportion of owner-occupied households declined from 71.7 per cent in 1970 to 49.9 per cent in 1990. In 2000, the rate of owner-occupation was 54.2 per cent, just four points higher than the 1990 level.

Table 4.2 Households by tenure, 1970–2000 (unit: 00; percentages in brackets)

	1970	1975	1980	1985	1990	1995	2000
Owner-Occupied	3,996	4,260	4,672	5,127	5,667	6,910	7,753
	(71.7)	(64.1)	(58.6)	(53.6)	(49.9)	(53.3)	(54.2)
Chonsei Rental*	1,457	1,171	1,904	2,201	3,157	3,845	4,040
	(26.1)	(17.6)	(23.9)	(23.0)	(27.8)	(29.7)	(28.2)
Monthly Rental	not	1,049	1,231	1,893	2,173	1,876	2,113
	available	(15.8)	(15.4)	(19.8)	(19.1)	(14.5)	(14.8)
Others	123	167	162	350	358	328	406
	(2.2)	(2.5)	(2.0)	(3.6)	(3.1)	(2.8)	(2.8)
Total	5,576	6,647	7,969	9,571	11,354	12,958	14,312
	(100)	(100)	(100)	(100)	(100)	(100)	(100)

* *Chonsei* is a rental agreement where the tenant pays a lump sum deposit to the landlord in lieu of rent for two years. The entire deposit (excluding any interest earned) is returned when the household moves out at the end of the tenancy. The amount of the chonsei deposit ranges from 30 per cent to 70 per cent of the housing unit's market price, depending on market conditions. Technically, the chonsei contract combines two separate transactions. The first is a loan made by the tenant to the landlord; the second is a lease by which the landlord grants the tenant use of the residence for imputed interest payments on the chonsei deposit. Landlords are not restricted in their use of the deposit and frequently the chonsei money is used as leverage to invest in additional housing units.
Source: National Statistical Office, Five yearly Population and Housing Census.

cent of the nation's population lived in the SMA, but by 2000 this figure had increased to 46.3 per cent. As a result, there is an excess of households over dwellings in SMA.

    4   Compared to western European countries where housing tenure is usually classified into four types – public rented, private rented, owner-occupied and other – in Korea a different classification is used, reflecting the lack, until recently, of permanent public rental housing. In Korea households normally are classified into two groups, owner-occupiers and tenants, with two forms of rental: '*chonsei*' and monthly rental. Thus, the standard tenure classification is owner-occupation, *chonsei* rental, monthly rental, and other.

Comparing owner-occupation in urban and rural areas, Table 4.3 shows that for urban areas, the rate was 54 per cent in 1970, declining to 43 per cent in 1990. By 2000, it had risen to 50 per cent, reflecting in part the improvement in the 1990s in the housing supply ratio (Figure 4.1). It is said that the declining owner-occupancy rate in urban areas until 1990 was a consequence of rapid urbanization and an insufficient supply of housing in urban areas (Son, Won and Moon 2001). But considering that about six million housing units for sale were built from 1988–2000, the home ownership rate should have increased substantially. In fact, the rate increased by only 4 per cent from 1990–2000, suggesting that the better-off who could afford to buy had purchased most of the newly constructed units for investment purposes.

Even if many more new housing units could be provided, the level of owner-occupation could not rise significantly without the government's financial support for low-income families who do not own a house. Moreover, the decline in ownership in rural areas since 1970 reflects the trend in rural-urban migration that has been such a major feature of Korea's recent development.

Table 4.3 Owner-occupation in urban and rural areas, 1970–2000 (percentages)

Area	1970	1975	1980	1985	1990	1995	2000
Nation	71.7	64.1	58.6	53.6	49.9	53.3	54.2
Urban	53.8	48.9	46.5	44.3	42.7	48.1	50.2
Rural	90.8	87.6	87.3	85.9	84.2	83.8	79.7

Source: National Statistical Office, Five yearly Population and Housing Census.

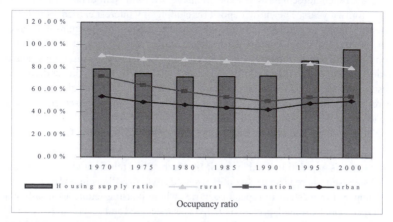

Figure 4.1 The housing supply ratio and owner-occupation, 1970–2000

Source: National Statistical Office Five yearly Population and Housing Census.

In the absence of a well-defined and balanced housing policy, disparities between income groups and regions have become wider. According to the statistics of the Ministry of Home Affairs, in 2002, 8.32 million households owned 13.7 million housing units, while a further 8.43 million households lived in rented accommodation. Just 50 per cent of households were home owners. Considering that public rental housing accounted for only 2.3 per cent of the housing stock in 2002, the majority of tenants had to live in the private rented sector. In Korea many tenants have to move every two years, if they cannot pay the increased rent required by landlords when the time comes to renew a two year rental agreement. The average period of residence for a tenant in the same property is 3.7 years, while for an owner-occupier it is 10.2 years (Korea Statistics Office 2004). This frequency of movement results in high transaction costs for tenants. Moreover, since 2000, many *chonsei* tenancies have been converted to monthly rental because the decrease in interest rates has made *chonsei* unattractive to landlords. Some landlords now charge one per cent of the old *chonsei* deposit as the new monthly rental.

Housing prices and rents

From the 1960s to 1986, housing prices for owner-occupation rose faster than real incomes or general inflation because housing demand exceeded housing supply. According to the official housing and rental price statistics survey done since 1986, housing prices rose almost 50 per cent between 1988–90 as shown in Figure 4.2. Such factors as trade surplus and the inflow of foreign currency created a huge and fluid liquidity; the stock market continued to break records and assets of all kinds, including housing, increased in value. At that time, many low-income families could no longer afford rising rents and they began demanding higher wages. Housing prices (for home-ownership) and *chonsei* rents fell dramatically in 1991 and housing prices remained relatively stable until 1997.

This trend in housing prices from 1991–95 was due to the Two Million Housing Construction Plan from 1989–93. After the completion of that plan, a further 600,000 housing units were constructed every year until 1998, which contributed to the stabilization of housing prices. As a result of the 1998 economic crisis, average housing values decreased by 12.4 per cent over the previous year, while *chonsei* values decreased by 18.4 per cent. In the Seoul Metropolitan Area, housing prices decreased by 13.2 per cent and *chonsei* prices fell by 22.7 per cent. In 1999 when the economy began to recover, with a 10.9 per cent GDP growth rate, the housing market also started to recover. Housing prices rose by 3.4 per cent, and *chonsei* rents by 16.8 per cent. *Chonsei* rents continued to increase by two-digit numbers from 2000–02 as shown in Figure 4.2. Housing prices also increased from 2001–03.

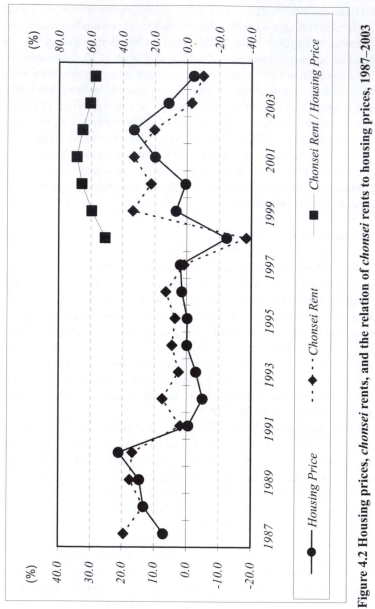

Figure 4.2 Housing prices, *chonsei* rents, and the relation of *chonsei* rents to housing prices, 1987–2003

Source: Kookmin Bank, Statistics of Housing Market since 1986.

This rapid increase of rent from 1999 gave rise to the formulation of the One Million Rental Housing Project in 2002, while the rapid increase of housing prices from 2001 resulted in strong anti-speculation measures for real estate, introduced on 29 October 2003. This led to an immediate fall in housing prices, followed by a decline in *chonsei* rents in 2004. Figure 4.2 shows the changing proportion of *chonsei* rent to housing price from 1998–2004 according to the statistics of Kookmin Bank.

Because of the nature of the *chonsei* system, Korean *chonsei* tenants are putting down as a rental deposit up to (and sometimes more than) 50 per cent of the money that would be needed to buy a house. This does not seem a good use of their resources. If the Korean government had established a housing finance system to provide *chonsei* tenants with long-term, low interest mortgages, while at the same time creating a sufficient supply of new housing to enable renters to buy, then home-ownership could have increased and the difficulties of realizing the 'my home dream' could have been lessened. The Korean government, however, focused not on housing finance but on housing supply. As a result, the majority of *chonsei* tenants could not catch up with increasing house prices. Newly constructed housing was sold to those who could afford to buy without a housing loan.

The Development of Housing Policy in Korea

The 1960s: housing under the military regime

The military coup d'état which occurred in 1961 in the name of national security and economic development resulted in a highly centralised government system in place of the previous parliamentary one. Housing development by the public sector was initiated in 1962 (see Table 4.4 for a summary of this and other policy developments) as part of the first Five Year Economic Development Plan (1962–66). During that period the Korean government borrowed funds from overseas for infrastructure and industrial plants,[5] while only limited resources were allocated for housing. In 1962 the Korea National Housing Corporation (KNHC) was established as a government agency to construct public housing. However KNHC was set up as a self-financing public enterprise and was unable to build housing that families on low incomes could afford. In this respect, it could be said that KNHC was providing for middle-income households rather than those in housing need. Moreover, KNHC housing was for sale rather than to let. Those considered eligible were household heads who had not owned any houses for one or more years at the time the new houses were advertised for sale. This regulation was part of the Public Housing Act of 1963. The Act also gave local government a responsibility to provide public housing, especially for the lowest income families.

---

5   In 1965 the Korean government agreed with the Japanese government the amount of indemnity relating to the colonial period from 1910 to 1945. Part of the settlement enabled Korea to obtain loans from Japan to assist economic development in Korea.

Table 4.4 Housing policy developments in Korea, 1950–2003

Year	What happened?	Policy Issue	Consequence
1950	Outbreak of the Korean War	Housing destruction by war	No priority for housing
1953	The end of the Korean War	Many refugees	
1962	The First Economic Development Plan	The Establishment of KNHC The Public Housing Act (PHA)	
1963		The Land Readjustment Act	
1966		The Korean Housing Bank established	
1967	The Second Economic Development Plan		Housing as political propaganda
1972	High priority of industries	Ten Year Housing Construction Plan 1972–81	
1978	Rapid urbanization	Housing Construction Promotion Act (the repeal of the PHA)	Severe housing shortage
1981	'One house per household' policy	Price control of newly built housing; Residential Land Development Promotion Act (1980) National Housing Fund created (1981)	
1982	Rapid rise of land and housing prices		
1984		Rental Housing Construction Promotion Act (1984)	Serious housing disparities
1988	Seoul Olympic Games		
1989	Two Million Housing Construction Plan		
1997	Asian Economic Crisis		
2000	National Basic Livelihood Guarantee	Korea Housing Finance Corporation	
2002			Shortage ended (2002)
2003	One Million National Rental Housing Plan	The Minimum Standard of Living	

In the Second Five Year Economic Development Plan period (1967–71) housing policy continued to be a low priority for the Korean government. The main focus was on reconstructing the economy. The government had no capital to invest in the housing sector. Laws to facilitate land development and housing finance were passed. The Land Re-adjustment Law of 1966 was to encourage the development of the urban periphery. The Korea Housing Bank[6] was established in 1967 as a state-owned specialized bank for housing finance. KHB raised funds by taking contractual savings from potential homebuyers, for example under the Housing Subscription Savings scheme (HSS)[7] and the Housing Subscription Deposit scheme (HSD).[8] KHB also took general deposits in the retail savings market; and issued debentures in the capital market. Priority for loans was given to individual savers according to the amount saved and the length of time they had been saving. During the decade from 1962–1971, 866,000 housing units were constructed, but the public sector's share was only 12.5 per cent.

1972–1979: challenges to mass production under the Yushin[9] Government

In 1970 the Korean economy slumped because of overcapitalization and the increase of foreign debt. Labour disputes reflected the unrest resulting from what was felt to be the dominance of financial cliques. Externally, the Shanghai Communiqué of 1972 presaged a normalization of relations between the USA and China and changing economic and political relations in East Asia. All these events had implications for the Korean government. In October 1972, President Park suspended the existing constitution and established the Yushin Constitution[10] based on the concept of an imperial presidency. 'Yushin' was said to be the new coup d'état, aiming to strengthen Park's position against those who opposed him. At that time, in connection with housing policy, government adopted the slogan 'one house per household'. A Ten Year Housing Construction Plan was established to build 2.5 million housing units

---

6   In 1997, KHB was converted from a state-owned housing bank to a private commercial bank named the Housing and Commercial Bank (HCB). In 2001, HCB was merged with the Kookmin Bank to form the largest commercial bank in Korea. The new Kookmin Bank is a commercial bank and does not have to specialise in housing finance. However, it remains a dominant force in the housing finance market and its share of housing business has been maintained since the merger with HCB.

7   By joining the HSS scheme, a head of household was eligible to apply for new public housing, including housing for owner-occupation.

8   HSD is a savings scheme enabling depositors to apply for new private housing.

9   'Yushin' means to reform institutions and political ideologies. The President claimed to be following the model of *ishin*, or reformation, from the period of the Emperor Meiji (sometimes referred to as the Meiji restoration) which in Japan, from 1868, restored Imperial rule and began the process of modernizing and reforming the country.

10   According to the Yushin Constitution, the President was to be elected not by the people but by an electoral college. Local administration was reduced to the status of being a local branch of the national administration.

from 1972–81. The Public Housing Act was repealed and was replaced by the Housing Construction Promotion Act of 1972. The new Act gave momentum and the government assumed a pro-active attitude towards solving the housing shortage. The Act was characterized by the simplification of procedures and the cutting out of various permits and approvals, which had to be applied for only when building more than 50 housing units[11] simultaneously. Private developers organized themselves in response to the Act, and large construction companies started building large-scale housing estates. From that time, apartment houses began to prevail in Korea.[12]

By the mid-1970s, the government was under increasing pressure to distribute the fruits of development to working class and low-income families. In 1977 the Special Law for National Housing Stabilization was introduced. According to this law, the government planned to construct 15,000 public rental apartments annually for low-income families and special rental housing for the working class in large scale industrial complexes, even though the housing would be let for only one year before having to be sold. The plan was not realized, however, because of financial constraints (Lim 2002, 96–7).

Although spending on housing had become a low priority for the government,[13] housing supply continued to increase. Ironically, more than 300,000 units were constructed in 1978 when real estate speculation became a national phenomenon, and housing prices increased very rapidly. In response, the government introduced the Comprehensive Anti-Real Estate Speculation Measures.[14] The measures were strongly enforced and prices began to fall. In 1978, the government introduced a price ceiling system for newly constructed housing in multi-family units, requiring builders to sell at a regulated price determined by government. Demand was controlled by restricting eligibility to those with contractual savings but even then, the number seeking housing at regulated prices was so great that allocations for sale were made by a lottery which only eligible households could join. The Korean government thought price control a good policy to help those who wanted to own a house. As the gap between the market price and the regulated price amounted to a windfall gain, competition for new housing remained very high until housing price control was eventually ended. Not surprisingly, most of the windfall gains were made by middle and upper class buyers, since the supply of housing finance was insufficient for the needs of lower-income households. At first, the price ceiling system resulted in a decrease of housing supply. The initially negative impact on builders, however, was short-lived, since they made many quick sales at a small profit, which was a good opportunity for their business.

---

11 Later the number was reduced to 20 housing units.

12 The number of apartment dwellings increased from 33,372 in 1970 to 5,231,319 in 2000. By contrast, the number of single detached houses remained almost the same, at 4,359.000 in 1970 and 4,337,000 in 2000.

13 In the early 1970s, the government did not make any investment in housing because the oil-shock hit the economy.

14 Typical measures were the land transaction permit system and heavy taxes on capital gains, particularly when the properties being sold were not registered.

During the ten years from 1972–81, nearly 1.88 million units of housing were constructed, fewer than the target of the 2.5 million housing project. Seven hundred and twenty-four thousand of these units were constructed with support from the government.[15]

1980–1987: ambitious plans under the new military regime

In October 1979 the Director of the Korean Central Intelligence Agency assassinated President Park. In May 1980 military leaders seized power and established the Legislative Council of the National Defence Emergency Measures Board. The new regime, though it had only *de facto* authority, endeavoured to solve the problems of daily life under the slogan of Korea as a 'developed welfare nation'. As one strategy to achieve this, the Residential Land Development Promotion Act was enacted in 1980. Using this law, public sector developers such as KNHC and the Korea Land Development Corporation (KLDC)[16] prepared land for development through a procedure called 'public development'. The public developer first acquired all the land in the project area, using compulsory purchase powers if necessary; drew up a comprehensive land use plan; installed various infrastructures; and undertook other engineering works. As the price of land in the project area was determined by government valuation rather than the market, the price was effectively controlled; and when the prepared sites were sold for development, any capital gain accrued to the public sector. Prepared land was usually sold to house builders and commercial property developers, sometimes at subsidized prices. This kind of land supply mechanism contributed to the mass production of housing. Such 'Promotion Acts' as the Housing Construction Promotion Act and the Residential Land Development Promotion Act were enacted under martial law and it could be said that a regime lacking popular support tried to improve its standing by implementing populist policies of this kind.

Also in 1980, the Legislative Council of the National Defence Emergency Measures Board put forward a programme to solve housing shortage by building five million housing units in the ten years from 1982–91. If the programme could have been achieved, it would almost have doubled the national housing stock from its level of 5.3 million in 1980 (see Table 4.1). There were those, including government officials, who thought the cost of this programme to be excessive, given that others (for example the International Bank for Reconstruction and Development) were recommending tight monetary control, reduced government spending and price stabilization as appropriate economic policies, especially for a country seeking

---

15 Between 1971 and 1980, about 65,000 apartments were constructed for public rental, on condition that they would be sold to their occupants within a mandatory period of one or two years (KNHC 1992, 234). The aim was to recover the cost of construction within a relatively short period.

16 KLDC was established in 1979. In 1996, its name was changed to Korea Land Corporation (KLC).

loans from the IBRD (Lim 2002, 102). It was clear the government could not fully implement this programme. The target figure was reduced several times and in the end was quietly forgotten. In reality, between 1980–90 (Table 4.1) the housing stock nationally was increased by about two million dwellings.

In 1981 the Government created the National Housing Fund (NHF)[17] through an amendment to the Housing Construction Promotion Act. The NHF has been a very important policy instrument in housing supply. At first, it specialized in providing low interest loans for the production of small dwellings for sale: they were to be less than 60 sq m.[18] The loan is made initially to the developer and then passed to the buyer, for repayment over 20 years.[19]

Also in 1981, the Housing Lease Protection Law was enacted to assist *chonsei* tenants. According to the law, rent increases were to be limited to a maximum of 5 per cent of the rent in the previous year. However, as there was not a concept of renting as a long-term tenure in Korea at that time, the idea of relating current rent to previous rent levels was not useful. In the early 1980s, the normal lease was for only one year.[20] If a landlord were to go bankrupt, the serious problem for the tenant was: who would be responsible for returning the *chonsei* deposit – or lump-sum rent? Under the 1981 law, those who acquired a house following a bankruptcy became responsible for returning the tenant's *chonsei* deposit, either on the termination of the lease or sooner, if the new owner wished for vacant possession. But even this was not straightforward since the *chonsei* rent paid as a deposit could be more than the *chonsei* to be repaid at the end of the agreement; the amounts also varied according to criteria applied in different regions of the country. Despite these complexities, the significance of the 1981 law was in the willingness of government to protect the interests of *chonsei* tenants in the hope of greater stability in this part of the housing market.

---

17 This fund was to be managed by the Ministry of Construction through the Korea Housing Bank (KHB). The NHF mainly comprises National Housing Subscription Savings Deposits, National Housing Bonds, loan repayments, Housing Lottery funds, and loans and other contributions from the government. The National Housing Bond is compulsory and is sold to those who are in the process of gaining permission to buy or who are registered for new purchases, including housing and other items such as automobiles. The interest rate on bonds was 5 per cent until 2001 and is 3 per cent at the time of writing. The repayment period for bonds is five years. The contribution of the government is a modest 0.9 per cent from the NHF. By 2003, nearly 3.5 million housing units had been built with the assistance of the NHF (Ministry of Construction and Transportation 2004, 16).

18 In 1984, temporary five year public rental housing began to be provided in Korea. The housing could be rented for five years but at the end of that time, tenants were expected to buy it.

19 The maximum loan per household is approximately 30 to 40 per cent of a unit's construction cost. With regard to the financing of newly built housing, 3.04 million housing units, or almost 36 per cent of the total housing units constructed between 1981 and 2000, were financed through the NHF.

20 The minimum period for a housing lease has been two years since 1989.

From 1982–83 the government relaxed anti-speculation measures with a view to revitalizing the housing market. These measures, combined with a general improvement in the national economy, fuelled an increase in housing demand. In 1983 when housing prices began to go up, government introduced a 'bond-bidding' system as a device to discourage speculation in the regions where the disparity between the market prices and the regulated prices of newly built houses was high. Would-be purchasers were required to enter a competitive bidding process for buying new housing. Sales were awarded to the highest bidders and the profit, in effect the bond paid by the purchaser, was credited to the National Housing Fund.

In 1984 the Rental Housing Construction Promotion Law was enacted to promote the construction of rental housing by private builders. Private builders were permitted to buy land prepared by 'public development' and to borrow money from the banks. Under this law, 'rental' meant five years not permanent rental. The level of deposit and the rents charged had to follow Ministry of Construction guidelines. Through this law, the construction of five year rental housing increased from 1984–87.

Until 1986, rents continued to increase but housing prices were stable and the government did not put emphasis on housing supply. During the period 1980–87, the housing industry built about 220,000 houses annually, roughly 150,000 dwellings a year short of the estimated need for new housing.

By the mid-1980s, there were signs of growing economic prosperity because of lower oil prices, the lower prices of raw materials and the weak domestic currency, which benefited international trade. In June 1986 students and other citizens demonstrated to fight for constitutional reforms, demanding a more democratic political system with direct presidential elections. The government could not resist these claims and began the process of amending the Constitution. In addition, in 1987, there were labour disputes in support of free trades unions and the right to collective wage negotiations. Housing became a political issue, partly because the growing trade surplus was attracting foreign investment which in turn led to speculation in housing and land prices, both of which increased sharply. During the Presidential election campaign in late 1987, the candidate of the ruling party pledged to build four million housing units within five years. After his election, the figure was reduced from four million to two million: still a formidable target and equivalent to one-third of the existing housing stock in 1987.

1988–1992: the successful mass supply of housing under a quasi-democratic government

From 1988–92, 2.7 million housing units were added to the housing stock, equal to what it had taken the previous decade to produce. The annual average of 600,000 new units outpaced the rate of household formation, which averaged 400,000 per year. Owing to the massive housing supply produced by the so-called 'Two Million Housing Construction Plan', spiralling house prices were halted and the housing supply ratio began to improve.

Previous housing plans had never been achieved in their entirety. The reasons for the attainment of the Two Million Housing Construction Plan were, first, that housebuilders could buy land at a relatively cheap price. The government designated 68 million *pyung* (3.3 sq m) of land for residential development, mostly less expensive agricultural land and other green-field sites. In addition, the government decided to develop five new towns[21] near Seoul with a total planned population of over 1.5 million. An important incentive for house-builders was the relaxation of the normal price ceiling for house sales, to allow for the lower price of land in the areas designated for development.[22] As a result, many builders bought land prepared as 'public development' schemes and sold at regulated prices. As another incentive, the Government relaxed land use regulations, for example, density control and builders were able to use the land to build multi-story housing. This enhanced their profits and at the same time helped the government building targets to be achieved.

Second, government provided financial assistance by increasing the National Housing Fund from which builders could obtain loans. The size of the NHF quadrupled in less than four years from 1.3 trillion *won* in 1987 to 5.32 trillion *won* in 1990 (Koh 2002, 261). Therefore, builders constructed as many housing units as they could and the capacity of the construction industry increased accordingly. More than 600,000 housing units were constructed from the completion of the Two Million Housing Plan to 1997. One third of the housing built at this time was funded by the NHF.

The Two Million Programme included projects to provide public rental housing. The term 'public rental' was first used in 1971 and five year public rental housing was introduced in 1984. According to the plan at that time, there were to be three types of public rental housing: five year public rental housing, employees' rental housing and permanent public rental housing. Five year public rental housing, usually of about 60 sq m is let for a five year mandatory rental period, as a condition of the preferential NHF loans through which it is funded; it is then sold to the tenant who has to be a saver in the Housing Subscription Scheme (HSS). The reason for the sales is to ensure a rapid turnover of housing funds, which can then be re-used to support further construction. The government has encouraged private companies to build this type of housing through NHF loans and tax incentives. This type of housing has had limited success, largely because of the few building companies willing to invest in rental dwellings; and the financial difficulty for tenants in buying the dwelling after the five year rental period comes to an end (Chung 1995, 327).

Employees' rental housing is sold by its developers to an employer who employs at least five persons. The employer then lets the housing to its employees for the five year mandatory rental period, before selling it in the same way as happens with five

---

21 The new towns are located within a radius of 20 km from the centre of Seoul. Their sizes ranged from 5 sq km to 20 sq km and their target populations from 170,000 to 390,000.

22 Normally this would not have been allowed. The price ceiling for house sales would be fixed without regard to the price paid for the land. Thus, in areas of high land prices, it could be difficult to build at a profit within the designated price ceilings.

year public rental housing. Recently, this type of housing became unpopular because employers did not wish to continue to provide company housing.

Permanent public rental housing is rental housing in the true sense of the term. This type of housing was intended to accommodate extremely poor households, such as the recipients of Livelihood Benefits in 1988 when the Two Million Housing Construction Plan was initiated. The government budget allocated 3.5 trillion *won*, which was 85 per cent of the total construction costs. The aim of the subsidy was to bring the rents within the means of lower income households but the housing proved unpopular among its intended beneficiaries, even though its quality and amenities were a great improvement on their previous housing. There were at least three reasons for this weak demand. First, the space was very small, less than 30 sq m in size. Second, the housing units were located in high-rise apartments. Third, the units were generally located far from where the intended residents were living. In addition, many poorer households felt they could not afford the monthly rent, even though it amounted to no more than their present housing costs. For these reasons, some of those who were on social welfare benefits cancelled their housing applications. The government then proposed widening the eligibility to include Housing Subscription Scheme depositors but finally decided in 1992 not to construct this type of housing. By 1995, the total number of permanent rental units was just over 190,000.

The two million housing programme was successful in increasing the supply of housing and in achieving improvements in the overall quality of the housing stock. The programme was not based on social welfare considerations but on the seriousness of housing problems, especially housing shortage, that the government could no longer neglect. The problems were typified, at the extreme, by a number of well-publicised cases where people committed suicide because of their inability to pay increased rents.

Constructing 2.7 million housing units within five years produced negative side effects such as increases in wages and the price of raw materials. People worried about the safety of what was built, by possibly unqualified workers using low quality building materials but these worries generally were unfounded. As mentioned before, however, the numerical success of the programme was not matched by a corresponding increase in the level of home-ownership. Those who tended to benefit directly from the programme were those who could afford to leave their existing homes and move into the smart, newly-constructed housing that had been provided, while others filtered into the older housing that was vacated, or became tenants of those prosperous enough to acquire investment properties among the 2.7 million that had been built.

1993–1998: A free market under a civilian government

In 1993 a new civilian government developed the New Economy Plan, advocating minimum intervention in the free market. Housing policy focused on the deregulation of development permits, density and land use controls, and redevelopment and reconstruction procedures. Especially, the government used the deregulation of land use control as a new means of land supply and relied heavily on the private sector to supply new housing. In 1994 the 'semi-agricultural area' was introduced as one of the five categories of national planning zones. This enabled private builders easily to develop semi-agricultural areas around Seoul, helped by the fact that the previous categories of permitted land uses were replaced by a list of non-permitted uses. For example, residential land development and housing construction in the semi-agricultural areas were allowed if the area of the site was less than 30,000 sq m. As a result, many housebuilders rushed out to develop, leading to a housing construction boom with 3.12 million housing units being constructed from 1993–97. Forty-four per cent of them were in the Seoul Metropolitan Area.

By contrast, during this period, most of the government subsidized housing programmes for low-income families were either eliminated or under-budgeted into gradual extinction. Instead of permanent public rental housing, 50 year public rental units, each less than 40 sq m, were supported. These were government financed and thus they remain rental units over the long term. Eligibility was limited to housing subscription depositors and subsequently to tenants of squatter areas, for example, areas undergoing redevelopment or renewal. Initially, the government planned to build 100,000 of these units but only 30,000 were completed because of budget cuts. At that time, the public sector's role in providing housing became unclear.

The new government relaxed some of its tight restriction and regulation of financial institutions such as banks and life insurance companies. The measures included interest rate deregulation, the abolition of money supply control, deregulation of fund management and the broadening of the business scope of financial institutions. It was widely assumed that the public would benefit greatly from this shift to a 'free market' and that the finance system would become much more efficient. However, the deregulation of the finance system was the main cause of Korea's economic crisis in 1997. In 1998, record-high interest rates and unemployment led to a severe decrease in the construction of new housing. Housing starts declined from 596,000 in 1997 to 306,000 in 1998 as shown in Table 4.9.

1998–2002: beginning of the One Million National Rental Housing Plan under the 'People's Government'

The new government that was elected shortly after the financial crisis was called the 'People's Government' and was headed by President Kim Dae-Jung. The revitalization of the private housing market was seen as a useful method, not only of reducing unemployment but also of stimulating the economy. Therefore, the government tried to support the private housing market by various measures.

- First, the government abolished sale price regulation and the 'bond-bidding' system. House builders were free to determine the price of housing for sale.
- Second, to increase housing demand, the government exempted from acquisition and registration taxes those who bought new or unsold apartments.
- Third, the government set a mortgage ceiling at 70 per cent of housing price

for genuine first-time buyers with an interest rate 2–5 per cent lower than the market rate. The aim was to create demand as well as to lower the cost of house purchase. Three hundred billion *won* of the NHF construction funds were converted into consumer loans with a 7–9 per cent interest rate, a three year grace period (no repayments for the first three years) and a 10–20 year repayment period. Two hundred million US dollars borrowed from the World Bank were to be used as seed money to extend credit of up to 900 billion *won* in order to help new home buyers meet their instalment payments on time and thereby to help the ailing housing industry (Koh 2002, 267).

- Fourth, the government extended credit of up to 200 billion *won* for landlords who were unable to reimburse *chonsei* deposits to tenants because the rent/ *chonsei* price had declined by as much as 15–20 per cent, as a result of the economic crisis. At that time the Korea Housing and Commercial Bank was authorised to issue additional housing credit of up to 600 billion *won* with terms slightly lower than the market rate to help middle income home buyers meet their instalment payments.

- Fifth, to raise low-cost funds on a long-term basis, the government in September 1998 established a legal framework for issuing asset-backed securities (ABS). In January 1999, mortgage-backed securities (MBS) were introduced. In April 2001, the Real Estate Investment Trusts Act was enacted. These measures enabled the issue of MBS either by a Special Purpose Company set up under the ABS Law or by a specialised mortgage pooling company. As an example of the latter, the government in September 1999, in partnership with major financial institutions, established KoMoCo, the Korea Mortgage Corporation. KoMoCo could buy mortgages from primary lenders, pool them and issue various forms of MBS in the capital market. Such activity was intended to provide funds to enable primary lenders to make additional housing loans; and although KoMoCo had difficulty at first in finding lending institutions that would sell mortgages, by August 2003, it had issued MBS's valued at 2.87 trillion *won* based on funding from the NHF loans (Social Research Institute of Kunkuk University 2003, 37). With the introduction of this secondary mortgage market, the housing finance system became a fully-fledged system, similar to that of the USA (Kim and Kim 2002, 112).

- Sixth, in an effort to increase housing demand, eligibility to establish a subscription deposit to buy a new apartment was granted to all household members aged 20 years and over.

Policy on public rental housing also began to change from 1998 under the 'People's Government' of President Kim Dae-Jung. Ten year and 20 year National rental housing began to be built. An initial programme of 50,000 units, with a maximum size of 50 sq m per unit, was planned for the period from 1998–2002. This housing was to be provided by the private sector with a government contribution of 30 per cent of the construction costs. The other 70 per cent was to come from the NHF (40 per cent), tenants' deposit (20 per cent) and KNHC (10 per cent).

In 2001 the government placed special emphasis on building more national rental housing and declared that 200,000 units would be completed by 2003. Eligibility for the ten year units was to be limited to subscription depositors with an income less than 70 per cent of the average urban household income. Eligibility for the 20 year units was for low-income families with an income less than 50 per cent of the average urban household income. The aim was to achieve rents 40 per cent cheaper than for equivalent private rental housing in the same type of neighbourhood.

By the year 2000, housing prices and rents were tending to recover as shown in Figure 4.2. As the national economy improved, the housing market gained stability. The financial crisis however, had dented the confidence of landlords, especially *chonsei* landlords whose investment income had been badly affected by the crisis. They could see the benefits of the stable income flow from monthly tenants. To compensate for the perceived new risks of *chonsei* rental, *chonsei* rents increased sharply. Moreover, the high conversion rate of tenancies from *chonsei* deposit to high cost monthly rental was so great that many tenant households could not afford to pay. In 2002, faced by growing concern about the future affordability of private rental housing, the government announced a One Million National Rental Housing Construction Plan for ten years from 2003–12, (Table 4.5).

Table 4.5 The One Million National Rental Housing Construction Plan, 2003–2012 ('000s per year)

Year	2003	2004	2005	2006	2007	2008	2009	2010	2011	2012
Units planned	80	100	100	110	110	100	100	100	100	100

Source: Ministry of Construction and Transportation.

Under this plan, the rental period of two types of National Rental Housing was to change to 30 years and government assistance was to vary according to the size (floor space) of housing unit. It can be said that, at present, the One Million Plan for National Rental Housing is the most important housing policy for low-income families. And the government has begun to think of public rental housing as the most appropriate housing tenure for people on low-incomes.

2003–present: welfare oriented housing policy under the 'Participatory Government'

The 'People's Government' was succeeded in February 2003 by the election of the self-styled 'Participatory Government'. The new government was committed to the building of national rental housing and took a strong line against real estate speculation, to reduce the widening gap between rich and poor resulting from rapid increases in housing prices. Anti-speculation policies included imposing an additional tax of up to 3 per cent of holdings whose total value is more than 0.9 billion *won*, raising the tax base for houses and land to reflect market value,[23] and imposing a heavy tax on capital gains. These measures helped to stabilise housing prices. The government also introduced a new price control system for newly built housing for sale of less than 60 sq m that is partly financed by NHF. These small apartments were to be sold at regulated prices from March 2005. However, there were criticisms of these strong restrictions, on the grounds that they might lead to a contraction in housing supply, with adverse effects on the construction industry in what are still seen as difficult economic circumstances. The dilemma for policy-makers is that while many people think a property bubble is bad, the prospect of market collapse is seen as much worse, especially after the experience of the 1997 economic crisis.

In an important policy change, the government revised the housing finance system with the aim of supporting home purchase by those in middle-and lower income brackets. A new law affecting the Korea Housing Finance Corporation (KHFC) was promulgated in December 2003. As a result, KoMoCo and the Credit Guarantee Fund were merged with KHFC in March 2004. This created a fund enabling KHFC to lend up to 300 trillion *won* to individual borrowers including first-time buyers) over a period of ten years with a fixed interest rate[24] to finance the purchase of houses priced at 600 million *won* or less. The interest rate of 5.95 per cent is lower than that for loans from commercial banks. According to KHFC, about 47,000 people in 2004 took out mortgages valued in total at 3.3 trillion *won*. However, it seems the main beneficiaries have not been low-income families but those on moderate incomes because the average annual income of the new borrowers, at 34.2 million *won*, was much higher than the average income for households in manual occupations.

Another important policy of the Participatory Government in June 2004 was to redefine the national minimum housing standard in terms of net floor space, the number of bedrooms by household size and the provision of basic amenities such as a water closet, a shower or bath and a modern kitchen.[25] The government then suggested that to reduce the number of people living below the minimum housing standard would require more emphasis on policies such as national public rental housing and the redevelopment of areas of substandard housing. Time will tell if these policies can achieve the government's objectives.

---

23 In 2005, the average taxable value of houses and land was set at around 30 per cent of their market value.

24 The amount borrowed nationally for home financing was estimated at 220 trillion *won* at the end of 2002, 77 per cent of which was accounted for by loans maturing within the next three years (Korea Herald, 23 December 2004).

25 The first attempt to define a minimum housing standard was in October 2000. At that time, the government wanted to include another goal: the attainment of a 100 per cent housing supply ratio. This goal was announced by MOCT, but was not applied in practice by the government and was not included in the 2004 redefinition.

Evaluation of Housing Policy

While government policies have led to some improvements in housing, they have not solved the housing problem. Indeed, in some respects they have intensified the housing problem of low-income families. As a result, even though the quality of housing has improved, large numbers of urban and rural poor still live in slums without inside w.c.'s, plumbing, and other basic amenities. In addition, the unequal distribution of income and wealth leaves many people with jobs and incomes that are inadequate to meet the rising cost of housing and rent, while others remain well off. According to the research of Son, Won and Moon (2001), the proportion of income spent on housing is much greater for the lower income than the higher income groups. A typical household in the lowest income group spends about 25 per cent of its total income and 30 per cent of its cash income on housing, whereas a higher income household spends between 5 and 10 per cent of its income on housing. One reason that poor families suffer from inadequate housing and pay too much of their income in rent is that the Korean government has not tackled directly the problem of housing need, nor really considered who needs or deserves housing assistance. Instead, past government policy has placed emphasis on the supply of new housing, in the belief that the benefits would 'trickle down' to those in need through a filtering process. In Korea there is still no system of rent allowances, even though *chonsei* rent could now be financed by the National Housing Fund.

Another failure of housing policy is that, despite the large volume of housing built for owner-occupation, the percentage of home-owners has not increased. In Korea successive governments have tried to increase home-ownership by regulating the sale price of housing and by suggesting eligibility criteria, often income-related, for housing purchasers. Nearly 13 million dwellings were built, mostly for sale, in the 39 years from 1965–2003. Yet the rate of owner-occupation declined throughout much of that period (Table 4.3), especially in rural areas, even though housing there has not been in short supply. Governments wishing to increase home ownership in their countries need to consider how best to make it affordable to those on lower incomes; and how to ensure that development takes place in areas where people need to live, including rural areas.

The mass supply of new housing has widened disparities between the rich and the poor. As many scholars have pointed out, rising incomes and wealth increase the ability to pay and thus the demand for housing and ownership. Wealthy households are more likely to be owner-occupiers than the poor (Werczberger 1997, 337–8). Even though owning one's home is widely believed to be a basic human desire, in Korea where housing finance for low-income families has not been readily available, new housing units provided at regulated prices were often owned not by those on lower incomes but by the wealthy. Consequently, the benefits of government policy were given to many middle and upper middle-income households.

The most serious problem of Korean housing policy was insufficient attention to rental housing policy. It can be said that public rental housing, often called social housing, is generally regarded as the most appropriate housing tenure for low-income families or individuals. This is especially the case in Korea, where, with rapid urbanization, public housing is particularly necessary for low-income households. However, Korean governments have not provided sufficient public housing. In 2003 the public rental sector, including temporary rental housing,[26] was 7.8 per cent of the total housing stock; while the proportion of permanent rental housing was only 2.2 per cent of the total housing stock.

Table 4.6 Distribution of public rental housing units[27] in 2003 (number and percentage)

Total Housing stock	Total Public Rental Stock*	Five year Rental Housing	Fifty year Public Housing	Permanent Rental Housing	Employees' Rental Housing	National Rental Housing
12,669,000 (100%)	986,000 (7.8%)	640,000 (5.0%)	93,000 (0.7%)	190,000 (1.5%)	42,000 (0.3%)	21,000 (0.2%)

Notes: * The Korean government normally includes certain rental housing units owned by registered private landlords in the number of public rental housing units. Table 4.6 excludes these 59,994 units because the housing is leased at market value and can not be regarded as 'social housing'.

Currently, there are five different types of public rental housing in Korea: (1) five year public rental housing; (2) 50 year public rental housing; (3) permanent rental housing; (4) employees' rental housing; and (5) national rental housing. The distribution is shown in Table 4.6.

Public rental housing in Korea can be criticized on a number of grounds. Firstly, its provision ignores some households who cannot afford even minimum housing costs. Secondly, five year public rental housing has been provided mainly through private companies that are entitled to make a profit; there is a potential conflict of interest here. Third, the central government is significantly involved, perhaps too much involved, in the direct supply of public rental housing. For example, KNHC which is an agency of central government owns and manages 286,000 public rental units and has played the main role in providing National rental housing. By contrast, local governments own and manage 125,000 public rental units, including 50 year

---

26 That is, housing that must be sold after periods of, for example, 5 or 50 years.

27 The term 'public rental housing' should be clarified in the context of the Korean housing market. In Korea, public rental housing means housing whose construction costs and rents are subsidized by the NHF or public expenditure. However, one peculiar characteristic of public rental housing in Korea is that the period of public rental differs according to the kind of funding.

rental and National rental housing. Recently, many have been unwilling to construct National rental housing in their administrative areas. By the end of 2004 only 8.6 per cent of National rental housing had been built by local governments. There are no non-profit, non-governmental social housing organizations in Korea. Fourth, the eligibility for and provision of public rental housing can be easily changed and is therefore insecure, since government subsidies are given without the support of any legal articles. As a result, the provision of public rental housing has been subject to manipulation for short-term political considerations, including economic regulation or revitalization.

Table 4.7 Housing quality trends in Korea, 1980–2000

		1980	1985	1990	1995	2000
Quantitative Indicators	Dwellings per 1,000 population	14.2	15.1	17.9	20.7	24.9
	Housing supply ratio (%)	72.8	71.7	72.4	86.0	96.2
	Average habitable floor space (sq m)	68.4	72.6	80.8	80.5	83.8
	Rooms per dwelling	3.3	3.5	4.0	4.3	4.4
Living space	Average floor area per household (sq m)	45.8	46.4	51.0	58.6	63.1
	Average floor area per person (sq m)	10.1	11.8	14.3	17.2	20.1
	Average number of rooms per person	0.5	0.5	0.7	0.9	1.1
Amenities	Dwellings with hot water supply (%)	10.0	20.0	34.1	74.8	94.1
	Dwellings with flush toilet (%)	18.4	33.6	51.3	75.1	87.4
	Dwellings with modern kitchen (%)	18.2	35.1	52.4	84.1	93.9

Source: National Statistical Office, Annual Population and Housing Census.

Conclusion

Housing is a major capital resource that affects every aspect of national life. How people live and how much they pay for shelter have a significant effect on their personal well-being. For these reasons, all nations, regardless of their orientation towards free markets or central planning, intervene in the housing market. The Korean government has intervened extensively in the production, consumption, financing, distribution and location of housing. Especially in the political context, government often regards housing policy as a tool for political stabilization.

The Korean government has always pursued housing policies designed to foster economic growth in the conviction that the ensuing economic prosperity would filter down to the poorest members of society. The country has achieved considerable improvement in the supply and quality of housing, as shown in Table 4.7. Looking at the period from 1980–2000, many households now are living in larger and better housing than ever before. Notwithstanding this, behind the improvements in housing supply and consumption many low-income people still live in overcrowded and poor quality housing. They suffer from high housing costs and rent increases due to the lack of affordable housing. In this regard, Korean housing policy has strongly favoured higher-income housing over lower-income housing. It could be said that Korean housing policy is not welfare policy but a policy that puts economic development first.

Appendix

Table 4.8 Housing supply and demand in Korea, 1965–2003

| | Housing Stock ('000) | Housing Starts ('000) | | | Housing Supply Ratio (%) | Housing Starts/ Population ('000) | Housing investment (% of GDP) | GNI/per Person (US$) | Unemployment rate (%) |
		Public	Total	Private					
1965	3,932	8	70	62		2.4	1.50		
1966	3,867	12	93	81		3.1	1.90		
1967	4,097	10	95	85		3.1	2.30		
1968	4,183	20	96	76		3.2	3.00		
1969	4,229	38	105	67		3.4	2.70		
1970	4,360	12	115	103	78.2	3.6	4.24	289	
1971	4,427	24	130	106	77.3	4.1	3.81	319	
1972	4,484	17	110	93	76.3	3.4	3.06	396	
1973	4,558	44	143	99	75.5	4.2	3.74	541	
1974	4,640	43	158	115	74.8	4.6	5.51	594	
1975	4,734	63	180	117	74.4	5.1	5.16	799	
1976	4,822	62	170	108	73.3	4.7	4.77	1,009	
1977	4,927	78	204	126	72.6	5.8	5.43	1,399	

1978	5,082	115	300	185	72.5	8.2	6.85	1,636	
1979	5,211	118	251	133	72.0	6.7	5.81	1,598	
1980	5,319	106	212	105	71.2	5.6	5.45		5.2
1981	5,450	78	150	72	70.5	3.9	4.20	1,749	4.5
1982	5,640	68	191	123	70.2	4.9	4.88	1,847	4.4
1983	5,852	82	226	144	70.2	5.7	5.77	2,020	4.1
1984	6,061	114	222	108	70.1	5.5	4.87	2,190	3.8
1985	6,104	132	227	95	69.8	5.6	4.61	2,229	4.0
1986	6,303	153	288	135	69.7	7.0	4.86	2,550	3.8
1987	6,450	167	244	78	69.2	5.9	4.79	3,201	3.1
1988	6,670	115	317	202	69.4	7.6	5.30	4,268	2.5
1989	7,032	162	462	300	70.9	10.9	5.96	5,185	2.6
1990	7,357	269	750	481	72.4	17.5	8.76	5,886	2.4
1991	7,853	164	613	449	74.2	14.2	8.88	6,810	2.4
1992	8,631	195	575	381	76.0	13.2	7.81	7,183	2.5
1993	8,798	227	695	469	79.1	15.8	8.23	7,811	2.9
1994	9,133	258	623	364	83.5	14.0	7.47	8,998	2.5
1995	9,570	236	619	391	86.0	13.8	7.43	10,820	2.1

Table 4.8 Continued

	Housing Stock ('000)	Housing Starts ('000)			Housing Supply Ratio (%)	Housing Starts/ Population ('000)	Housing investment (% of GDP)	GNI/per Person (US$)	Unemployment rate (%)
		Public	Total	Private					
1996	10,113	232	592	360	89.2	13.0	7.13	11,380	2.0
1997	10,627	219	596	377	92.0	13.0	6.48	10,307	2.6
1998	10,867	131	306	175	92.4	6.6	6.02	6,742	7.0
1999	11,181	151	405	253	93.3	8.6	5.17	8,581	6.3
2000	11,472	140	433	293	96.2	9.2	4.32	9,628	4.1
2001	11,892	128	530	402	98.3	11.2	4.69	10,162	3.8
2002	12,357	124	667	543	100.6	14.0	4.89	11,493	3.1
2003	12,669	86	585	499	101.2	14.0	4.94	12,646	3.4

The Bank of Korea National Accounts 2000 http://ecos.bok.or.kr
The Statistics Office, KOSIS, http://www.nso.go.kr
Note: Housing investment in GNP before 1995 is based on constant prices in 1995. Housing investment in GNP from 1996 is based on 2000, per capita GNI (Annual, at Current Prices).
Source: Korea National Housing Corporation, Yearbook of Housing Statistics.

Chapter 5

Housing and State Strategy in Post-War Japan

Yosuke Hirayama

Introduction

In Japan, since the end of the Second World War, the state has consistently emphasized economic development and the maintenance of social solidarity. The housing system, reflecting the basic course of the state, has focused on the creation of the 'social mainstream' by expanding home-ownership (Hirayama 2003a). The post-war economy developed at a rapid rate and an increasing number of middle-class households were encouraged to purchase their own homes. Mass-construction of owner-occupied housing was accelerated in order to address the demand for housing and, more importantly to the state, to stimulate the economy. Since the prices of land and housing rose noticeably and continuously, owning a house, which was accompanied by a capital gain, became an effective means of accumulating an asset. A system was formed where the promotion of home-ownership was closely linked with economic development and the growth of the middle class.

The government played a key role in operating the mainstream-oriented housing system. Japan aspired to catch up with the western 'advanced nations' following the war, which led to accelerated economic development and the prioritization of industrial productivity (Murakami 1992). However, the state in Japan has completely differed from the European welfare states which emerged in the immediate post-war period, in terms of the formation of housing provision strategies. It has never set out to expand the social housing sector nor accepted the concept of universal citizenship rights for housing (Harada 1985; Hirayama 2003a; Izuhara 2000; Ohmoto 1985; Ronald 2004). In post-war Japan, while education and health services have developed relatively universally and comprehensively among various public welfare provision programmes, direct provision of housing welfare has remained small scale. Nevertheless, the fact that Japan did not adopt European welfare state models does not imply that the Japanese government has not been concerned with housing provision. The relationship between the state and housing, in post-war Japan, developed in a very particular context. Since the period immediately after the war, the Japanese government has nurtured the creation of a society and an economy orientated around the middle classes and middle class home-ownership.

The housing system in Japan has essentially been shaped and rationalized under the conditions of economic growth and social stability. Over the past two decades, however, the housing context has been transformed by a more volatile, uncertain economy and the increasing fragmentation of society. The so-called 'bubble economy', which started with a tremendous rise in housing and land prices in the latter half of the 1980s, collapsed at the beginning of the 1990s. Ever since the bubble burst, Japan has been in the grip of a long and deep recession, characterized by the destabilization of the middle class. Land and housing prices fell sharply for the first time since the end of the war. Owner-occupied housing has come to generate capital losses and the security of residential property as an asset has been undermined (Forrest, Kennett and Izuhara 2003; Hirayama 2003b). The demographic structure has also been undergoing dramatic changes due to an unprecedented increase in the elderly and a drop in the fertility rate. The proportion of conventional family households is in decline and single, elderly-only and couple-only households are increasing. Consequently, the consistency of the social mainstream has become increasingly irregular and the traditional housing system has begun to lose ground.

It is, therefore, becoming a critically important challenge to find an alternative direction for housing in present-day Japan. However, whether or not the housing system will develop a clear new course and how it will function in shifting circumstances remain to be seen. This chapter will explore, in a chronological arrangement, the context in which the state has developed its housing strategy (see Table 5.1 and Table 5.2). The housing system not only provides housing but also is deeply implicated with the wider economy and social structure. It will be demonstrated in the following discussion how vividly the state's housing strategy reflects and reinforces social and economic conditions.

Table 5.1 Key figures for Japan

Land area	377,899 km²	(2003)
Population	127,716 thousand persons	(01 Nov 2004)
Number of households	49,838 thousand households	(31 Mar 2004)
GDP	4,302,557 million dollars	(2003)
GDP per capita	33,727 dollars	(2003)
Unemployment rate	4.7 %	(2004)

Source: Cabinet Office, Ministry of Land, Infrastructure and Transport, and Ministry of Internal Affairs and Communications.

Table 5.2 Transformation of housing policy

	Housing conditions	Policy direction
1945–50	End of WW2 Acute housing shortage	Emergency measures
1950–55	Persistent housing shortage	Three pillars of post-war housing policy
1955–73	High-speed economic growth Rapid urbanization	Primacy of economic development Emphasis on owner-occupation Residualization of public housing
1973–85	Low-growth period Quality and affordability issues	Japanese style welfare society Mass-construction of owner-occupied housing as an economic booster
1985–90	The bubble economy Upsurge of house prices End of housing shortage	Mass housing construction to stimulate domestic demand
1990–2000	The 'lost decade' after the bubble burst Long-standing recession Devaluation of housing properties	Mass housing construction to recover the economy Emphasis on urban regeneration
2000–	Socio-economic uncertainty	End of the three pillars Emphasis on the deregulation of the housing and mortgage markets

Housing and the Social Mainstream

Rising from the ashes

There was an overwhelming housing shortage when the Second World War ended in August 1945. The Department of Post-War Reconstruction estimated the housing shortage immediately after the war at as many as 4.2 million dwellings. It was more than one fifth of the total number of existing dwellings at that time. Particularly in urban areas that had been devastated most by intensive air raids, housing was desperately short. Moreover, the impact of rent regulation during and initially after the war discouraged the provision of private rental housing (Miyake 1985). The wartime government enforced the first Rent Regulation Ordinance in 1939 and the second one in 1940, in order to control social unrest by keeping rent from rising. Before the end of the war, rental housing accounted for most of the dwellings in the large cities. According to the 'Survey of Housing in Large Cities' conducted by the government in 1941, the ratio of rental housing to total housing was 73.3 per cent in Tokyo, 89.2 per cent in Osaka and 80.3 per cent in Nagoya. The rental housing market, however, did not respond to the housing shortage after the war due to the impact of rent regulation. The third Rent Regulation Ordinance came into force in 1946 to cope with the post-war confusion. It was in 1950 that the order was removed thereafter for newly built rental housing. The Rent Regulation Ordinance, which was effective for some ten years, largely suspended private rental housing provision.

Immediately after the end of the war, the government was pressed into providing housing programmes as emergency measures to address the tremendous demand for housing (Hayakawa and Ohmoto 1988). It was decided in August 1945 to build temporary housing for winter in the main war-devastated cities. The construction work, however, did not make any progress due to the lack of materials. Consequently, facilities formerly for military use, factory accommodation and burnt-out buildings were turned into living quarters by the Emergency Housing Order in November 1945, and some large houses were compulsorily handed over to war-affected households in May 1946. A state subsidy was initiated for the construction of new housing in 1946. There were, however, only some 300,000 dwellings built by the government and other public bodies between 1945–50. The series of emergency programmes was, in reality, barely effective where housing was in exceedingly short supply.

The government established post-war housing policy based on a patchwork of emergency measures. The Ministry of Construction was founded in 1948 and given jurisdiction over housing policy. It systematized post-war housing policy on the so-called 'three pillars': the GHLC (Government Housing Loan Corporation) Act in 1950, the Public Housing Act in 1951 and the JHC (Japan Housing Corporation) Act in 1955. The GHLC, a state agency, mainly provides individuals with long-term, fixed, low-interest loans for the building and acquisition of their own home. Public housing, which is subsidized by the national government, and constructed, owned and managed by local governments, is provided for low-income households at subsidized rents. The JHC was founded as an agency of the state to develop multi-family housing estates for middle-income households in large cities.

Although the government began to implement housing policy with its three pillars, priority was put on the reconstruction of the economy along with various other domestic issues and consequently poor living conditions and the shortage of housing stock were left to wait. The fundamental course of housing policy did not expand the direct provision of housing by the public sector but relied, as much as was possible, on the unaided construction of private housing (Harada 1985). Though the public provision of a minimum amount of housing and other welfare services was regarded as being necessary in order to subdue the growing social unrest, the dominant idea was that economic reconstruction rather than the improvement of people's lives was the way to facilitate the rebuilding of the country. The enormous housing shortage did not ease swiftly enough and many people suffered from the wretched dwelling conditions for an extended period. Even ten years after the end of the war, according to the Housing Survey carried out in 1958, the number of households having housing difficulties was 4.8 million, or more than 26 per cent of total households. Households with difficulties were defined as those who lived in non-housing places such as buses and hen houses, in other people's houses, in dilapidated housing or in overcrowded conditions where, for example, four or more members lived in a space of less than 20 sq meters.

Critically, the government operated a housing policy in order to construct a social mainstream. In other words, housing policy aimed not at improving housing conditions for all the people, but predominantly for the core members of society (Hirayama 2003a). Japan addressed fundamental reforms centring on demilitarization and democratization under orders of the U.S. General Headquarters. Industries and the economy had completely collapsed and people were living in extreme poverty. Support for the people thought to make up the mainstream of society was given priority in housing policy in order to form the state's new direction and to encourage the rebuilding of industries and the economy. In the last half of the 1940s, the government also attached importance to the improvement of living conditions for coal-workers in order to rebuild the coal industry, which was a key industry at that time (Hayakawa and Wada 1968). Most of the public funds and materials for housing were used for housing construction in the coal mining districts.

Essentially, the three pillars of housing policy helped mainly middle-class households to secure housing (Hirayama 2003a). It was considered that such households would play a bigger part in the reconstruction of the nation. The GHLC encouraged middle-income families to build their own homes and the JHC constructed housing for an increasing number of white-collar worker households in large cities. Single people were excluded from most of the housing policy measures, since it was presumed that they had no problems in terms of overcrowded living conditions and, furthermore, they did not count as members of the main part of society. Only once they were married and had children could they benefit from housing policy. The government sector constructed some public housing for people on low incomes. However, those on the lowest incomes were not included in the public housing measures. The calculation of rent was based on construction expenditure and did not vary according to the dwellers' incomes. Public housing was provided for households with the ability to pay rent. A high ranking government official, who had been involved in the formation of the public housing system, said later about the legislation process, 'People in the bottom bracket were left behind. Those who could not afford a certain amount of rent could not live in public housing. The poor were to be abandoned. It was a matter of course, wasn't it? There was an absolute shortage of housing. The thing was where to start. Putting priority on such burdensome people, leaving those who could contribute to the reconstruction of the nation, would not lead to the rebuilding of Japan' (cited in Ohmoto 1991, 275–6).

It was also noticeable that the proportion of home-ownership rose rapidly over a short period during and after the war. In Tokyo, the rate of owner-occupied housing, which was less than 30 per cent in the early 1940s, rose to approximately 60 per cent by 1953 (Miyake 1985). During the first few years after the war, there was an increase in temporary shack buildings (barracks) built by war-affected people themselves, which added to the stock of owner-occupied housing. As rent regulation severely limited potential profitability for rental property owners, an increasing number of landlords sold their properties to their tenants, which also pushed up the proportion of owner-occupied housing. As a result, the structure and pattern of tenure and housing stock in the post-war period was unrecognizable compared to that of the pre-war period.

Expanding home-ownership

The Economic White Paper in 1956 declared that the era of post-war confusion had come to an end, and indeed, industry and the economy began to develop at a striking pace. The conservatives formed the Liberal Democratic Party in 1955 and have held power almost exclusively ever since. Backed by strong connections in business circles, they took a clear line oriented towards economic development. The government in 1960 confidently announced a plan to double national income in a ten-year period, firmly showing that its policy focused on economic growth. During the period from 1955 to the oil crisis of 1973, the average annual GDP growth was as high as 10 per cent.

The mass-construction of housing was regarded as a booster for economic growth. The quantity of new housing starts increased consistently and rapidly throughout the 1950s and the 1960s (see Figure 5.1). Rapid urbanization put increasing stress on the demand for housing. According to the Population Census, the proportion of the population in urban areas rose from 37.7 per cent in 1950 to 63.9 per cent in 1960, and to 72.1 per cent in 1970. With this movement, the pace of increase in the number of households also rose. The average annual increase in the number of households swelled from 185,000 in 1950–55, to 466,000 in 1955–60, to 682,000 in 1960–65, and to 758,000 in 1965–70. There remained a great shortage of housing until the middle of the 1970s. Large-scale housing construction, which was complemented by the high demand for housing, came to occupy a pivotal position in the economy. Mass housing construction was also accelerated by the 'scrap and build' system[1] (Hirayama 2003b). With this approach construction demand is maintained by the repetition of construction and demolition, which, in turn, supports economic growth. Together with the increase of new housing starts, housing demolition also increased. The proportion of the number of demolished dwellings to that of new housing starts rose from 27 per cent in 1968–73, to 42 per cent in 1973–78, and to as much as 51 per cent in 1978–83 (Yamada 2000).

---

1   It has been customary in Japan for single-family houses to be rebuilt on the same site at intervals of 20–30 years. This has a bearing on the size of the market for 'second-hand' housing.

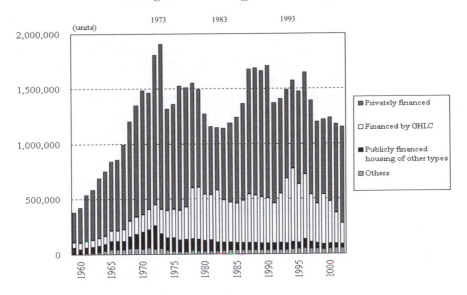

Figure 5.1 New housing starts, 1959-2003
Source: Ministry of Land, Infrastructure and Transport.

Table 5.3 Housing tenure, 1963–2003

Year	Owned houses (%)	Public rented houses (owned by local government) (%)	Public rented houses (owned by public corporation)* (%)	Private rented houses (%)	Company houses (%)	Total housing units (including tenure not reported) N
1963	64.3	4.6		24.1	7.0	20,374,000
1968	60.3	5.8		27.0	6.9	24,198,000
1973	59.2	4.9	2.1	27.5	6.4	28,731,000
1978	60.4	5.3	2.2	26.1	5.7	32,189,000
1983	62.4	5.4	2.2	24.5	5.2	34,705,000
1988	61.3	5.3	2.2	25.8	4.1	37,413,000
1993	59.8	5.0	2.1	26.4	5.0	40,773,300
1998	60.3	4.8	2.0	27.3	3.9	43,892,100
2003	61.2	4.7	2.0	26.8	3.2	46,862,900

Note: * Japan Housing Corporation (1955–81), Housing and Urban Development Corporation (1981–99), Urban Development Corporation (1999–2004) and local public corporations.
Source: Statistics Bureau, 1963 Housing Survey of Japan – 1993 Housing Survey of Japan, 1998 Housing and Land Survey of Japan, and 2003 Housing and Land Survey of Japan.

Among the three pillars of housing policy, the government most vigorously encouraged the building of owner-occupied housing by means of GHLC loans (Hayakawa 2002; Hirayama and Hayakawa 1995; Hirayama 2003a). Economic development led to an increase in the number of middle-class households who could own their own homes. The ratio of owner-occupied housing remained at around 60 per cent between 1963–2003 (see Table 5.3). Despite rapid urbanization and the increasing number of households, the ratio of home-ownership was kept at a certain level due to the measures used to accelerate housing acquisition. The ratio of private rental housing has been the second highest at around 25 per cent. However, housing policy has not supported private rental housing. There has been little assistance for the construction of private rental housing and absolutely no provision of rental subsidy. Direct provision of rental housing by the public sector has been positioned as a residual measure. The ratio of public rental housing to total housing has been very low, at around 7 per cent.

Home-ownership policy was operated as a means of stimulating economic growth, and the promotion of housing acquisition by the GHLC supported the development of construction and housing related industries. Private financial institutions, which had concentrated on the provision of capital for business enterprises in the immediate post-war period, began lending for the acquisition of owner-occupied housing in the 1960s. In order to acquire a house, households generally utilized a combination of loans made available by the GHLC and banks. The GHLC's low-interest loan withdrew capital from family finances and expanded the bank's financial market. The government thus structured a system which increased investment in housing using the GHLC as a lever.

Since 1966, a Five-Year Housing Construction Plan has been drawn up periodically as a foundation for housing policy. Under these plans the greater part of the projected number of housing units has always been occupied by privately funded housing. The majority of subsidy or public funding for housing construction has mostly taken the form of GHLC loans. The government's concern was focused on stimulating the mass-construction of housing, especially owner-occupied housing, by indicating a targeted amount of housing construction. The conservative administration was politically supported by the construction, real estate and housing industries and in turn facilitated housing construction and pushed economic development forward. The Five-Year Housing Construction Plans have thus clearly reflected the fundamentally politically orientated features of housing policy.

Home-ownership as asset ownership came to play a salient role in supporting the household economy. Between 1955 and 1980, while average consumer prices went up by 4.46 times and average income rose by 14 times, the average land price jumped by 32 times in the whole nation's built-up areas and by 58 times in the six biggest cities (Hirayama 2003b). The prices of land and housing kept on rising rapidly and home-ownership offered considerable potential capital gains. This strengthened the so-called 'land myth' – where land prices are assumed to rise in perpetuity. An increasing number of households, therefore, recognized the need to purchase a house at an early stage in life in order to build a valuable asset. Many households also bought their own homes as a means of obtaining social security for their old age. As the level of public pensions and social services for the elderly is low, and as older people are often rejected as tenants for private rental housing, by accumulating assets in the form of housing, people sought to ensure a secure place to live and a hedge against financial risk in their old age.

Middle-class family households who owned and lived in their own homes increasingly constituted and propagated the social mainstream. Home-ownership was not only defined in a material sense, but was also symbolic of the new social status and attitude of its owner (Hirayama 2003a). Single-family housing in a suburb was regarded as the 'Japanese dream'. It represented a middle or high level of income, a stable job and credibility. Home-owners were supposed to respect the order of society, work hard, and take care of their family. The government aimed at forming social solidarity and stability by increasing the level of home-ownership. Owner-occupied housing, suburban single-family housing in particular, symbolized that the owner possessed a certain position as a core member within society, and home-ownership was increasingly considered the social norm.

The first oil crisis of 1973 marked a turning point in housing policy and state intervention in the housing market expanded. Although the business climate recovered after a short recession caused by the crisis, the era of high-speed economic growth came to an end and a period of low growth began. The government further geared housing policy towards the mass-construction of owner-occupied housing in order to revitalize the economy, and put more stress on encouraging people to acquire their own houses with a loan provided by the GHLC. Immediately after the second oil crisis in 1979, mass housing construction was again promoted. Associated with the combination of measures to stimulate the economy in unstable conditions, the level of new housing starts, which had increased steadily, became volatile in the 1970s (see Figure 5.1). There appeared a new pattern of housing construction, that is, a repetition of ups and downs in new housing starts. Within the three pillars of housing policy after the 1970s, public housing and JHC housing were further residualized and only the construction of owner-occupied housing was promoted. Between the 1971–75 fiscal period and the 1991–95 fiscal period, the percentage of new publicly-funded housing starts increased from 26.2 per cent to 40.4 per cent, and of these publicly funded new starts the proportion using GHLC loans rose noticeably from 56.1 per cent to 84.1 per cent (see Figure 5.1).

By the middle of the 1970s, it had become progressively less affordable for renters to purchase their own homes due to the rapid rise in house prices. The programme of economic stimulation, which directed a huge amount of investment into the housing market, further pushed up the prices of residential property. In response to rising house prices, the GHLC increased the loan limit and lengthened the repayment period to improve lending conditions. A series of new programmes to promote housing acquisition was also created by the GHLC. The Step Repayment System, in which the amount of repayments was set at a low level for the first five years, was introduced in 1979. A housing loan system for two generations was also established in 1980, enabling children to take over their parent's loan (Hirayama and Hayakawa

1995). In addition, the Supplementary Loan Programme, which augments the basic loan, was also launched in 1985. The GHLC, in the 1980s, began providing loans for single households, which previously had been excluded from most housing policy measures, in order to maintain the large quantity of housing construction. A cycle appeared where the improvement of loan conditions encouraged house acquisition, expanded demand for owner-occupied housing and boosted housing prices, which then again necessitated the improvement of loan conditions (Hirayama 2003b).

Two-tiered Housing System

Manipulating social inequalities

The Japanese housing system, which concentrated public funds on middle-class families and encouraged them to purchase their own homes, generated a large disparity between those on low incomes and those with higher incomes; between single and family households; and between renters and home-owners. The difference in size and quality between rental and owned homes is also substantial, and the average floor area of an owner occupied house is around three times more than that of a rental house. While the consistent rise in land and housing prices meant an increase in asset value to those who already owned a house, it also meant that the purchase of housing would become unaffordable for rental housing dwellers.

Social inequality in relation to housing grew larger by the 1970s. However, a housing ladder system, which encouraged people to move from a rental house to an owner-occupied house, or from a condominium to a single-family house, was developed to manipulate social inequalities and rationalize the concentration of public funds on middle-income groups (Hirayama 2003a). Even if it was a burden to purchase a house, as income generally increased with the advance of age, repayments of the loan were expected to ease and the value of the house rose. To justify growing housing inequalities the following rationales were asserted: a) while rental housing residents might suffer poor housing conditions, they should eventually be able to climb the housing ladder and become a home-owner; b) single people, normally excluded from housing policy, could utilize various public systems once they got married; c) a household who bought a small house could move to a bigger house utilizing capital gains. In this context, support for middle-income households was thought to improve the condition of housing for low-income people through a chain reaction of moves.

Despite the fact that social stratification and greater social differentiation had actually developed, there was a 'middle-class myth' that most Japanese people belonged to and thus formed a 'middle-class society'. According to the Public Opinion Survey conducted by the government every year since 1958, the proportion of those who answered that they belong to the middle class increased from 72 per cent in 1958 to 87 per cent in 1963, and exceeded 90 per cent in the 1970s. This is because, though the society was stratified, people in each stratum believed their future life would improve. Even those in the low strata did not doubt that their living conditions would be better, and considered themselves members of the middle class. The housing system reinforced the 'middle-class myth' by promoting the assumption that people can climb up the socio-economic ladder via home-ownership.

It is necessary to consider that major companies played an important part in systematizing the housing ladder. Japanese society is often called a 'company society' – many companies have adopted a lifelong employment system and a seniority system for wages and promotion to form a model of 'company as a community' and 'company as a family'. In the company society, major companies have provided systems for employee housing, rental subsidy, internal saving for housing acquisition and low-interest loans for employees who buy a home (Ohmoto 1996). These systems were embedded in the housing ladder. Employee housing and rental subsidies were supplied for young employees, while employees at a later stage on the housing ladder made use of the company loan system to purchase a house. According to research conducted by the Japan Federation of Employers' Associations in 1984, the proportion of companies, with over 5,000 employees, which implemented a) employee housing provision, b) a savings programme for house purchase and, c) provided housing loans, was 96 per cent, 90 per cent and 100 per cent, respectively (Japan Federation of Employers' Associations 1984).

From the 1970s through the 1980s, a dispute emerged over whether or not European welfare state models should be applied in Japan, in context of Japan's growing affluence, as a stark contrast between economic prosperity and poor public welfare provision had been developing. According to the 'post-war intellectuals', who were generally liberals or socialists, no 'middle-class society' had been established and social inequalities were growing in Japan. They argued that it was necessary for Japan, an 'underdeveloped nation' among industrialized countries, to follow the western 'advanced welfare states'. Despite growth in GDP, improvement of housing conditions had been delayed, houses were small and housing costs were high. Hayakawa (1979), a leading housing scholar in Japan, emphasized that the social housing sector had developed on a large scale in the immediate post-war period in European countries and insisted that Japan should follow suit and adopt universal citizenship rights for housing. Harada (1985) and Ohmoto (1985) among others also suggested that the government's role in housing provision should be reconsidered in the light of developments in the post-war housing situation.

With the beginning of a low growth period in the 1970s, however, the conservative administration began to emphasize the necessity of forming a 'Japanese style welfare society'. The basic concept was to revitalize the traditional Japanese spirit and practice of mutual-help, and to characterize families, companies and local communities as principal welfare providers. In the conservatives' view, western welfare states were 'inferior' in the sense that increased dependency on public welfare spoils economic activity, and that Japanese traditional society and its value system were 'superior'. The government supposed that, as long as the economy continuously developed, a 'middle-class society' could be maintained and government expenditure for welfare could be controlled. The 'post-war intellectuals' and the conservatives were thus in

direct confrontation regarding welfare provision. However, they had the same attitude
to the extent that neither of them intended to deepen their insights into the differences
and commonalities in the socio-cultural, politico-economic and institutional contexts
of western countries and Japan, and both of them focused on social value systems
as 'superior' or 'inferior'. Although discussion concerning welfare states provided
opportunities to reconsider the Japanese welfare system, it did not lead to significant
changes in the housing system. The government, as before, encouraged the mass-
construction of housing to develop the economy and manipulated social structures
via the ladder system.

Neglecting public housing

Japanese housing policy can be described as a two-tiered system (Hirayama 2000).
While there has been generous support for middle-class groups in order to become
home-owners by using GHLC loans on one tier, support for those on lower incomes
has become increasingly residualized and the target group for the direct provision of
public housing has been strictly limited on the second tier. The government created
a system that defined home-ownership as the social norm and placed public housing
provision as a marginal measure.

Public housing has been located outside of the social mainstream. Although the
new starts of public housing increased until the end of the 1960s, they have been
dropping continuously since the beginning of the 1970s. According to the Housing
Survey in 2003, the proportion of public housing is currently as little as 4.6 per
cent (see Table 5.3). When the Public Housing Act was introduced in 1951, public
housing was available for a wide range of households including the middle-income
group. However, the government has increasingly emphasized the marginal nature
of the public housing system since the period immediately after it was launched,
and has progressively limited its target recipients to the lowest-income groups. The
government sector often constructed public housing on large-scale developments on
the fringes of cities, where people on low incomes were housed together. The two-
tiered housing system separated public housing from middle-class neighbourhoods
socially and spatially.

In order to residualize public housing systematically, income criteria for moving
into public housing have been progressively narrowed (Hirayama 2000, 2003a).
At the time of the 1951 Public Housing Act, the majority of households, or the
lowest 80 per cent of all income groups, qualified for public housing. However,
the percentage dropped to 33 per cent in the 1970s and to 25 per cent after the
amendment of the Act in 1996. In addition, a series of discriminatory measures in
relation to households whose incomes rose after moving into public housing have
been developed. The 1959 amendment established a system in which a household
whose income exceeded a certain amount was required to make an effort to move out,
and the 1969 amendment made it possible for local governments formally to request
those with higher incomes to move out. Although the system of rent calculation was
originally based on the cost of building construction and site acquisition, the 1996

amendment introduced a new system of rent calculation based on a set of factors that included tenants' incomes. As a result, many residents with improved incomes have increasingly been pressured to move out of public housing since they have been required to pay market-level rents and have lost any economic advantages of living in public housing. Lastly, welfare categories have been revised in terms of more restrictive criteria and necessary qualifications to move into public housing. Although overall public housing provision has been reduced, special public housing provision, exclusively for the elderly, people with disabilities and single-parent households, has been increased.

Public housing has been for the 'deserving poor' and has been justified as long as it has been residualized. It has become increasingly difficult to be regarded as worthy of the title 'the deserving poor' simply by being a low-income earner. By not only limiting the income criteria but also using welfare categories for residents, a means of procuring agreement for the justification of public housing has been established. Provision of public housing until the 1960s was aimed at supporting young households who were recognized as the 'deserving poor' since they were expected to move out of public housing after a short period and acquire their own housing eventually as their incomes increased. In this context, public housing was embedded in the housing ladder and used as a stepping-stone to the social mainstream. Since the 1970s, however, the government has separated public housing from the mainstream of society. Public housing, which was removed from the housing ladder, has increasingly formed an isolated domain where the lowest income classes, older people and the disabled live for a long time.

A factor that has enabled the government sector to avoid constructing public housing sufficient for meeting the housing needs of low-income groups has been the continued buoyancy of the private rental sector. The proportion of private rental housing has been kept at approximately one quarter of the total (see Table 5.3). The provision of private rental dwellings has not been significantly profitable. However, many individuals or families who hold land have continued to construct and manage rental housing as a sideline business without investment in site acquisition. Although the physical condition of many private rental dwellings, particularly wooden ones, has remained substandard, private landlords have provided substantial numbers of low-income households with a place to live. The government has thus relied upon the private rental sector, and has been able to evade housing responsibilities by substituting private rental housing for public housing.

In the early post-war era the Japan Housing Corporation developed multi-family housing estates for white-collar worker households. New starts of JHC rental housing, however, have been decreasing since the beginning of the 1970s, and according to the 2003 statistics, the proportion of JHC rental housing owned by the corporation is now as low as 2 per cent (see Table 5.3). The difficulties the corporation was confronting in developing housing estates had grown by the 1970s. In the context of the rapid increase in land prices, development sites became more and more distant from city centres, rents rose sharply and a large number of housing units became vacant. Local governments began refusing to give permission for developments by the JHC as they had neither the intent nor the ability to bear the responsibility for providing residents in JHC estates with road infrastructure, utilities and schools. Although the JHC was established as one of the three pillars of housing policy, its accomplishments have been limited.

The Changing Context of Home-ownership

Destabilizing the housing economy

Since the 1980s, the condition of home-ownership has been eroded by an increasingly uncertain economy. Economic globalization, financial deregulation and the formation of a more competitive business environment have re-shaped the economy. The tendency of the home-ownership-based housing system to reflect and amplify the instability of the economy has been growing, and the system of home-ownership promotion has become increasingly shaky.

The rise and fall of the bubble economy played a key part in restructuring the economic environment surrounding home-ownership (Forrest, Kennett and Izuhara 2003; Hirayama 2003b). The bubble swelled with an abnormal upsurge in land and housing prices in the latter half of the 1980s and burst in the beginning of the 1990s (Muramatsu and Okuno 2002; Oizumi 1994). Fluctuations in the real estate market were particularly noticeable in big cities (Yamada 2001). A tremendous rise in land and housing prices started in Tokyo and rippled to Osaka and Nagoya. The bubble collapse also began in Tokyo and spread to the other big cities. Before the bubble developed in the 1980s, a sharp increase in land prices was observed at the beginning of the 1960s and the beginning of the 1970s. It spread all over the country, including both the big cities and the provincial cities. Industrial development was centred on heavy industry during the high-speed growth period. Factory districts and industrial complexes were opened up in many regions of the nation, and this promoted investment in land in provincial cities. By contrast, the swelling of the bubble economy in the 1980s occurred prominently in the big cities and the tendency for Tokyo to instigate new waves in the land and housing markets became stronger. From the 1970s and during the 1980s, the focus of industry shifted from heavy industry to urban area based industries consisting of services, finances and real estate, resulting in a concentration of real estate investment in big cities.

A direct cause of the bubble was the deregulation of finance (Tanaka 2002). As a result of the easing of monetary control, surplus capital was injected into the real estate sector. In the context of Japan-US trade friction, the Japanese yen immediately appreciated and interest rates were rapidly lowered after the Plaza Accord[2] of September 1985. Although banks mainly had been financing investment in plants and equipment, they increased the amount of finance for real estate as major companies began to obtain capital from equity finance in the 1980s. Once land prices

---

2   The so-called 'Plaza Accord' was an informal agreement among the Group of Seven industrialized countries to allow the yen to appreciate against the US dollar.

began to rise, all kinds of enterprises joined the real estate related corporations in a rush to invest in real estate.

After the bubble burst in the early 1990s, Japan experienced a long recession, associated with a chain reaction of enterprise bankruptcies and a rising unemployment rate. The Asian financial crisis, which started in 1997, was an additional blow to the recession in Japan. It has become uncertain whether or not the 'company society' can be maintained. Major companies have been restructuring by downsizing and abandoning the lifelong employment and seniority wage systems as a more competitive business environment has emerged. The security of employment has become increasingly fragile and the stability of incomes has weakened. There are more part-time workers and employees on temporary contracts. As the economic climate deteriorated, social disparities expanded and the stability of the middle class began to weaken (Sato 2000; Tachibanaki 1998). The 1990s, consequently, are often referred to as Japan's 'lost decade'.

Real housing prices have fallen continuously since the beginning of the 1990s, and this devaluation of housing property can be directly attributed to the burst of the bubble. However, the over-construction of owner-occupied housing has further pulled down house prices. During the bubble period, the government promoted housing acquisition with the intention of easing the Japan-US trade friction by expanding domestic demand. The GHLC's lending conditions were repeatedly improved. After the bubble collapsed, the government accelerated housing construction even more and increased the provision of GHLC loans in order to revive the economy. Tax reduction for those who purchased their own houses was greatly expanded in the 1990s and housing loan interest was reduced to a record low.

The housing shortage was critical immediately after the end of the war through to the 1970s. In the 1980s, however, the imbalance between housing demand and supply was gradually reduced and a housing surplus appeared. Since the 1970s, when the total number of dwellings exceeded that of households for the first time, vacancy rates have constantly risen, from 7.6 per cent in 1978 to 9.8 per cent in 1993, and reached 12.2 per cent in 2003. Urbanization, which advanced furiously in the 1950s and 1960s, started to subside in the 1970s. Essentially, housing surpluses do not necessarily imply stability in housing conditions. In a situation where vacancies were steadily increasing, a policy of promoting the construction of housing accelerated the deflation of house prices.

Households who became home-owners during the bubble period have been suffering capital losses since the beginning of the 'lost decade' (Forrest, Kennett and Izuhara 2003; Hirayama 2003b). In the 1980s when the economic bubble swelled, the prices of all types of owner-occupied housing rose at a similar rate. However, in the 1990s after the bubble collapsed, the rate at which housing prices fell differed greatly according to the type of owner-occupied housing (see Figure 5.2). The fall was greater in second-hand housing than in newly built housing, and for condominiums rather than for single-family dwellings. In other words, the depreciation of second-hand condominiums has been marked, and capital losses generated on condominium properties are substantial. The Real Estate Information Network for East Japan

(2003) investigated the scale of devaluation of condominium assets in the Tokyo Metropolitan Area in 2003. According to their estimates, a household who purchased a condominium during the 1988–92 period is suffering, on average, a capital loss of over 20 million yen (US$182,000 approx),[3] and it is increasingly difficult for them to sell their housing properties.

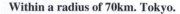

Within a radius of 70km. Tokyo.

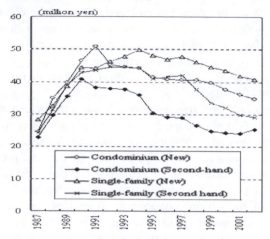

Within a radius of 50km. Osaka.

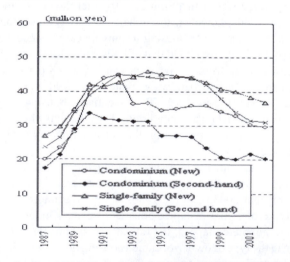

Figure 5.2 Nominal prices of housing with GHLC loan, 1978–2003
Source: Government Housing Loan Corporation.

---

3   ¥110 = US$1

The sharp drop in prices of second-hand condominiums in the 1990s was stimulated by the construction of a large quantity of new condominiums. As the market for new condominiums expanded, the prices of second-hand ones inevitably fell. The marketability of second-hand housing was further eroded by institutional factors. Housing policy for home-ownership is designed to encourage the purchase of new housing in order to promote and accelerate new housing construction. For example, while the longest repayment period for a GHLC loan is generally 35 years for new housing, it is 25 years for second-hand housing. Furthermore, the GHLC does not finance the purchase of second-hand housing which is over 25 years old. The taxation system also gives a number of advantages to purchasers of new housing.

The family budget of households with housing loans deteriorated in the 1990s. In the long recession, an increasing number of households found it difficult to repay their housing loans, and the number of loan defaults increased. Many households could only afford a small deposit because of artificially inflated prices during the bubble, and ended up taking out considerable housing loans because of the increased attractiveness and availability of GHLC loans and their periodically staggered low interest rates. Many households who bought housing at the height of the bubble, consequently, still have large loans and negative equities. The Step Repayment System was a main factor in the exacerbation of family budgets. Households who enrolled in this system had to repay suddenly at increased levels after the first five years of the low repayment period although their incomes did not commensurately increase. The system, criticized for unfairly enticing not only those with middle incomes but also those on lower incomes into acquiring a house beyond their means, was abolished in 2000.

Upsetting the housing ladder

The housing ladder system has become less effective in expanding home-ownership. Destabilization of employment and income has made it risky to take housing loans. Owner-occupied housing, which used to generate a capital gain, may now be accompanied by a capital loss and is increasingly insecure as an asset. While capital gains fuelled the ladder system, growing capital losses imply the reverse function. Consequently, there are now not only those climbing up the ladder but also those who are climbing down.

The fragmentation of society has also been a destabilizing factor in the housing system. Those who led a 'standard life course' and formed nuclear families, constituting a normalized form of 'standard household', established the social mainstream. The housing ladder system operated along the standard life course and encouraged standard families to become home-owners. However, the structure of household formation has been transformed with a rapid increase in the elderly and a decline in the birth rate. The characteristics of families have been changing greatly due to the postponement of marriage and a rise in the number of people who either choose not to marry or, if they do marry, do not have children. The divorce rate has also been increasing. Conventional family households have decreased and small households such as single-person, couple-only households and elderly-only households have increased. According to the Population Census, between 1970 and 2000, the proportion of nuclear family households decreased from 46.1 per cent to 32.8 per cent, and that of single households rose from 10.8 per cent to 25.6 per cent. The concepts of a 'standard life course' and a 'standard family', therefore, are declining in salience in the current housing context.

Changes in levels of home-ownership according to age are illustrated in Figure 5.3. This clearly indicates that the younger cohorts have obtained owner-occupied homes at a later age compared with older generations. The rate of home-ownership for those aged 30–34 was 46 per cent in the generation born in the period 1949–53, and 29 per cent in the generation born in the period 1964–68. The combination of a sluggish growth of income and changes in the patterns of household formation has been causing young people to delay entering into the home-ownership market. Housing trajectories have been increasingly differentiated according to generation. There is a growing tendency among the younger generation not to follow the straightforward path towards home-ownership that the older generation experienced.

The effects of the bubble economy on home-owners were also differentiated between different generations. Japanese baby-boomers were born between 1947 and 1949. The majority of them, climbing up the housing ladder at a time of robust economic growth, purchased housing before the occurrence of the bubble and thus did not suffer capital losses significantly. Baby-boomers as a generation symbolized the development of the social mainstream. In contrast, the following generation that entered the home-ownership market during the peak of the bubble has been affected by the serious devaluation of their housing properties and has experienced the erosion of the housing ladder.

In the 'company society', major companies created a series of internal housing programmes. An increasing number of companies in the 'lost decade', however, started to unload employee-housing properties and to abolish internal housing-related systems. Many employees, therefore, have begun to lose their footing on the housing ladder, which used to be reinforced by companies. The proportion of company housing, which was 7.0 per cent in 1963, decreased to 3.1 per cent in 2003 (see Table 5.3). The Research Institute of Employee Benefits carried out research into the benefits programmes of 1,561 companies in 2001–02. According to the results, 9.5 per cent of companies were intending to discontinue the provision of employee housing and 9.3 per cent were planning to abolish rental subsidy programmes. The research report emphasized the trend within many enterprises to withdraw from housing schemes for employees (Research Institute of Employee Benefits 2003). According to research conducted by the Japan Institute of Life Insurance on 2,014 companies and 1,802 full-time workers in 2002, 34.2 per cent of full-time workers answered that 'housing' is an issue on which they wish their company to place importance in the future, while only 9.1 per cent of companies answered in this fashion (Japan Institute of Life Insurance 2003).

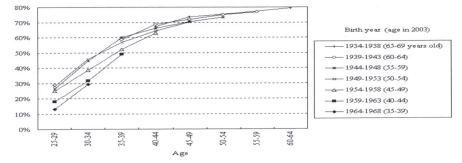

Figure 5.3 Changes in the home-ownership rate by age cohort
Source: Statistics Bureau, 1963 Housing Survey of Japan - 1993 Housing Survey of Japan, and 1998 Housing and Land Survey of Japan.

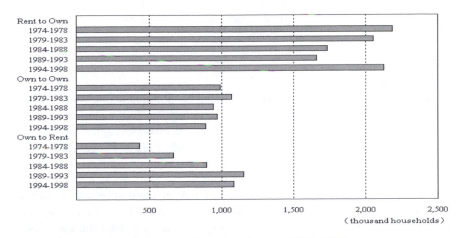

Figure 5.4 Household moves and tenure change, 1974–1998
Source: Statistics Bureau, 1978 Housing Survey of Japan - 1993 Housing Survey of Japan, and 1998 Housing and Land Survey of Japan.

The change in the pattern of housing tenure related to household moves is shown in Figure 5.4. The actual situation of such shifts concerning home-ownership implies that the housing ladder system has become dysfunctional. The number of moves from rental housing to owner-occupied housing dropped sharply between the periods 1979–83 and 1989–93. The jump in housing prices during the bubble period reduced the number of first-time home purchasers. Other factors relating to changes in family structure such as the increase in single households and the delay of marriage have also lessened demand from first-time buyers. Moves from rental housing to owner-occupied housing increased in the period 1994–98 because housing prices went down in the post-bubble period. The number of household moves within the owner-occupied housing sector steadily decreased from 1979–83 and 1994–98. One reason is that households who bought a condominium during the bubble period have become tied down by a capital loss. Many had anticipated a move to a better condominium or to a single-family house using the condominium as a stepping-stone. With the burst of the bubble, however, it became difficult for them to sell and move out of their condominiums.

It is important to note that moves from owner-occupied housing to rented housing increased greatly from the period 1974–78 to the period 1989–93, though they decreased slightly from 1994–98. The expected function of the housing system is to propel households up the ladder from a rental house to an owner-occupied house. An increase in the households that climb down the ladder implies that the functional integrity of the system is unravelling. The cause of this is not clear though some inferences can be drawn. Home-ownership may have so much pressured the finances of households buying homes during the bubble period that an increasing number of households have since sold their homes. The labour market may have become so unstable that many home-owners have now sold their houses and moved for reasons related to their occupations.

Dividing the urban housing market

The home-ownership market has been becoming even more complex and unsettled with the increasing restructuring of urban space (Hirayama 2005). During the period of high-speed economic growth, the construction of owner-occupied housing was combined with the simple force of expansion of urban areas. However, since the middle of the 1990s, the home-ownership market has been reflecting and promoting the spatial segmentation of urban areas.

The government has been emphasizing the redevelopment of big cities since the 1980s. Of all the big cities, Tokyo has been regarded particularly as having the status of a global city, and in response to the globalizing economy, the restructuring of Tokyo has been given top priority. Since the middle of the 'lost decade', the government has further accelerated urban redevelopment as well as housing construction in order to stimulate economic recovery. The Urban Planning Law and the Building Code have been deregulated repeatedly since the latter half of the 1990s (Harada 2001). The administration of Prime Minister Junichiro Koizumi, founded in 2001, has also been focusing on the revitalization of the big cities, especially Tokyo, and their deregulation of urban planning has been the most drastic ever (Igarashi and Ogawa 2003). The Urban Renaissance Special Measure Law came into force in 2002 to designate special zones where planning regulations could be relaxed. Essentially, the government has been trying to restore the economic strength of Japan by using the restructuring of Tokyo as a catalyst (Machimura 2003; Saito and Thornley 2003).

The combination of the economic downturn and the government's response to it has led to the division of urban space into 'hot spots', where the housing market is increasingly active, and 'cold spots', where the market is persistently inactive (Hirayama 2005). While the housing situation in the cold spots has been affected by the continuous devaluation of residential property, a new boom of housing construction has been generated in the hot spots. The spatial division caused by differentiated ups and downs in the urban housing market has created a novel context for home-ownership.

A construction boom of condominium towers of over 20 storeys propagated the growth of the hot spots in Tokyo. In the post-bubble period it has become possible to construct residential buildings in the central city areas where land prices have decreased, and with the persistent recession, many enterprises have begun to dispose of large tracts of land, which are now being utilized for new condominium developments (Ministry of Land, Infrastructure and Transport 2003). In the Tokyo Metropolitan Area, according to research by the Real Estate Economic Institute in 2003, 137 condominium towers, consisting of 35,697 units, were completed between 1987 and 2002. New starts of high-rise housing are expected to increase. As of January 2003, 336 condominium towers with 109,181 units were planned to be built in Tokyo Metropolitan Area. Critically, it has been the wide-ranging deregulation of urban planning that has enabled the construction of high-rise residential towers.

A condominium tower block forms a fortress-like space (Hirayama 2005). Not only does it create an economic and social differentiation of space, but also it is symbolic of the segmentation of urban space. A large-scale building complex is horizontally cut off from its neighbourhood and its higher floors are vertically segregated from the ground level. The complex produces a closed and self-contained space. Within the complex, residents are provided with hotel-like services and have access to various facilities such as fitness rooms, relaxation rooms, party rooms and retail shops. The security systems to protect the complex are tight. The architectural profile of the tower is alien to its vicinity, and those living in it rarely have contact with residents of the surrounding neighbourhood.

The average price of housing in big cities has been decreasing since the bursting of the bubble. However, pricing within tower-type condominium blocks in Tokyo follows its own course. There are lower-priced dwellings on lower floors, which are for those in the moderate to middle income bracket. The higher the floor on which the dwelling is located, the higher the price becomes. Dwellings on the top floors are for households on high incomes, and on the very top floor, expensive, luxurious dwellings for the very rich can be found. As Tokyo is strongly connected to the global economy, people with a high income such as elite workers at global enterprises, highly paid financiers and lawyers have been generating demand for expensive luxury housing. The top floors of the condominium towers, which form 'the housing market in the sky', symbolize the emergence of the new luxury hot spots. The spatial differentiation of the urban housing market is thus increasingly emphasized not only horizontally but also vertically.

Post-bubble housing devaluation spread to entire areas of many cities, and its impact was especially intense in some specific areas. Cold spots were formed mainly in the suburbs, where the market prices of 'suburban bubble condominiums' – condominiums built in the suburbs during the bubble period – have been greatly depreciating (Hirayama 2003b; 2005). Though households that move to the suburbs generally desire single-family houses, families with moderate incomes purchased condominiums in the suburbs during the bubble period, since housing prices had risen so dramatically. The marketability of a condominium unit of this type nose-dived in the post-bubble period. Households who bought a suburban condominium did not generally belong to high-income groups and they are now repaying massive amounts on the loans for their housing, which is rapidly declining in value.

Moreover, at the bottom of the second-hand housing market, the stock of 'bargain-priced condominiums' costing less than 10 million yen (US$90,909) has increased. Many of these are old, are located on the periphery of cities and have small floor areas. Some 'bargain-priced condominium blocks' are becoming increasingly dilapidated and losing market potential as vacancy rates rise, the amount of unpaid management fees accumulates, and the proportion of low-income residents increases. The cold spots were produced not only by the burst of the bubble but also by the formation of the hot spots themselves. The expansion of condominium developments in the central city areas has been accelerating the deflation of prices for the 'suburban bubble condominiums' and multiplying the quantity of 'bargain-priced condominiums'. In this context, the appearance of hot and cold spots in the urban home-ownership market are linked to each other, and the new boom in the housing market in the hot spots has been created at the expense of the cold spots.

The End of Traditional Housing Policy

The housing strategy of post-war Japan was associated with a clear social direction. Home-ownership was seen as the cornerstone of a life plan and many people climbed up the housing ladder with a view to eventually becoming a home-owner. The housing system, however, has begun losing its direction because of an increasingly uncertain economy and social fragmentation. People have lost confidence in the 'middle-class myth' and the generosity of the 'company society'. The 'land myth' is, after all, nothing more than a myth and home-ownership no longer promises asset formation. The housing ladder has begun to crumble and it has become less simple to plan a life course in relation to housing. Suburban single-family housing is no longer the 'Japanese dream' for young generations. The mainstream-oriented housing system is being shaken to the core.

The mass-construction of housing met the mass-demand for housing and played a significant role in economic development. However, it will be next to impossible to maintain the mass-production of housing. Pressure from the demand for housing will be lessened in the future due to demographic changes. According to the 2002 estimate by the National Institute of Population and Social Security Research, the total population of Japan which was 127 million in 2000 will decrease from its peak in 2006 to 101 million in 2050. The rate of increase in households will also decline significantly. Japanese society is ageing very fast. The proportion of elderly people to the total population, which was 17.4 per cent in 2000, is forecast to be as high as

35.7 per cent by 2050. In the future, investment in housing will inevitably decrease in this ageing society.

The strategy of the state for housing provision since the middle of the 1990s has clearly moved towards emphasizing the role of the market (Hirayama 2003b; Oizumi 2002a). The government began radically to deregulate the market economy, downsize the public sector and retreat from housing provision. The fiscal condition of the government has been deteriorating and this has restrained its financial expenditure on housing. The construction, real estate and housing industries, which have suffered the post-bubble recession, have increasingly put political pressure on the government to expand the sphere of housing businesses. Until the 1980s, Housing and Land Committee reports, which set out the basic course of housing policy, were based on the idea that interference by the government in the housing market was necessary. By contrast, the 1995 report clearly declared that housing principally be left to market forces and that housing policy should focus around a more deregulated market. The 2000 report even more clearly emphasized the necessity for market-based housing provision.

Since the 1980s, housing systems in the western societies, among other Anglo-Saxon societies, particularly Britain and the U.S, have been remarkably transformed by increases in private housing provision and the erosion of the social housing sector, which have been associated with the diffusion of the so-called neo-liberal ideology. The traditional welfare state model, which was formed in European countries in the early post-war period, was not influential in shaping the Japanese housing system. In contrast, changes in western housing systems and neo-liberal thought have more recently played a significant role in rationalizing the government's retreat from housing provision in Japan. The disposal of public housing by sale in Britain and the drastic cut backs in public expenditure on housing in the U.S. have repeatedly been referred to in Japan and have influenced the reorientation of housing policy. The tendency of the Japanese government to employ scholars and commentators who are fundamentally neo-liberal as core members of various policy-making committees has become remarkable.

The government has already started to break up the traditional three pillars of housing policy. The Ministry of Construction, which had jurisdiction over housing policy, was combined with the Ministry of Transport to form the Ministry of Land, Infrastructure and Transport in 2001. The new position of housing policy, among the various policies of this new ministry, has been notably marginalized. The Five-Year Housing Construction Plan, the basis for all housing policy, was discontinued in 2005. In terms of public housing policy, the existing stock may be reconstructed but no new housing will be constructed, and the role of public housing is being narrowed even more. The Japan Housing Corporation was reorganized into the HUDC (Housing and Urban Development Corporation) in 1981 and again into the UDC (Urban Development Corporation) in 1999. The UDC greatly reduced its housing programmes so as not to compete with housing businesses in the private sector. The UDC was further reorganized into the URA (Urban Renaissance Agency) in 2004, basically withdrawing from new construction of housing. The Housing Lease

Act was also amended in 2000 in order to deregulate the rental housing market and to make investment in rental housing businesses more profitable. Before this amendment, tenants' security of tenure was protected and landlords could not easily evict them. With this amendment, however, it is now possible for owners to rent their houses for more limited periods.

The government announced in 2001 that the GHLC would be abolished by the end of the fiscal year 2006/07 (Oizumi 2002b). This signified a substantial and historic shift in Japanese housing policy. One reason for this move is that national finances have been trapped in the housing finance system during the prolonged recession. The administration, therefore, judged it to be prudent to do away with the GHLC, which was a huge financial burden. The new corporate body replacing the GHLC is scheduled to retreat from the primary market of housing loans and will concern itself only with the secondary market in which housing loan securities are circulated. Private banks, having been affected by the economic downturn, have been calling for the expansion of the private mortgage market as a new financial market. Financing for housing purchase, which has been supported by housing policy, is now expected to be met by market forces. It remains to be seen what will come from the abolition of the GHLC.

A policy trend that is becoming noticeable is the de-socialization and individualization of housing issues. The government has set down a clear social target of housing policy every five years along with the Five-Year Housing Construction Plan. The goals were clear: the goal set in 1966 was that housing for all families was to be ensured; the one set in 1971 was that a room for every household member in each housing unit should be guaranteed; the one set in 1976 was that substandard housing would be eliminated by 1985. However, housing policy since the 1990s, emphasizing reliance on market forces, has not shown an explicit social target. Market forces are now the critical mechanisms in the production, provision and consumption of housing. It is not clear, however, what kind of housing should be provided and what kind of problems should be addressed with this mechanism. Instead, 'individual choice' and 'self-reliance' have become the key terms in forming housing policy.

The traditional framework of state-run housing policy in post-war Japan has come to an end. The housing shortage immediately after the end of the war was serious but the necessary housing policy to address the situation seemed straightforward. The state played a leading role in setting forth a clear direction for the housing system. A critical point in understanding the erosion of conventional housing policy is the fact that the housing shortage was long ago resolved and vacancy rates have subsequently risen substantially. On the other hand, the necessity for the state to elaborate a new institutional framework for the housing system is arising since there is a notable tendency for the changes in the housing sphere to become increasingly influential in the transformation of the socio-economic structure. The expansion of the mortgage market is deepening the linkage between housing and the wider economy. The way in which housing is provided is increasingly intertwined with the reorganization of society. The new question, therefore, is whether or not the government is able to cope with the unpredictability of shifting socio-economic conditions in deciding new directions for housing policy.

Concluding Remarks

Successive post-war Japanese governments built up a system characterized by a particular set of orientations – that is, orientations towards the production of the social mainstream, the expansion of home-ownership, mass housing construction, and reliance on the paternalism of the 'company society', as well as the residualization of public housing. The state has consistently placed significance on economic productivity and social solidarity, which has been reflected in the organization of the housing system.

Post-war Japan strove to catch up with the western 'advanced nations' and achieved this goal in terms of economic development. Modernization was often regarded as westernization in Japan. However, Japan never adopted the housing provision model of the European welfare states. The nature and function of the state in operating the housing system developed within a distinctive and particular context in Japan. What the Japanese government imported from the 'advanced nations' was some skill in employing housing instruments. Experiences of social housing in Britain and other European countries were referred to in the legislation process for Japanese public housing. The U.S. General Headquarters in the late 1940s suggested the Japanese government set up a special financing body for housing, which was translated into the foundation of the GHLC. Policy makers in the Japanese government researched European housing institutions in order to establish practicable Japanese definitions for housing related factors such as substandard housing. Contextual reference to housing models in the European welfare states, however, was never intended.

Over the past decade, together with the erosion of the social mainstream, the state strategy for housing has moved sharply towards deregulation and emphasis on market mechanisms. In an increasingly globalized environment, the housing system in Japan, as well as in many other countries, has been experiencing volatile economic conditions, greater social fragmentation and pressure to cut back on social spending and public subsidies. In the context of the broader structure of change, there have been similar trends between Japan and other industrialized countries in terms of attempts to promote market-based housing provision. The decline of the traditional welfare model in European states and the increasing influence of neo-liberal thought have encouraged the reshaping of the Japanese housing system.

It is misleading, however, to regard the housing system of each society as converging on a specific course. The effects of the wider changes on the housing situation are subject to the social, cultural, economic, political and institutional contexts of particular countries. The combination of broader changes and indigenous contexts are leading to the production of more diversified housing systems. The Japanese housing system is undergoing drastic changes due to the increasing uncertainty of economic conditions and the fragmentation of the social structure, and its new direction is unclear at present. If a new housing system emerges in Japan, it will be influenced by wider trends but with localized effects, and will move along a new trajectory radically divorced from the earlier context of policy and system development.

Chapter 6

From Socialist Welfare to Support of Home-Ownership: The Experience of China

Ya Ping Wang

Introduction

Housing provision in Chinese cities has experienced many important changes since the Communists came to power in 1949. Before 1949, most urban housing was private rental, provided by landlords. This was changed through a socialist transformation in the 1950s, in which the majority of properties owned by big landlords were nationalized. Public housing was built by government owned enterprises and institutions (the work units) and distributed directly to their employees as part of a comprehensive welfare provision system. Other elements of this welfare system included free education, health care and pensions. By the late 1980s, a public sector dominated housing provision system was established in all cities and large towns. This system was based on socialist principles but there were many problems, including severe shortage, lack of investment, unequal distribution, corruption, inefficient management and maintenance (Wang and Murie 1996). To solve these problems, the government put forward new policies to reform the urban housing system. After several years of experimentation, comprehensive housing reform policies were implemented in the early 1990s. These policies included the sale of existing public housing, increasing rents and encouraging individual savings for housing. Arrangements were also made in the area of housing finance, mortgage lending and home insurance. House building was carried out by commercial developers rather than by public sector employers. An urban housing market was established gradually in all cities and towns.

The Chinese pre-reform urban housing system differs in many ways from that in other Asian countries or regions. Recent reforms have brought the Chinese system closer to the others in the region. The emerging housing market in Chinese cities now shares many features of that in operation in other East Asian market economies. The government largely relies now on the market for housing supply to the majority of urban residents and direct housing provision has become a very minimal, residual public service. The socialist package of public housing and welfare support to the mainstream of urban society has given way progressively to a new system, which supports home-ownership with different policies and arrangements for different social and economic groups (Lee, J. 2000). Table 6.1 summarizes the nature of housing policies and services during each period.

Housing system reform was also accompanied by changes in other social welfare services. Under the planned economic system, over 98 per cent of urban residents were employed either by the state or by the collective sectors. Apart from housing, all public employers also provided comprehensive welfare services, including job security, health and children's education. Under this arrangement, government had effectively decentralized the whole canon of social welfare services to employers. The functions of local government were related more to production management than service provision. With the introduction of the market economy, welfare services provided by work units were reduced substantially in order to improve production efficiency. From the middle of the 1980s, new social support policies were introduced to replace some of the work unit welfare services. These included the establishment of several social security systems aimed to protect the weak and unemployed. New 'pay-as-you-go' style social insurance systems were introduced, which cover five main areas: retirement insurance (pensions), health insurance, unemployment insurance, employment accident insurance, and maternity leave insurance. (Wang 2004) This system normally requires people to make contributions when they are in employment and apply for benefits when they are in need. New housing policies work more or less independently from these social security systems.

This chapter will discuss urban housing policy and practice in China since 1949. It will firstly explain the origins and development of public housing, which will be followed by a brief examination of the reform and privatization processes. The remaining parts will then discuss the key features of the emerging urban housing system. In the conclusion, problems associated with housing privatization and the new system will be discussed. China is a very large and populous country. Housing provision differs substantially between rural and urban areas. In rural areas, traditional family ownership of houses has been maintained, though very different types of houses at various standards have been built during the reform period. The discussion in this chapter is concerned only with urban housing.

The Development of Socialist Welfare Housing

Nationalization

Private housing was the major form of tenure in Chinese cities when the Communists came to power in 1949 and most urban housing was controlled by large landlords (Table 6.2). Although this private ownership of urban housing was allowed to continue for several years, communist control and political uncertainties effectively stopped private house building. In the meantime, the rapid expansion of the urban population after the war resulted in serious overcrowding problems in many large cities. Average housing floor space per person across urban areas at this stage was

Table 6.1 Urban housing policies at different periods

	Major policy periods since 1949				
	1949–1956	**1956–1976**	**1977–1991**	**1992–1998**	**1998–**
House Building	Stagnation of private sector and small scale public building	Modest expansion of public building through work units	Large scale public (work unit) and commercial building	Commercial and private building	Large-scale commercial house building with various standards
Key Policy Instruments	Confiscation and regulation of private rental market; Establishment of housing distribution system	Socialist Transformation: Nationalization of private rental housing from large landlord ownership	Consolidation of distribution system; Experiments in housing reform	Systematic privatization of urban publicly owned housing	Establishment and consolidation of housing finance system, real estate management system, new social housing provision system
Shift of Direction	From private to public housing and establishment of the comprehensive socialist welfare system		From public to private home-ownership and re-establishment of urban housing market		Formalization of urban housing market and social housing system; Segmentation and diversification

only around 3 sq m. The new government made some investments to build new houses in many large cities, but the increase in stock was much slower than the growth of urban population (Ministry of City Service 1957b).

The first public housing in Chinese cities came mainly from nationalization and confiscation of private houses owned by the previous government, its senior civil and military officials and other 'anti-revolutionaries' – the enemies of the Communists. This small stock provided the basis of public housing. This public housing was mainly distributed among senior government officials and army officers. In the period immediately following 1949 there were limited resources to devote to housing development. In order to concentrate new investment on industry, it was necessary for the private housing stock to be managed effectively to solve the housing problems of urban employees.

Table 6.2 Proportion of private housing in ten major cities, 1955

City	Percentage of private housing
Beijing	54
Tianjin	54
Shanghai	66
Jinan	78
Qingdao	37
Shenyang	36
Harbin	42
Nanjing	61
Wuxi	80
Xuzhou	86

Source: CCP Central Committee 1956.

In 1957, when the urban political and economic situation stabilised, the government began to review housing problems. It proposed policies to reform the urban housing system according to socialist principles. These policies included:

- Building public housing. This was seen as the main way to solve the problem of urban housing;
- Encouraging individuals to build family housing, but not for renting or speculation;
- Control of rural to urban migration;
- Better protection of the existing housing stock;

- Improving housing distribution and management;
- Implementation of socialist housing transformation and regulation of private housing. (Ministry of City Service 1957a)

Although the socialist housing transformation appeared as the last policy, it proved to be the key element among these new policies. In the same year, central government issued an instruction, which urged local authorities to transfer the management of private rental housing from landlords to the municipal housing authorities. The specific means of transformation included: a) Joint state-private ownership; b) Unified management; c) Rent Retention with State Supervision (Wang 1992). Data published by the central government showed that the transformation had been carried out in all officially defined cities and one third of county towns over a period of several years. About 624,100 landlords were affected and the transfer involved a total housing area of 116.5 million sq m (Ministry of Urban and Rural Construction and Environmental Protection 1982). This transformation had given government more control of the urban housing market over allocations, rent levels, property tax collection, repairs and maintenance. This control of rents in both private and public sectors enabled the government to keep wages in the public sector at a very low level and to free up more investment for industrial development. The Cultural Revolution (1966–76) saw more changes in the declining private housing sector. Landlord ownership of properties was finally abolished, and landlords' rental housing stock, both under the joint state-private ownership and the unified management system, was transferred to public ownership (State Housing and Property Management Bureau 1967).

Building Public Housing

The 1950s saw the public dominated housing provision system established. Although nationalization of private housing was a key feature during this period, public building made an important contribution as well. Between 1949 and the end of 1956, the government had invested 4.4 billion yuan in housing development. This enabled the construction of 81 million sq m of housing. 65.2 million sq m of which were built during the first four years of the First Five-Year-Plan period (1953–57). This level of housing investment was about 9.3 per cent of total capital investment (Zhang 1957).

Public housing management was disorganized during the first few years. Housing responsibility was shared by different municipal government departments in many cities (Ministry of City Service 1957b). In large enterprises, institutions and other public establishments (work units), housing offices were set up to organize house building and distribution, to collect rents and carry out maintenance. These housing offices were accountable to the directors of work units rather than to a municipal housing authority. This practice resulted in two different types of public housing in Chinese cities: houses managed directly by the municipal housing departments and those managed by individual work units. In most cities, the first type of housing was a result of transferring private housing into the municipal ownership, while the second type consisted of mainly new houses built from government investments.

Several efforts were made to regulate public housing management and to centralize properties controlled by work units within the municipal housing management department. In 1957, for example, central government had issued a policy calling for unitary management of urban public housing stock by housing authorities at city level (Ministry of City Services 1957a). Under this policy, most public sector properties owned by individual institutions were to be transferred to the municipal housing department. Apart from some local experiments, this centralization attempt was disrupted by other events. In later years, more houses were built by work units.

Toward the end of the 1950s, steady economic development gave way to a series of political movements starting with the 'Great Leap Forward' (1958), economic adjustment (1963), and the Cultural Revolution (1966–76). Not many new houses were built in urban areas and housing policies experienced a period of stagnation. At the end of the Cultural Revolution period, urban housing conditions remained very poor; the average housing floor space per person was still around 3 sq m (the standard observed in 1949), and it was common to find urban families crowded in one small room, using various makeshift beds.

Public spending on housing production increased dramatically after the Cultural Revolution. This was prompted not solely by the concern with housing conditions, but also by the realization that ostensibly 'unproductive' investment in housing can have a multiplier effect. During the Fifth Five Year Plan period (1976–80) nearly 30 billion yuan investment went into urban housing construction. This was increased to over 100 billion yuan for the Sixth Five Year Plan (1981–85). The share of total capital investment reached a historical high of 25.4 per cent in 1982 (Tables 6.3 and 6.4). These new investments resulted in a dramatic increase in housing floor space in cities, particularly in the public sector. Between 1981–85, a total of 648 million m² of new housing was added in urban areas. About 81 per cent was constructed through state investment. The collective[1] and individual sectors contributed 5.5 per cent and 13.2 per cent of new housing respectively during this period.

Tables 6.3 and 6.4 indicate that urban housing development was dominated by state capital and technical upgrading investments in the 1980s and the early 1990s. This, however, does not mean that all resources came directly from central and local government. Changing economic policy increased the financial management power of enterprises and other government organizations and enabled them to retain some funds for housing development. Public sector housing development was again dominated by the work units. Between 1979–85, about 60 per cent of housing investment came from enterprises and institutions.

---

1   Collective enterprises were set up by local governments or large work units to produce goods or services outside the state economic plans; they also provided jobs to non-skilled workers who had difficulties in gaining a permanent position in the formal state sector.

Table 6.3 Urban housing investment in China, 1976–1990 (billion yuan)

Year	National Five Year Plan	Total housing investment (all sectors)	State capital investment for housing	State technical upgrading investment used for new housing	Collective sector housing investment	Private (family, non-agri. only) housing investment	State housing capital investment as per cent of total capital investment
1979	Fifth	7.8	7.7			0.2	14.8
1980		12.7	11.2	0.8	0.3	0.4	20.0
1981	Sixth	14.5	11.1	2.0	0.6	0.8	25.1
1982		18.8	14.1	2.9	0.9	0.9	25.4
1983		18.8	12.5	4.2	1.1	1.0	21.1
1984		19.6	13.6	3.4	1.2	1.4	18.3
1985		29.1	21.5	3.3	1.7	2.6	20.0
1986	Seventh	29.1	18.9	5.3	1.9	2.9	16.1
1987		32.0	18.1	7.5	2.1	4.2	13.4
1988		38.5	19.8	9.4	2.6	6.7	12.8
1989		33.1	18.9	6.4	2.1	5.6	12.2
1990		29.7	17.0	6.1	1.8	4.8	10.0

Source: Real Estate Management Department of Ministry of Construction 1995.

Table 6.4 Urban housing completions in China, 1979–2002 (floor space: million square metres)

Year	National Five Year Plan	All sectors	State capital investment	State technical upgrading investment	Collective sector	Private families*	Average cost**
1979	Fifth	74.8	62.6	8.0	1.7	2.5	100
1980		102.1	82.3	10.5	2.8	6.5	113
1981	Sixth	110.7	79.0	14.4	4.3	13.0	128
1982		131.5	90.2	21.1	6.6	13.6	135
1983		129.4	81.2	26.5	7.9	13.8	151
1984		123.5	77.0	22.1	7.7	16.7	160
1985		153.2	95.7	20.2	8.9	28.4	177
1986	Seventh	148.4	89.2	21.8	9.7	27.7	196
1987		137.2	64.5	29.0	8.8	34.9	213
1988		140.0	60.1	30.5	9.0	40.4	241
1989		109.5	50.6	20.5	7.0	31.4	290
1990		97.2	48.2	18.4	6.4	24.2	316
1991	Eighth		56.9	16.9	6.4	68.1	
1992			69.2	17.5	7.5	85.9	
1993			79.9	17.5	11.3	98.1	
1994			89.6	20.3	11.3	122.7	
1995			92.5	19.9	32.9	133.3	
1996	Ninth		95.9	18.4	29.4	145.2	
1997			100.9	17.7	30.1	151.7	
1998			125.5	15.7	34.9	182.3	
1999			160.3	15.2	37.4	192.5	
2000			131.5	8.0	38.5	189.3	
2001	Tenth		116.5	4.3	37.2	194.7	
2002			104.2	2.8	34.2	194.4	

* Non-agricultural only   ** Yuan/m² floor space

Notes: Table does not include housing built by real estate development companies (Commercial housing). Since the early 1990s, commercial developers began to build a significant proportion of new houses in cities. There are differences between data provided by different sources, particularly in relation to the family house building activities.

Source: Real Estate Management Department of Ministry of Construction 1995 (For data up to 1990). State Statistics Bureau 1998 (For data between 1991–96). State Statistics Bureau 2003, (for data from 1997).

Although housing floor space increased dramatically after 1976, housing shortages were far from solved by the mid 1980s. Other housing related problems also became more prominent. The housing conditions associated with different work units were very unequal. Housing improvement was very slow in small work units, particularly the small enterprises in the urban collective sector and some non-profit organizations, such as schools. The standard of some new housing was thought to be too high. Many larger units were built for the powerful and high status groups, and this resulted in less housing for general workers. Corruption in the distribution of housing was widespread. Housing investment was maintained at a high level, but it became a heavy fiscal and management burden on government.

Housing Reform and Privatization

Policy Development

At the beginning of the 1980s, the Chinese government planned to address these problems through housing reform. During the 1980s, a series of reform programmes were tested at various locations.[2] These included: the sale of new housing to urban residents at construction cost (1979–81), subsidized sale of new housing (1982–85), and comprehensive housing reform (1986–88) (Wang 1992). The publication of the central policy document, *Implementation Plan for a Gradual Housing System Reform in Cities and Towns* (State Council 1988) marked the turning point of housing reform from pilot experiments to overall implementation in all urban areas. The objective of this Plan was to 'realize housing commercialization according to the principles of socialist planned market economy'. Reform policies included rent increase, housing subsidies, and sale of public housing (Wang and Murie 1996). This plan was interrupted in 1989 by economic and political problems.

The housing reform programme was resumed in 1991 with the publication of another central government resolution, *On Comprehensive Reform of the Urban Housing System* (General Office of the State Council 1991). This document reinforced the 1988 resolution and required all urban authorities to carry out housing reform. Although there were no major changes in the overall objectives of housing reform, this resolution led to the large-scale sale of existing public housing at very low prices. In 1994 new policies were issued in the document, The Decision on Deepening the Urban Housing Reform (Housing Reform Steering Group of the State Council 1994). These policies focused for the first time on the establishment of an urban housing market. Strategies aimed to change the housing investment, management and distribution systems and to establish:

---

2   See Bian and Logan (1996); Chen (1996); Chiu (1996, 2001); Lau, (1993 and 1995); Leaf (1997); Li (2000a, 2000b); Logan et al (1998); Wang and Murie (1996, 1999a and 2000); Wang (1992, 1995, 2000, 2001, 2003); Wu (1996 and 2001); Zhou and Logan (1996).

- a two track housing provision system with social housing for middle and low income households and commercial housing for high income families;
- a public and private housing saving system;
- housing insurance, finance and loan systems which would enable both policy oriented and commercial developments;
- a healthy, standardized and regulated market system of property exchange, repair and management.

Apart from rent changes and the sale of public housing, this document formalized several special arrangements to help ordinary urban household to participate in the new housing market. The first important arrangement involved the establishment of a housing provident fund system based on the Singapore model, through which the urban employer and employee each made a contribution to the employee's housing saving fund. The savings were to be used to purchase housing or for housing repairs. They could be used for other purposes only when the employee retired. The other important changes included the introduction of subsidized commercial housing for low and middle income families. Central government loans and free land allocations were used as the main mechanism for the development of affordable housing (the *anju* – peaceful living projects; and later *jingji shiyong fang* – affordable housing).

Taken together, these policies resulted in important changes in housing construction, distribution and management, and significant improved housing conditions after 1992. Individuals' share of housing costs has increased substantially compared with the beginning of the reform. Rent for example had increased many times although it had not reached the desired level. These reforms however, had not managed to shift the system away from the work units. House sales, rent increases, and setting up various housing funds were all done within established work units. While work units sold their existing stock to employees at a heavily subsidized price, they continued their house-building programme or purchased new housing from commercial developers at full market prices for distribution to employees at the front of the housing queue. Most commercially built housing during the 1990s, particularly the expensive units, actually ended up in the old welfare system. The proportion of direct sales to individual families was very low. The creation of a housing market was slow, and housing provision was still very expensive for employers (Wang 2000).

New housing policies were introduced by the central government in July 1998 (State Council 1998). These included three main objectives:

- to end direct housing distribution by employers and introduce housing cash subsidies;
- to create a diversified housing supply system with state supported affordable (low cost) commercial housing as the main form;
- to set up a new housing finance system to help developers and individuals with loans and mortgages to facilitate the urban housing market.

Table 6.5 Commercial housing development and sales, 1997–2002

Year	Floor space of buildings completed*	Average cost of buildings completed+	Total floor space sold*	Average price+	Villas, high-value apartments: Floor space*	Villas, high-value apartments: Average price+	Affordable housing: Floor space*	Affordable housing: Average price+
1991			27.5					
1992			38.1					
1993			60.4					
1994			61.2					
1995			67.9					
1996			69.0					
1997	158.2	1175	78.6	1790	2.5	5382	11.1	1097
1998	175.7	1218	108.3	1854	3.5	4596	16.7	1035
1999	214.1	1152	130.0	1857	4.4	4503	27.0	1093
2000	251.0	1139	165.7	1948	6.4	4288	37.6	1202
2001	298.7	1128	199.4	2017	8.8	4348	40.2	1240
2002	349.8	1184	237.0	2092	12.4	4154	40.0	1284
2003				2413				
2004				2724				

Notes: * million m^2 + yuan/m^2
Source: State Statistics Bureau 1998, 236. State Statistics Bureau 200, 244–6.

Under this new policy, the future housing requirements of public sector employees in work units would be met directly through the housing market. The employers were allowed to issue housing subsidy to their employees but not to be involved directly in housing construction, distribution or management. To reduce the commercial housing price and support the public sector employees, 'affordable housing' was to be built with government support for low and middle income groups (see below). The government planned to make this type of housing accessible to most urban residents (70–80 per cent). The higher income households in urban areas (the top 10–15 per cent) were to be encouraged to obtain high standard commercial housing through the market; and poor urban families (the bottom 10–15 per cent) were to be given subsidized rental housing by their employers or the city government (State Council 1998). These reform policies introduced important changes in urban housing provision. In the 1990s, most new commercial housing was bought by employers and distributed to their employees. In 2003 about 95 per cent of new housing was sold directly to individual families.

Commercialization of the housing construction process was particularly successful. From the late 1980s, commercially built housing provision had been increasing throughout the country. During the first half of the 1990s, commercial housing played a supportive role in comparison with public sector housing development (Table 6.5). Since 1998 commercial house building has surpassed the public sector housing construction and become the main source for market housing.

Privatization of public housing

Housing privatization was a main element of the reform programme during the 1990s and significant progress was made in this area. By 2002, 80 per cent of public housing had been sold to its occupiers. This included most purpose-built housing units owned by work units. Though it is difficult to estimate how many units have been sold in the country, the sale of public housing was thought to be the largest privatization project ever implemented. In 1981, over 82 per cent of urban housing was in public ownership (53.5 per cent was controlled by work units and 28.7 per cent by the municipal housing authorities); and private housing declined to 17.8 per cent. (Almanac of China's Economy 1983, IV–103). Most of the remaining private housing was of poor quality and was demolished during the urban redevelopment process in the 1980s and the 1990s. By 2003, home-ownership had become the most common tenure in cities, and over 82 per cent of urban families owned their home. In Beijing city by 2003 nearly 87 per cent of public sector tenants had bought housing from their employers or the municipal housing authority through privatization (Beijing Municipal Housing Reform Office et al. 2003). This dramatic increase in home-ownership also altered the distribution of urban assets. Government statistics showed that in 2001, average household asset in urban areas was 228,300 yuan, and 47 per cent was in the form of properties (Liu 2003).

Only a very small proportion of public housing was not sold. The main reasons included:

- Properties were not suitable for sale;
- Occupiers were too poor (usually retired) and could not afford to buy;
- Occupiers were not employees of the work unit (offspring or relatives of the employees) and were not eligible to buy;
- Work units (mainly poor performing state-owned enterprises) were too slow to produce housing reform plans and had missed the deadline set by local government. In Shenyang city, for example, state-owned enterprises were banned from selling houses in 2001 when new policies were introduced to transfer work unit housing to special property management companies.

House sales in the early 1990s were offered at government-determined standard price and sales only involved the transfer of the use right of the property from employer to purchaser with some limitations on resale. After 1997 public houses were privatized at cost price (the real costs for new housing or discounted costs for existing housing) and purchasers were granted full property rights. Subsequently, special arrangements were made to convert the use rights to full property rights. Early purchasers were given the option to make an extra payment to cover the differences between the standard price and the cost price.

After sale, most work units continued to provide some support and services to the privatized housing estates. While the costs of minor and internal repairs were paid by residents, major repairs, particularly external repairs, were paid by work units. During the pre-reform period, water, gas and electricity supply, for households in work unit owned housing estates, was provided by work units. In most cases, during the reform process these services were transferred to special supply companies.

Support for Home-ownership

After more than two decades of reform and commercialization, some of the key features of the new urban housing system had become clearer. The socialist idea of universal housing benefit provided through public sector employers had been abandoned. The new housing polices shared many of the features of the market economy and focused on two main areas:

- Support for home-ownership for the middle and high income families through financial arrangements; and
- Support for low-income households through a remodelled social housing provision system.

Support for home-ownership included several financial and subsidy arrangements. The major ones were the housing provident fund system, mortgage finance, building affordable housing, and housing subsidy. These are discussed in turn in this section. The new social housing approach is examined below.

Housing provident fund

A housing provident fund based on the Singapore model was first introduced in Shanghai in the early 1990s and was later adopted as a national policy in 1994. The system required both employer and employee to make a contribution to the employee's housing fund each month. This fund was held in special bank accounts or at housing fund management centres. It could only be used for housing. Other uses could be made when the employee (account-holder) reached retirement age. Though the initial contribution level was left to local government to decide, central government recommended a level of 10 per cent of the employee's salary (shared equally between employer and employee). The employee's contribution could be deducted from salary each month and the employer had to find resources for their contribution. The housing provident fund account was expected to accompany a person for their entire employment life. It could only be closed if the account-holder had left the city, died or retired. When an account-holder died, the family members could inherit the fund. Work units played a very important role in managing individual housing provident funds at the initial stage. They made the deposit on behalf of individuals, passed information between the fund management centre and employees, and arranged for withdrawals or mortgages.

Initially the housing provident funds were used mainly as short term loans to work units, housing co-operatives, and developers for the development of affordable housing. Subsequently, housing provident funds were used more in line with their original purpose – to help individual employees with housing. The specific uses included:

- House Purchase: Subject to approval by housing fund management authorities, account-holders could withdraw a lump sum to pay for house purchase within the limit of their savings, or obtain a mortgage. Mortgages were promoted vigorously after the initial participation period and individuals could borrow from the fund, at a lower interest rate than applied to commercial bank loans to purchase a home.
- Private House Building: Because private family house building was the main form of housing provision in rural areas, urban employees who married rural partners were allowed to withdraw their fund for house building in rural areas.
- Paying Rent: If rent was more than five per cent of total monthly household income, provident funds could be withdrawn to pay rent.

By 2001, over 67 million urban employees (about half of all those in employment) had joined the saving system. Most of them were public sector employees. In 2003, the average contribution had been increased to 16 per cent. The Ministry of Construction reported that the fund had helped 2.4 million families to buy their home through low interest mortgages. The housing provident fund system was claimed by government officials as one of the most successful elements of urban housing reform in China (Liu 2003).

Although the housing provident fund system was aimed at all urban employees, those who benefited most tended to be public sector employees, especially government officials, civil servants, academics and professionals. The public sector employers were funded by government and it was not difficult for employers to budget for the required contribution to be made to the individuals' housing fund. There were also steady increases in salaries in these sectors. The monthly contributions were substantial for employees. In contrast, private and other employers were not required to set up this fund for employees, and only some very high performing firms did so. In the private sector, most employees, and especially the manual and unskilled workers, stayed out of the system.

The housing provident fund practice in state owned enterprises varied substantially. In general, the level of contribution to the housing provident fund in state-owned enterprises was lower than in other parts of the public sector, and was less steady. State-owned enterprises involved in modern businesses and services had higher housing fund contributions than old manufacturing enterprises. Many poorly performing state-owned enterprises had to stop their fund contributions from time to time due to financial difficulties. The use of this fund by industrial workers also varied between enterprises. In rich enterprises, the amount of accumulated funds was larger and more employees (mainly managers and professional staff) benefited from low interest loans. In poor enterprises, contributions to the fund were not continuous and the amount in the accumulated fund was small. Comparatively few industrial workers borrowed from the fund.

Home loans

Housing privatization during the 1980s and the 1990s involved substantial discounts. Most public sector employees were able to pay off the asking price from family savings. Occasionally, some families had to borrow from relatives or friends. Since the middle 1990s, housing prices, particularly commercial housing prices, increased very quickly. This made any outright purchase of housing beyond the reach of most ordinary urban residents. Home loans become an important kind of financial arrangement in the emerging urban market. Three different types of home loan were promoted toward the end of the 1990s: housing provident fund mortgage, commercial bank mortgage and a combination of the two. Provident fund mortgages were related to the amount of funds accumulated and had relatively low interest rates. All major banks were owned by the government, and although functioning according to commercial principles, the government had strong control over them in relation to mortgage interest rates.

The Municipal Housing Fund Management Centre in Beijing for example has been providing home mortgages since 1994. A local regulation was issued to guide the process. The borrower must have a personal provident fund account with the Municipal Housing Fund Management Centre and must be a permanent resident in the city. There are differing terms for loans for the purchase of the existing public (work unit) housing by the sitting tenants and the purchase of new commercial housing. For work unit housing, the initial amount of the loan could be up to 90 per cent of the purchase price and 15 times the housing provident fund deposited by the borrower. The maximum period of the loan could be 30 years. For the purchase of commercial housing, the amount of the loan was limited to 80 per cent of the purchase price and ten times the value in the provident fund of the borrower. The maximum period of borrowing was shorter (20 years). While the provident fund savings of public sector employees (the main purchasers of work unit housing) were more or less similar, contributions by private sector employees had varied substantially. Some private or joint venture firms paid very high housing provident fund contributions to their employees. Although the borrowing limit for non-public sector employees – ten times savings – was smaller than that for public sector employees, the private sector employee could borrow a substantial amount. Initially, private sector employees were the major borrowers from the system and the key players in the commercial housing market in the early years when most public sector workers had not got used to the idea of borrowing.

Housing provident fund mortgage lending progressed slowly. In Beijing, between 1993 (when the fund was established) and June 1998, only 3,592 individual loans (0.2 per cent of the contributors) were made. About 62 per cent of these were made during the first six months in 1998. The total amount of lending was only about eight per cent of the provident fund held by the Municipal Housing Fund Management Centre.

Funds held by the Municipal Housing Fund Management Centres were not the only resources for mortgage lending. State owned banks also provided loans to house buyers. However, the scale of mortgage lending by banks during the 1990s was not large. The China Construction Bank (one of the major banks providing mortgage services) had only issued 11,000 individual loans in Beijing by the end of 1998. Most borrowers were from the wealthier group in the city, and very few were from ordinary salaried groups. Research also revealed that 70 per cent of these people bought housing as an investment, such as renting out, rather than as family homes (*Beijing Economic Daily*, 1 June 1999).

Low demand for mortgages and over supply of commercial housing has presented the Chinese government with a very difficult economic task. To encourage borrowing, the government reduced the bank interest rate seven times between 1996–99 and adjusted the terms and conditions on mortgage borrowing in the hope of pushing the urban housing market forward. China's central bank, the People's Bank of China, decided in November 1999 to reduce the interest rates on home mortgages and to extend the period of loan for commercial housing (including affordable housing) from 20 years to 30 years (http://www.realestate.cei.gov.cn/g00/C991122c.HTM). Commercial banks also relaxed their rules on borrowing. The China Construction Bank increased the amount of loan from 70 to 80 per cent of the purchase price.

To encourage spending on housing, central government introduced a 20 per cent tax on bank interest payments in 1999. Other policies were also introduced to encourage the re-sale of privatized housing (the so-called secondary housing market). Policy makers hoped that some families might move up the housing ladder and sell their smaller and older houses to lower income groups. There was also provision for combined home mortgages by both the Municipal Housing Fund Management Centres and commercial banks for those who could not borrow enough money from one source. In the second half of the 1999, mortgage lending activities by both the Municipal Housing Fund Management Centres and commercial bank sectors have increased. However, the main borrowers were still the better-off households. The majority of urban households, particularly traditional public sector employees, chose to stay in their current family homes.

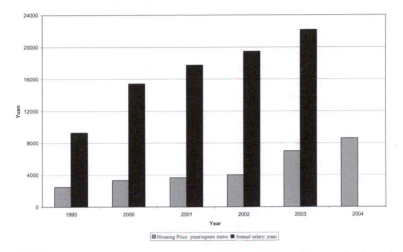

Figure 6.1 Average price for new commercial housing and annual salary in Shanghai

Sources: Various sources from internet and newspapers.

These policies eventually worked. Coupled with major increases in earnings in cities (particularly in the mainstream public sectors) and a change in attitude towards borrowing, home mortgages became an established feature in all cities by the turn of the century. The number of mortgages increased substantially in both housing provident fund and banking sectors. In some cities, residents queued for several days and nights to buy new completed houses. This has led to a continuous increase in the urban housing price. In large cities such as Shanghai, housing prices more than doubled in a short period of three years from 2002 to 2004 (Figure 6.1). This dramatic increase in housing costs put great pressure on the middle to low-income households which experienced serious affordability problems. At the same time it led some observers to worry that the property market in Chinese cities might be heading toward a big crash. Though there was no sign of this happening immediately, the government took steps to cool down the housing market. In March 2005, the first interest rate increase was announced (from 5.31 to 5.51 per cent). For large cities with excessive housing price increases, the government also demanded that lending be limited to 70 per cent of the value of the house.

Affordable housing

House prices in Chinese cities were very high in comparison with average salaries throughout the 1980s and the 1990s (Table 6.5). In 1997, the price of ordinary housing in the inner suburban areas of Beijing was over 4000 yuan per square metre. For high standard apartments near the centre and cottage houses in suburban areas, prices could be well over 10,000 yuan per square metre. This was more than one year's average salary in the city (the average annual salary in the city was 11,000 yuan in 1997) (Beijing Municipal Construction Commission 1997).

Beijing Municipal Government began to address this problem in the early 1990s. It initiated a *kangju* (healthy living) project to build low cost housing. Under this scheme the cost of housing for middle and low income public sector employees was to be shared by the state, the work units and individuals (*People's Daily*, Overseas Edition, 2 February 1995). This policy and experiments in other cities led to the idea of subsidized commercial housing for low and middle income families – the peaceful living [*anju*] project in 1995 (Wang and Murie 1999b). The target groups were low and middle income urban households (traditional public sector employees). The initial capital investment for *anju* projects was shared by central government and the cities. The investment was to be recovered through the sale of the completed houses. Central government would provide 40 per cent of the investment through bank loans. The remainder was provided by city governments from municipal housing funds, work units' housing funds, individual housing savings and pre-sale payments. The city government organized construction and the products were sold to qualified households (official residents of the city) at a cost recovery price.

Anju projects have a rather narrow scope, and they were targeted only at middle to low income groups (such as teachers) who worked for a small employer who could not afford to build employees' housing. In the 1998 housing reform policy, the *anju* project was replaced by a new approach – affordable housing [*jingji shiyong fang*]. The key differences between affordable housing and ordinary commercial housing are the way in which the land is allocated and government control of the profit made by the developers. For any projects approved by the local authority, for affordable housing, the land is administratively allocated without charging for land use. The developers' investment profits were controlled at a level of no more than three per cent (State Council 1998). Further instructions were issued by the Ministry of Construction to reduce other costs in the building process. Government controlled banks and the municipal housing fund management centres were instructed to allocate funds and issue loans to developers for affordable housing. The affordable housing idea came when the government shifted its economic development emphasis from export to internal consumption in response to the Asian financial crisis. Affordable housing development was promoted as a major sector of the urban economy, and designed to tap into the savings held by urban households.

Local government organized affordable housing schemes were not the only cheaper housing projects. The 1998 policy also made the provision for other types of affordable housing development. Large work units were allowed to organize their own affordable housing schemes and smaller work units were encouraged to develop affordable housing projects jointly. Although government policies had banned free housing distribution in 1998, work units were allowed to build housing on land under their control and sell new houses to their employees. This building for sale approach following the affordable housing provision was very popular and many work units, especially state-owned enterprises, adopted it. Work unit organized building for sale projects could reduce housing prices substantially in comparison with local commercial housing. By following the affordable housing policy provision, this building for sale could save land use fees and other government charges. Some work units also subsidized infrastructure construction. Normally, work units could build houses for about half of the cost of local commercial housing. Qualified employees had to buy the house and pay a deposit before the building process began. To be qualified, one had to satisfy the work units' housing allocation policies in relation, for example, to years of service, technical grade and status. Some work units used the old housing waiting list to determine which employees were qualified to buy.

Housing cooperatives forced another approach to affordable housing. Similar to building for sale schemes, housing cooperatives used spare land under work unit control. Smaller state-owned enterprises, for example, were encouraged to develop joint affordable housing schemes under the name of cooperatives. Housing cooperatives were also encouraged to form partnerships with property developers. Some property development companies were given housing cooperative status to help land-rich work units to build houses. In this case, work units usually cleared and prepared the land and provided necessary facilities. The housing cooperative then built housing for the participating work units' employees. The cooperative might sell some units to other purchasers outside the work unit to subsidise the cheaper prices offered to work unit employees.

Housing subsidy

In 1998 the reform policies banned public sector employers from direct housing allocations. The housing requirements of all public sector employees were to be met through the market. Public sector employers, however, were entitled to issue cash subsidy to help employees to buy their houses from the market or through the government-supported affordable housing schemes (Wang 2000). The implementation of this policy was slow, and in most cities detailed implementation plans were only made for the administrative sectors financed directly by the government. State-owned enterprises were encouraged to follow the practice in the administrative sector, though most state-owned enterprises did not attempt to apply this new policy.

Housing subsidy was available only in the public sector, and practice differed from city to city. Subsidy policies normally emphasized official status and related to housing entitlement, current salary, and years of employment. The level of subsidies differs between employees who started their employment before 1998 and those who started later; and between those who already had access to public housing and those who had not. Different subsidy calculation formulae were produced for each city. Housing subsidy policies in Guangzhou city for example were based on official status and housing entitlement. The system recommended a monthly subsidy scale for different groups of employees. The lowest monthly subsidy for those who had no access to public housing was 233 yuan and the highest was 4 times the level of the lowest subsidy (at 933 yuan) in 2003 (Table 6.6). The total length of subsidy was set at 25 years.

Table 6.6 Housing subsidy policy in Guangzhou

Cadre: Official Rank	Professional: Scale and No. of years in that scale	Technical Workers: Grade	Ordinary Workers: Year of employment	Municipal Subsidy Standard (Yuan/ Month)
Office assistant	Ordinary	Initial Grade	< 5 years	233
Officer	Assistant	Middle Grade	6–10 years	280
Assistant senior officer	Middle < 3 years	Higher Grade	11–18 years	327
Senior officer	Middle > 4 years	Technician	> 19 years	373
Deputy departmental head	Mid-higher < 3 years	Senior Technician		420
Departmental head	Mid-higher > 4 years			467
Deputy bureau director	Higher < 3 years			513
Bureau director	Higher > 4 years			607
Deputy Mayor				747
Mayor				933

Source: Guangzhou Municipal People's Government 2000.

Housing subsidy was aimed at those who either had not benefited or had not benefited enough from public housing. The principle was good because it gave equal housing rights to everyone employed by the state sectors. In the past, because of housing shortage, some employees lived in public housing while others waited in the queue. Cash subsidy theoretically speaking avoided this inequality. However, housing subsidy is different from salary-based income distribution. The level of subsidy is based mainly on office status, which was a key feature of the pre-reform housing distribution system. Housing subsidy in fact is an extra income given only to well-positioned managers and professionals. Most general workers had no access to such subsidy. In the government and public funded institutions, housing subsidies were financed through public money, while housing subsidy in state-owned enterprises had to be financed by their production profits. State-owned enterprises performed differently in the market with some becoming rich companies while most others struggled to balance their books. For the poor ones, housing subsidy was not a consideration at all.

New Social Housing for the Urban Poor

Housing commercialization and privatization in urban areas over the last 20 years has substantially changed the nature of housing distribution. Most public housing has been sold to sitting tenants. New employees (in both public and private sectors) have to buy their housing in the market. This approach, however, does not meet every urban resident's housing need. Apart from the high housing price problem discussed above, the widening gap between the rich and poor became a more important problem in cities. Recent economic reform and restructuring of the state owned enterprise sector had brought a stagnation of incomes among industrial workers. While the salaries of enterprise managers, professionals and high skilled workers increased substantially over the years, the wages of the non-skilled workers stayed low. From the mid 1990s onwards, state owned enterprises were allowed to lay off their workers. Many millions of industrial workers became either unemployed or 'laid-off' by their employers. When other living expenses (such as education and health care) increased steadily, these households found it difficult to think about making any housing improvement.

There were calls to include new social housing in the reformed social security system. The housing policies introduced in 1998 envisaged that about 15 per cent of low income urban families would rent social housing [*lianzu fang*] from the municipal government. Although the reintroduction of the social housing idea reflected an improved understanding of the urban housing market, its provision developed very slowly in most cities. By 2003, few provinces had produced local regulations for social housing. And local practice had moved away from the originally anticipated 15 per cent coverage and focused increasingly on a very small group of extremely poor families. There were also variations in practice in different cities. Some local government provided free or low rent housing to poor families, while others provided means tested rent allowances and cash subsidies.

In 2000, Beijing municipal government carried out a housing survey. It identified 32,000 households (about 1.4 per cent of the total households in the city) which required government's help with housing (Yang 2003). The number of households actually benefited from social housing was very small. By the end of 2002, the municipal authority only paid rent allowances to 998 households (Xie 2003). Shanghai, one of the frontrunners of social housing provision in the country, issued rent allowance to 3,366 households in 2003. Based on early experiments in two districts, the Shanghai Housing and Land Resources Management Bureau produced a policy document to guide the development of social housing in the city. The document made provision for households that met all the following conditions to apply for government support for housing:

- Monthly per capita income below the municipal poverty line, and family has received income support from the Civil Affairs authority for more than six months.
- Housing living floor space per person is less than 5 sq m.
- All household members have Shanghai residence registration status for over two years.
- At least one member of the households had local permanent non-agricultural *hukou* registration for more than five years.
- Family members have legal care or foster relationship between them.

According to these rules, the number of households qualifying for social housing was very small. In Changning District, of the 220,000 households, 3,651 (1.7 per cent) had an income under the poverty line, only 121 households actually qualified for social housing (Ying 2001). In Zabei District, 8153 out of 261,000 households were below the poverty line and 184 of them met the condition for housing support (Liu 2001). Households which met all conditions could apply to the District Social Housing Office [*lianzuban*] for support. The housing subsidy standard was set at 7 sq m floor space per person. If a household was assessed and qualified for support, rent allowance would be given to cover the cost of renting the difference between 7 sq m and the current per capita floor space used by the family. Rent levels were set according to the location in the city, with 40 yuan per square metre per month (2001 standard) in central areas, 30 yuan in near suburban districts and 20 yuan in counties and further districts. For example, if a family of three lives in a house with only 10 sq m floor space in the central area and meets conditions for social housing support, it would be entitled to a rent allowance for 11 sq m or 440 yuan per month. To ensure that a rent allowance is used for housing purposes, the Social Housing Office pays the allowance directly to the landlord, rather than to the family. This means that a family can only get this support when it improves its living conditions by moving to more spacious accommodation. Some households of elderly or disabled people could be allocated housing. These households are required to pay five per cent of their income as rent. The funding for this social housing programme is provided half and half by the district and municipal authorities. Because of limited funds and availability of housing, applicants wait in a queue arranged by date of application. Lists of successful households would be published in local media, and any objection from the general public or neighbours could lead to disqualification. Households which secured support have their income and housing situations re-assessed every half-year. If a household does not meet the conditions any more, the rent allowance payment is stopped. In case of direct housing allocation the household will be asked to move out of the social housing within six months. If the housing and income conditions of the household deteriorated, there will be no automatic increase in allowance. These families have to apply for an increase and wait in the queue again for their turn (Shanghai Property and Land Resource Management Bureau 2001).

Social housing provision was seen as an important part of the social protection system by the central government. However, the implementation of this policy was slowed down by the lack in most cities of a stable fund. As a result, the coverage of this support was very narrow. As in Shanghai, most other cities also linked social housing provision with the local minimum living standard and only provided help to families below the poverty line. Households with per capita income above the poverty line but living in poor conditions were not included. For convenience in operation, most local authorities preferred rent allowance rather than direct provision of low rent public housing. Rent subsidy could avoid the concentration of poor into specific areas. When direct allocation was necessary, only old empty public houses were used. In a few cities local housing authorities purchased difficult to sell commercial housing for this purpose.

Subsidized rental housing was seen by many local officials as a temporary measure to solve a short-term problem. Authorities had to evaluate the financial situation of the families every year to make sure only these still eligible stayed in the social housing provision system. However, most of these families' situations were determined by their educational background and personal quality, which may not change very much. With increasing unemployment, there were signs that the number of household actually requiring help was increasing rather than declining.

Conclusion

Progressive housing reform policies over a long period have made fundamental changes to the urban housing provision system in China. They have gradually changed the comprehensive socialist welfare housing provision into an urban housing market dominated by private home-ownership. The government has shifted its role from a direct provider to an enabler to support home-ownership and asset building. While early experiments had been exploratory, the 1998 housing reform policies prescribed a basic model of urban housing system for China based on home-ownership. Policy makers anticipated that urban housing would be provided through three different routes: social housing, affordable commercial housing and normal commercial housing. The initial idea was that 15 per cent of low income households would live in low rent social housing [*lianzu fang*]; 70 per cent middle to low income households would live in government supported affordable housing [*jingjishiyong fang*]; the remaining 15 per cent high income households would live in commercial housing [*shangpin fang*].

Over the last a few years, important changes have happened in the urban economic system and the housing market. Household incomes have become more unequal. The rich have become much richer and the poor remain very poor. This has led to some changes to the interpretation of the 1998 policies. Firstly, the target group of the new social housing has become much smaller. No housing officials expect that this will embrace as many as 10–15 per cent of the urban population. In most cities that implemented this policy, fewer than five per cent of households actually received some help under the policy. The nature of help also shifted away from direct public housing provision with a low rent, and most municipal housing authorities preferred to provide a rent subsidy rather than housing itself. The implementation of affordable housing polices also experienced some problems. It was difficult to define the 'middle to low income' households. In some cities with an over supply of new housing, as long as the purchaser was not obviously rich, he or she would be qualified to buy affordable housing. In some other cities, there were strong objections toward the affordable housing idea and very few affordable housing schemes were approved. Residents were encouraged to buy commercial housing directly from the market. Recently, some agreement emerged that the original target of 70 per cent for government supported affordable housing was too high. Some cities, Qingdao for example, have divided the original targeted residents for affordable housing into two different groups: a low income group which will qualify for affordable housing (about 30 per cent of the urban population above the urban poor); and middle income groups which will not qualify for affordable housing, but are given access to a new category of housing – ordinary commercial housing. Affordable housing development will receive the same level of government support as before (e.g. free land allocation, controlled development profits and reduced government charges), while ordinary commercial housing will benefit from a reduced land use fee and government charges. The idea of diversification in the housing market was also reflected in changes in the commercial housing development industry. More and more developers began to target different groups for their products. The range of commercial housing available in cities did not only include standard flats; it also included a higher proportion of luxury villas, terraced town houses and high standard penthouse apartments, which used to be found only in large cities such as Shanghai, Beijing and Guangzhou, where many foreigners live (Figure 6.2).

The change in urban housing provision has important implications for different social and economic groups. The emerging housing market provides the new rich with an excellent opportunity to improve their living conditions and to build up their assets and financial resources. In many large coastal cities, the housing market has become a good place for investment. Wealthy residents not only purchase high standard houses for their own consumption, but also as investments. In Guangdong Province, it was reported that more than 18 per cent of households owned more than one house. They rent these properties out to earn extra income. The dramatic increase in housing prices over recent years has helped many of these people to build their household wealth. These developments enabled local high income households to invest in housing, but also provided opportunities for outsiders. The proportion of new houses bought by outsiders in 2004 was 20 per cent in Shanghai and 60 per cent in Beijing. In Taiyuan, the capital city for the coalmining province of Shanxi, 80 per cent of new houses were sold to non-local residents. (www.xinhuanet.com, news pages on 24 March 2005).

In the transition from a socialist planned economy to a socialist market economy, housing reform, like other economic changes, benefited enormously the mainstream of the urban society. Government and party officials, academics and professionals employed by public institutions all benefited in one way or another from housing reform policies. They were able to purchase their home under the privatization programme during the early stages of reform. More recently, they received large increases in salaries, which enabled them to increase their housing investment. Government support for home-ownership was largely targeted at these groups. Housing provident fund contributions, regulated mortgage interest rates, affordable housing programme, work unit build for sale schemes and cash subsidy, in practice, all helped the mainstream of society more than the poor and the real urban low income groups. In this sense, the capitalist housing market has been adopted to serve the socialist elites.

Urban economic reform has increased the gap between the rich and the poor in Chinese cities; and housing reform and the market played an important part in the process of social and spatial stratification. As the urban poor have been marginalized into poor areas and locations, the rich and the new middle class have emerged as the key players in the housing market. The majority of these people already have a home. To move the market forward, everyone is encouraged to move up the housing ladder. While the upper level of the market became very active the bottom end of the market was relatively cool. Local low-income residents and working class families found it more and more difficult to participate. The ratio of the average price for a small flat of 70 m² to the average annual household income had reached 12 in Shanghai and 9.3 in Beijing in 2004. This means that for most ordinary urban residents, new housing was not affordable. Many cities relied on newcomers to fill the gap in the property market and international and outside investors sustained some of the major cities housing market in the coastal areas.

Although home-ownership and asset building is a better approach than the socialist welfare provision, the style of the new houses may cause some problems in the future. A detached or semi-detached stone or brick built house can last a very long time. It is also easy to maintain and repair. A house associated directly with a piece of land will also enhance its value. However in China, multi-storey flats, often in high-rise tower blocks, are the main form of new housing. These buildings are difficult to maintain, have very high running costs and very complicated ownership structures. Often built in haste sometimes with poor quality construction materials, they might have to be demolished at some stage. If the current trend continues with the rich moving toward the suburban cottage and town house areas and lower income households moving into the high-rise buildings, this type of housing will lead to serious social and environmental problems in the future. The current practice of demolishing low rise and traditional houses and relocating and compensating the

Figure 6.2 Urban housing provision, 1998 model and current trend

1998 central policy provision

Social housing for Low Income Group

Affordable housing Middle Income Groups

Commercial housing High Income

| 5 | 10 | 15 | 20 | 25 | 30 | 35 | 40 | 45 | 50 | 55 | 60 | 65 | 70 | 75 | 80 | 85 | 90 | 95 | 100 |

(per cent of population)

Low income group

High income group

Trend of future housing provision

Social housing

Urban Poor

Affordable housing

Low Income Groups

Government controlled ordinary commercial housing

Middle Income Groups

Commercial housing

High Income

original residents may not work for high density and high-rise buildings. The fast changing fashion in house design and the dramatic increase in housing price and inflation may mean that much of the household asset build-up in the high–rise areas is not sustainable. It may be lost by market adjustment and fluctuation similar to the 1997 Asian financial crisis.

House building in the last ten years has been dominated by commercial property developers. New housing estates were built to differing standards. This practice has resulted in serious spatial segregation between the new and the old and between the rich and the poor. The policymakers seem to accept this spatial differentiation and social divisions. Policies for the development of the secondary housing market will have profound effects on further social and spatial stratification. The original public sector tenants who bought their houses through privatization are seen as a major force that can push forward the urban housing market. Various policies (reducing the restriction on resale, salary increases, issuing housing subsidies, providing housing loans through the housing provident fund, simplifying the mortgage lending procedures) are promoted to encourage them to sell their existing low quality small flats to low-income families and to buy new and bigger houses in the well designed estates. This secondary market is still at a very early stage of development and most owners of privatized flats have found the commercial housing unaffordable. The existing pattern of residence preserves the relatively equal distribution and social mix of the socialist society. Once the secondary market has become active, we will see another major social and spatial re-organization of Chinese cities. When a more mature urban housing market is established, a series of new social problems involving a large proportion of population will also emerge.

One of the key features of the Chinese urban housing system is its quick transition from a public provision dominated system to a commercialized urban housing market. The socialist housing provision in the past made China very different from its neighbouring countries and the wider region included in this book. From the beginning of the 1980s, alongside the open door policy, Chinese governments began to learn from the experience of other countries. Large property developers based originally in Hong Kong, Singapore and Taiwan started to operate in China. This changed the approach to housing development. The privatization policies that followed drew on the experience of a wide range of countries in both the West and East Asia. The sale of public sector housing to sitting tenants was similar to the privatization process in Britain, and the introduction of the housing provident funds was based on the Singapore model. The promotion of the housing finance system centred on mortgage lending is common practice in many market economies. The speed of the transition in China is fast, though it has not adopted the big bang approach. The speed of housing privatization (sale of work unit housing), for example, is faster than that experienced by Britain, Hong Kong and Singapore. In less than a decade, most saleable houses owned by work units have been sold. The direct involvement of government and work units in house building and distribution has been reduced dramatically. The proportion of urban residents who now own (or partially own) their houses is higher than in either Singapore or Hong Kong. This fast track transition and commercialization will make China once again different from its neighbours. It has moved from one extreme to another.. In the near future, China could claim to have a more privatized urban housing market than that in some of its neighbouring countries, but the diminishing social housing sector may pose serious problems for the stability of urban society.

The movement from a socialist economy built on state owned enterprises and employment by the state to a market based economy has not meant that China has adapted the welfare regimes associated with the old welfare states. Rather it has adopted an asset based welfare system built on home-ownership and more in tune with system changes in Singapore. The approach has involved privatization subsidy and state support for developers to facilitate the development of the market especially among middle and higher income groups and established urban residents. Redistributive welfare objectives have been largely obscured by the opportunity to adopt a welfare approach that it is seen as contributing to the development of a modern competitive economy and cities that can compete internationally.

Chapter 7

Taiwan's Housing Policy in the Context of East Asian Welfare Models

Pui Yee Connie Tang[1]

Introduction

Taiwan, or the Republic of China (ROC), has a total land area of 36,006 square kilometres, which is about one tenth the size of Japan but has a population of 22 million people, which is about one fifth that of Japan. With an average population density of 622 persons per square kilometre in 2002, Taiwan is nearly as crowded as Bangladesh, despite the fact that more than half of the country's area is relatively mountainous. Hence, it is one of the most densely populated countries in the world. (*Taiwan Times*, 31 January 2005). With over 75 per cent of its people living in cities and towns, the island's western coastal area is one of the world's mostly densely urbanized areas. The capital city, Taipei, has a population of 2.6 million and its average population density rises to 9,720 persons per square kilometre (GIO 2004). Taiwan has few natural resources (no coal, minerals or oil) and experiences frequent earthquakes and typhoons. The country has borne a heavy burden in maintaining a high defence budget. Nevertheless, the island state has sustained rapid and strong economic growth for nearly five decades. The growth rate of gross national product (GNP) fluctuated around 10 per cent from the early 1960s to the 1980s, fell to 6–7 per cent in the 1990s, eventually dipping to 3–4 per cent at the beginning of the 2000s. Although per capita GNP fell from US$14,114 in 2000 to US$13,139 in 2004 (DGBAS 2005b), Taiwan is considered to be a high-income economy (per capita US$9,265 or more) by the World Bank classification. Economically, it is often regarded as one of the four Asian dragons/little tigers or Newly Industrialized Economies along with Singapore, Hong Kong and Korea.

As 96 per cent of the population is Chinese,[2] Taiwan is also described as a Confucian state, belonging to the group that also includes China, Japan, Singapore, Hong Kong and Korea. Politically, Taiwan is regarded as a developmental state

---

1 The author is grateful to Professor Chang Chin-Oh for comments on a draft of this chapter and for an explanation of the high vacancy phenomenon in Taiwan; and to Professor Yeung Yue-man for facilitating the author's appointment as a Visiting Scholar at the Hong Kong Institute of Asia-Pacific Studies at the time the chapter was written.

2 The indigenous population in 2000 was 398,000 persons, accounting for 1.8 per cent of the total population. Foreigners constituted another 1.8 per cent. Over the past decade,

(Johnson, 1982, 1987; Weiss, 2000) along with Japan and Korea. Thus, in the field of comparative social policy, the welfare system in Taiwan is seen as part of the regional cluster of the 'East Asian Model' of welfare states (Kwon 1997; Gough 2001), in contrast to the mainly western models described by Esping-Andersen (1990).

Both Taiwan and Korea were occupied by Japan for a long period of time. Taiwan was ceded to the Japanese following the Sino-Japanese war in 1895 while Japan annexed Korea in 1895 and colonized it in 1910. Japan occupied both countries until 1945. During the occupation of Taiwan, the Japanese established a number of vital institutions, educational, financial, industrial and political, which today still have much in common with Japanese contemporary systems.

While the last decade has seen the growth of literature on East Asian welfare regimes, little is known about the development of social welfare including housing policy in Taiwan. The main reason for this is that there is little material in English on this topic. Also, analyses of East Asian social welfare systems have been heavily dependent on western concepts. This chapter analyses housing policy in Taiwan in the context of the broad East Asian welfare model, as well as the relevant subsets within the model (see Chapter 1).

The chapter is divided into four sections. The first section traces the development of social welfare in Taiwan within the developmental welfare regime (for example, White and Goodman 1998; Holliday 2000; La Grange and Yung 2001). The second section provides a historical account of the post-war development of housing policy. This is followed by an examination of the housing situation and an assessment of the specific impact of the Asian financial crisis and the subsequent global economic recession in the early 2000s. The last section discusses current issues facing Taiwan and their implications for housing as well as social welfare.

Social Welfare under the Developmental Welfare Regime

A Japanese colony for 50 years, Taiwan experienced a brief moment of independence after being taken over by Chiang Kai-shek and the Kuomintang (KMT) government at the end of the Chinese civil war in 1949. As Chiang believed that he still ruled China and would eventually resume his authority there, he ruled Taiwan through an authoritarian military regime. In anticipation of an imminent invasion by the People's Republic of China (PRC), martial law was imposed in Taiwan until 1987. Despite the regime's shortcomings, Taiwan was successfully transformed from an agrarian economy to an industrial one in a very short period of time. Rapid industrial development was first started in the 1950s, as Taiwan was one of the major suppliers of American military goods during the Korean War (1950–53). The war also tied Taiwan and the United States closely together politically. Taiwan's industrialization was further speeded up by being given preferential treatment over imports into the United States. In the 1960s and 1970s, Taiwan became a major exporter of cheap

---

the number of foreigners has increased over 12 times due to the inflow of foreign labourers permitted by the central government since 1989 (DGBAS 2005a).

manufactured goods. The strategic alliance between Taiwan and the United States was severed after the American government granted the PRC formal diplomatic recognition on 1 January 1979. Taiwan's declining international status aroused public pressures for political liberalization. In order to build stronger support from Taiwan's residents to justify its political legitimacy, Chiang Ching-kuo, who succeeded his father in 1978 as President of Taiwan in a dynastic fashion, initiated the democratic reforms. Under his tenure, the government of the ROC, although still authoritarian, became much more open and tolerant of political dissent. Towards the end of his life, Chiang relaxed government controls on the press and speech, and put native Taiwanese in positions of power, including his successor Lee Teng-hui who furthered the course of democratic reforms. Lee became the first native-born President of Taiwan in 1988 and was reconfirmed as President in a direct election in 1996. During this period, the rise of wages and the strong currency forced Taiwan to shift to capital- and technology-intensive industries, particularly chemicals and electrical goods, and the island became one of the world's largest producers of computer-related products in the early 1990s. In 2000, Chen Shui-bian of the Democratic Progressive Party (DPP) succeeded Lee, ending more than 50 years of KMT rule in Taiwan.

During the first three decades of KMT rule, the Taiwanese government had little interest in providing social welfare. Family, and sometimes the local community, was the primary social welfare provider. Assistance to the truly destitute was in the form of charity and local mutual aid based on the combination of Buddhist and Confucian ethics. Obsessed by the goal of re-conquering and unifying mainland China, defence and economic development were given the highest policy priority. This was apparent from the enactment of the Military Servicemen's Insurance Law of 1953, the first piece of welfare legislation in Taiwan, which was targeted towards the military. On the economic side, the Taiwanese state adopted a Japanese style 'developmental state', and through control of the banking system, channelled all financial resources to export oriented industries. It also pushed industrial companies to adopt new technologies and new practices in order to maintain Taiwan's international competitiveness and improve its comparative advantages over the other tiger economies. The constant threat of communism and the sense of vulnerability, however, have persuaded the political elite and many of the population to support a developmental strategy (Jones, 1990; 1993). Thus, social welfare policy was the economic policy in which the authorities believed that the full employment created by economic growth could improve living standards, achieve an egalitarian society and enhance political stability in Taiwan.

Under this regime, the development of welfare policy was pragmatic and ad hoc, a response to immediate political needs rather than the needs of the people. The Labour Insurance Scheme in 1958, for example, was established as an appeasement measure to avoid potential worker revolts (Goodman and Peng 1996, 205). Pensions only covered Taiwanese people who were Mainlanders (soldiers and military officials who fled from mainland China to Taiwan) who typically worked in military and government positions, and who were mostly men (Ofstedal, Reidy and Knodel

2004, 167). Both programmes were aimed at consolidating the government's power base. There was no legislation to protect the rights of workers. Union strikes were prohibited, and labour unions were excluded from the decision-making process. Moreover, the government allowed the frequent exploitation of workers, particularly women. In free export zones, such as Kaohsiung and Mansan, some 80 per cent of the workforce were female; the majority were teenage girls from rural areas, who were paid at a third of the Japanese level and one-fifth to one-tenth of the level of comparable workers in the United States (Cummings 1987, 74–5).

The year 1980 marked the first phase of involvement of the Taiwanese government in social welfare. The 'three laws of social welfare' (for the elderly, the handicapped and the poor) were enacted and implemented during the same year. Also, three major systems of social insurance were established for labourers, civil servants and military servicemen, to cover the risks associated with death, disability, maternity, funeral expenses, medical care, old age, injury and sickness. By 1984, the Labour Standard Act was promulgated. This was designed to provide a minimum-working standard for labourers. It was obvious that the state was keen to play the role of a 'regulator' rather than a 'provider'; government involvement in social welfare was still marginal and hands-off, with a strong tilt towards meeting the nation's demand for a capable labour force. Also, those workers who were seen as most closely related to the stability of the Taiwanese state received the lion's share of central government welfare expenditure. In 1988, for example, the central government spent 0.1 per cent of its social welfare budget on labour welfare, while 63.1 per cent was spent on military welfare (Goodman and Peng 1996, 206). In 1991, 75 per cent of social welfare spending went to teachers, civil servants and the military (9 per cent of the total population) while 'the disadvantaged' (the aged, handicapped, women, the young and the poor), received only 3 per cent (Holliday 2000, 714). Indeed, the Taiwanese government successfully used the argument of its ultimate goal to unify with mainland China to forestall the development of welfare state schemes (Goodman and Peng 1996, 206).

1990 saw the beginning of the development of a social welfare system that was approaching the western model in providing livelihood protection and a basic safety net for Taiwanese citizens. The competition for political power after the establishment of the first opposition party, the DPP in 1986, the emergence of interest groups after the revision of the Civic Organization Law that removed the severe restrictions on the formation of non governmental organizations, and the rise of the people's political rights after the democratic reforms in the late 1980s all contributed to the expansion of social welfare services in Taiwan. The ROC government began to play the role of 'provider' in social welfare provision. Starting in July 1993, it has provided cash assistance, non-cash benefits and special subsidies to the disabled, low-income families, elderly farmers, and the medium- and low-income elderly. However, to restrict the use of government funds to the deserving poor, the government set an incredibly low poverty line – 60 per cent of per capita consumption expenditure in the previous year. It was estimated that only around 5 per cent of the total population was eligible for the cash benefit (Aspalter 2002, 74).

Then, in March 1995, it implemented the National Health Insurance programme, merging the medical care previously covered under the three insurance systems mentioned above. From the start, almost every Taiwanese was included under this scheme. Accordingly, government spending on welfare programmes more than doubled in five years from NT$145.8 billion to NT$291.2 billion[3] during 1993–98 (Hsieh and Hsing 2002, 521). Later, rising unemployment at the end of 1998 (3.1 per cent, the highest level of the past three decades) and the competition from the DPP for the presidential election forced the KMT government to install an unemployment benefit system in the labour insurance programme.

The scope of welfare services was further expanded after the DPP came to power in 2000. In contrast to the KMT's Chinese values and furtherance of the economy, the DPP was well known not only for its political argument for Taiwanese interests but also for its pro-welfare ideology. To match its public image for social reform, the DPP introduced a series of new welfare policies including the provision of an old-age allowance (NT$3,000 a month) to every elderly citizen over 65 years who had not received any pension, and low-cost mortgages at a 3 per cent interest rate for young, first-time homebuyers. For the first time, the allocation to welfare services (18.9 per cent) in the 2001 national budget was more than for culture and education (16.4 per cent), defence (15.5 per cent) and economic development (14.8 per cent), (Chan and Lin 2003, Table 4). However, a lot of public funds had been spent by the KMT government in the fight against the Asian financial crisis, along with tax cuts in favour of private investment.[4] The gap between governmental revenue and expenditure has been increasing remarkably in the early 2000s. The accumulated public debts officially admitted were about NT$3,289 billion in 2002, equivalent to 32.9 per cent of GNP in Taiwan, increasing from 25 per cent in 1997 (Ku 2004, 318). This forced Chan Shui-bian to change policy after just 100 days of his presidency, declaring economic development as the government's new priority and that social welfare programmes would be postponed. This announcement meant that further social welfare reform was uncertain. Overall, despite the marked increase in the size and coverage of social security programmes in the 1990s, Taiwan's welfare expenditure remains at a very low level. In 2002, (including retirement pension) it was 5.5 per cent of the Gross Domestic Product (GDP), well below the average 25 per cent that the European countries spent for social purposes. But Taiwan is ahead of other tiger economies such as Singapore and Hong Kong, which spent around 5 per cent (Hort and Kuhnle 2000, 164).

In summary, the essence of Taiwan's welfare system, like that of Japan and Korea, is social insurance that places the greatest importance on the enhancement of the productive element of society. In 2001, for example, the ROC government

---

3   The exchange rate in 2003 was NT$1,000 = US$34.

4   In order to counteract the adverse impact of the Asian financial crisis on Taiwan, the KMT launched many financial measures, such as tax cuts, bailouts and public purchases of company shares, to help business in trouble. The total costs were equivalent to 16 per cent of total government expenditure in 1998 (Ku 2004, 313).

allocated 64.4 per cent of its total welfare expenditure to social insurance but 27.7 per cent to welfare services (Chan and Lin 2003, Table 5). However, in terms of the commencement of its programmes, Taiwan is midway between the two. Japan enacted the daily livelihood protection law in 1947 while Taiwan established the labour insurance system in 1958 and Korea introduced a similar scheme ten years after Taiwan (Goodman and Peng 1996, 206). Japan began to adopt the 'western' type of social welfare in 1973 while Taiwan followed it in the early 1990s. Also, Japan and Korea have a strong emphasis on enterprise welfare in addition to the family welfare. Enterprise welfare is less obvious in Taiwan because its economy is characterized by a few large conglomerates with a huge number of small, family-oriented or medium-sized companies. Furthermore, the universal component in the Japanese welfare system is stronger than that in Taiwan and Korea. At the time of writing, contributory pension schemes are only available for some occupational groups. A national pension scheme has been planned for many years but it has not yet been realized. Nearly half (47.1 per cent) of the elderly were financially dependent on their children in 2000 (Ramesh 2004, Table 3.9). The primary role of the family to take care of the elderly is further strengthened by the civil laws that require people to care for their parents. Article 183 in the Criminal Law (1979) stipulates that adult children who refuse to perform their duties to support an aged family member will be sentenced to not more than five years' criminal detention. The 1996 law on Protection of the Rights and Interests of the Elder (Maintenance and Support by Families) also emphasizes the responsibility of adult children to support their parents and parents-in-law. Thus, despite the implementation of different types of social security schemes, the Taiwanese government still regards the family as the main provider of support and care for dependants, especially the elderly.

Housing Services Provision under Taiwan's Welfare Regime

Given the dominance of economic growth and political stability in the developmental welfare regimes, housing is rarely regarded as part of the social welfare programme. While governments in the western (or more precisely the Anglo-Saxon) countries have focussed traditionally on housing policy to improve the accessibility of low-income families to subsidized housing, the East Asian countries have focussed on housing production as part of economic strategies to increase the productivity of society (Doling 1999). Thus, all developmental states design their housing policies with the idea of 'economic policy first': housing programmes are driven by economic considerations rather than for a social purpose, and this is particularly obvious in Taiwan's housing services provision.

A residual mode in public housing provision

The Taiwanese government established its public housing programme in 1976. Before that, its involvement in housing was sporadic and targeted only to specific groups. It began in 1953 when a huge typhoon hit Taiwan, causing many people to become homeless, forcing the government to take some action. The government first established the 'Public Housing Committee of Executive Yuan' in 1954, and a statute was passed in 1957 to facilitate loans for public-housing construction. Yet, the progress of housing construction was slow; only 125,532 dwellings were constructed from 1959 to 1975, the majority of which were small and low quality (Yip and Chang 2003) and built for government officials and military servicemen (Ramesh 2004, 127). In Taipei City, the resident population exceeded one million in 1966 (Liu and Tung 2003, 15), and from 1968 to 1972, it continued to grow at an average increase of 76,000 each year (DBAS 2003, 12). To accommodate the growing number of migrants from other parts of the country, the city government started to borrow money from the Central Bank of China (CBC) and built houses, initiated urban renewal plans and developed new towns. During the period from 1968 to 1975, 10,370 housing units were built (DBAS 2003, 46).

Table 7.1 Number of dwellings constructed under the public housing programme in Taiwan, 1976–2002

Fiscal year[a]	Built by the government	Through government loans		Interest subsidies for individuals to purchase houses	Total
		Built by individuals	Built by private investors		
1976–81	67,565	3,670	-	-	71,235
1982–85	26,466	18,012	-	-	44,478
1986–89	2,596	7,640	432	-	10,668
1990–91	17,437	4,330	7,216	2,638	31,621
1992–99	51,794	8,684	27,383	94,027	181,888
2000–02[b]	-	1,665	-	6,986	8,651
Total	165,858	44,001	35,031	103,651	348,541

Notes: a) A fiscal year in Taiwan starts from 1 July 1 through to 30 June.
  b) It was up to the end of 2002.
Sources: Chen 2002, Table 5.1; MOI 2004, Table 8-3.

A series of political and economic events in the 1970s forced the government to act. The housing problems began when Taiwan was expelled from the United Nations in 1971. This was followed by the oil crisis of 1973 and the subsequent market slump. To address the problems, a six-year public housing construction programme (1976–81) was launched under the central government's 'Six-Year Taiwan Economic Construction Plan' in 1975. A number of public institutions were set up to supply public housing for middle and low-income families with an annual target of 25,000 housing units. As in Singapore, nearly all the public housing units were built for sale. Owing to difficulties in land acquisition, the housing programme missed its target by half (see Table 7.1). The public housing developed was either unpopular because of being built on cheaper but remote sites or expensive because of the high land price in prime areas (Yip and Chang 2003). Nevertheless, another four-year programme (1982–85) was implemented. However, when the property market went into a deep slump in the years of 1981 to 1986 (Figure 7.1), the government postponed the launching of the following four-year (1986–89) plan in order to prevent sales of public housing from falling even lower. Instead, the central government set aside a loan fund in its annual budget for the private sector to construct public housing. Provincial and city governments were allowed to borrow money from this fund. They were also permitted to levy a land tax so that they could use the money to purchase land and provide loans to individual households as a means to encourage private sector development. The domestic real estate market revived in 1989 and house prices soared. People rushed to buy public housing, which resulted in the shortage of public housing units. A waiting list for public housing was established in March 1989 to accord priority to different groups of applicants in buying the units (which was later suspended in April 1996). In 1990, a six-year plan (1992–97) was announced in which NT$176 billion was earmarked for the construction of public housing, plus NT$10 billion to subsidize interest payments on housing loans for people to buy houses on the open market (Ramesh 2004, 140–141). The subsidies were later replaced by the preferential-house-purchase-loans in 2003.

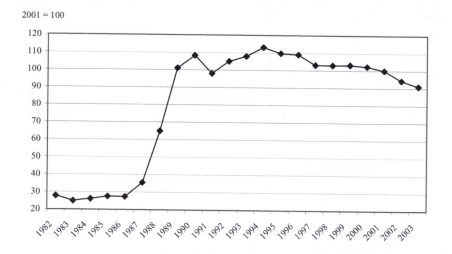

Figure 7.1 Housing price movement of newly constructed units in Taiwan, 1982–2003 (2001=100)
Source: Shih and Tsao 2004, Figure 3.

About 349,000 units were built under the public housing programme during the period 1976 to 2002 (Table 7.1). Of these, 47.6 per cent were directly built by the government, 22.7 per cent by individuals or private investors, and the remaining 29.7 per cent were private dwellings purchased on the open market by individuals with government interest subsidies. Before 1981, the proportion of government-built public housing units exceeded 90 per cent and then gradually dropped to around 60 per cent in the period 1982 to 1985. When the property market was in depression, the proportion of government housing fell dramatically to 24 per cent between 1986 and 1989, but bounced back to over 55 per cent when the market was overheated in 1990–91. After that, the emphasis of the public housing programme shifted from direct construction to offering incentives and subsidies. In 2000, in order to reduce the oversupply of new houses, the government imposed a four-year freeze on public housing construction projects. Overall, the direct intervention of the Taiwanese government in housing production contributed very little in terms of housing output compared to the public housing provision of not only Singapore and Hong Kong, but also Japan. The government of Japan, up to 1998, produced over 886,000 public housing units, and public housing accounted for 6.8 per cent of the total housing stock (Tang 2003, Tables 8.2–8.3). Public housing has played an insignificant role in the Taiwanese government's political agenda. Less than 1 per cent (0.87) of central government expenditure went to housing in the years of 1990 to 2000 (Croissant 2004, Table 1); thus, it is not surprising to find that only 5.5 per cent of total housing output was housing which was produced by the public sector (Table 7.2). However, this figure under-reported the actual extent of state involvement in housing. Between 1949 and 1989, 135,000 housing units were built by the Ministry of Defence for families of the armed forces, which were not included in any official statistics but represented more than one third of the public sector production (Yip and Chang, 2003). Nevertheless, since the overwhelming majority of public housing was built for sale, the number of public rented housing units, including those provided by social welfare departments but excluding those built by military establishments, amounted to less than 5,000, constituting 4 per cent of all rental dwellings in 2000 (ibid.).

The unregulated provision of owner occupied housing

Owner occupation is the major tenure in Taiwan. However, the growth of home-ownership is not the result of the government's deliberate pro-ownership policies such as those adopted by the governments in Japan, Singapore and Hong Kong. In contrast with the role of the state in relation to economic development, the Taiwanese government did not actually have much influence on housing. Rather the government had a negative perception of housing, seeing it as a non-productive consumption oriented good. It therefore imposed very strict controls on housing loans and channelled savings to economic development projects. Despite the absence of financial help from the government, Taiwan has achieved an extremely high home ownership rate – over 70 per cent in the 1980s (Figure 7.2). How was this possible when governmental and financial supports amounted to so little?

Table 7.2 Number of housing units completed in Taiwan, 1990–2000

	Private sector		Public sector		
	No.	%	No.	%	Total
1990	53,417	*79.0*	14,183	*21.0*	67,600
1991	68,410	*95.0*	3,606	*5.0*	72,016
1992	94,190	*92.0*	8,209	*8.0*	102,399
1993	140,655	*97.9*	2,994	*2.1*	143,649
1994	191,503	*96.9*	6,175	*3.1*	197,678
1995	184,037	*94.5*	10,725	*5.5*	194,762
1996	143,245	*94.1*	8,960	*5.9*	152,205
1997	105,597	*93.3*	7,545	*6.7*	113,142
1998	90,195	*92.2*	7,654	*7.8*	97,849
1999	85,233	*99.6*	333	*0.4*	85,566
2000	62,273	*100.0*	0	*0.0*	62,273
Total	1,218,755	*94.5*	70,384	*5.5*	1,289,139

Source: Yip and Chang 2003, Table 4.

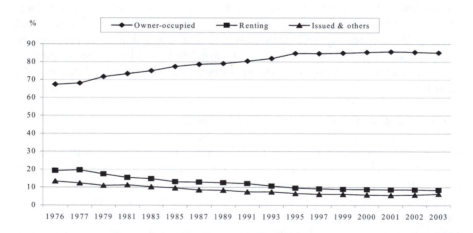

Figure 7.2 Housing tenure in Taiwan, 1976–2003
Note: 'Renting' includes households renting either from a private or a public landlord.
Source: DGBAS 2003, Table 20 (http://www.dgbas.gov.tw/public/Attachment/ 41141117871.doc).

The dominance of self-built housing in the 1950s to mid–1960s Taiwan in the 1950s was an agriculturally based society. Anticipating a Communist attack, the newly arrived KMT government used most of the available resources on military defence. Much of the housing was produced on a self-help basis, that is, the houses were built by the users themselves. Self-building activities were further boosted by land reform. In order to guarantee support from the peasants and to prevent a Communist revolution, a land reform programme was launched in three stages between 1949 and 1953. The results are many. First, peasants and tenant farmers acquired cheap land from the government, or from absentee landlords, at reduced rents and could therefore build their own houses, which were mainly low-rise simple structured dwellings. Second, the landlords, with compensatory capital in hand, were transformed from an exploitative class to urban entrepreneurs, concentrating their interest in industrial and property development. They were also the major providers of housing credits in the informal market for people wanting to buy land and build houses, before commercial banks were allowed to provide housing loans. Furthermore, the division of agricultural land into smaller plots and the subsequent large number of rural landholders aggregated these farmers into a powerful political lobby group which subsequently hindered the government not only in the acquisition of land for the development of public housing but also in the conversion of agricultural land to urban land in an attempt to cool down the property market during the late 1980s. Over 80 per cent of rural homeowners acquired their homes through building the dwellings by themselves or inheriting from the previous generation and the homeownership rate exceeded 93 per cent in 1995 (Li 2002, Table 2).

When industrialization began to take off in the 1960s, massive migration from rural areas pushed the population in Taipei from less than one million in 1960 to over two million in 1975 (Li 1998, Figure 10). Since housing provision was mainly achieved on the basis of self-help construction and the house building industry was underdeveloped, there was a relatively small amount of housing output. The large population growth, combined with little housing production, created a problem of housing shortage. It was estimated that there was a shortage of 200,000 housing units in Taipei city in the 1960s (ibid., 35). Overcrowding and squatting therefore became a feature of urban housing at that time.

The growth of pre-sale housing in the mid–1960s to 1970s Before the establishment of the public housing programme in 1976, the government response to the mounting squatting problem was to deregulate building standards and legalize self-constructed buildings. This boosted the industrialization of house building activity, and private housing production was further accelerated after the development of the pre-sale system. The system began to evolve in the late 1960s and became popular in 1973. In contrast to Hong Kong, the builder in Taiwan could begin to sell residential units, while still at planning stage, right after obtaining the building permits. Payments for house purchase were divided into stages. The buyer needed to pay the first 5 per cent of the sales price when he/she signed the contract, then another 35 per cent in stages during the construction period, and the remainder when the units were completed.

During the pre-sale period, usually three to six months, the builder could decide whether the project would be started or cancelled according to the sales result. The length of time from starting selling to project completion was about 24 months. The pre-sale arrangement therefore allowed the builder to overcome the shortage of funds from the market, and housing projects could be started even when the available funds were small. This also allowed investors with less capital to enter into the house building industry easily. So, in contrast to the large property developers in Hong Kong and Singapore, the construction of private housing in Taiwan was dominated by small builders. The housing industry enjoyed a golden age in the 1970s and 1980s. In Taipei City in 1969 there were only 188,728 houses (commercial and residential). This figure grew to 339,115 in 1976 and by 1986, reached 731,355 (Li 1998, 39). Houses built after 1970 constitute the main part of the existing Taipei housing stock, and they are predominantly low-rise condominiums (two to five storeys). However, the relative ease for small-scale developers to put units on the market, particularly during price booms, has led to excessively speculative house building. Since 1970, Taiwan has had a chronic problem of over-supply, with a vacancy rate continuously in the range 13–19 per cent.

For homebuyers, the pre-sale system reduced their financial burden by enabling them to pay the large amount of housing costs over a period of time. It also counteracted the limited availability of housing loans in the market. Before 1972, the total amount of mortgages and loans for housing was only about 3.7 per cent of the amount of finance available (Li 1998, 105). The restrictions on formal loans for housing boosted the development of the informal market, which provided around one-quarter of all housing credits until the 1980s despite interest rates of two or three times those charged by formal financial institutions (Ramesh 2004, 140). However, the massive rise of household income also compensated for the lack of mortgage finance. For example, the average monthly disposable income of Taipei households increased dramatically over 4.5 times from NT$5,806 in 1971 to NT$27,276 in 1981 (in nominal prices; DBAS 2003). Thus, during the first three decades of the post-war years, most homeowners were outright owners.

The growth of homeownership in the 1980s onwards   Although the overall homeownership rate in Taiwan in 1976 was 67.4 per cent (see Figure 7.2), the ownership rate in urban areas was much lower (around 50 per cent) because of the difficulty in obtaining housing loans. The urban homeownership rate started to pick up when the Taiwanese government began to deregulate the financial market in the 1980s.

In response to the market slump in the early 1980s and the existence of 0.45 million vacant properties that were built during the property boom in the late 1970s, the government first introduced a tax deduction on mortgage interest payment to promote homeownership. In 1982, restrictions on housing loans were relaxed which allowed commercial banks to provide homebuyers with a mortgage of up to 80 per cent of the house price. Finally, a private housing finance system was established. As banks began to make mortgages more easily available and repayment periods were extended to 15 or even 20 years, the homeownership rate in urban areas grew dramatically. For example, in Taipei, the private ownership ratio of housing climbed from 56.4 per cent in 1981 to 70.3 per cent in 1987 (Hsueh and Chen 1999, 367). In 1986, the government allowed the construction industry, for the first time, to secure credit facilities from the banks (Yip and Chang 2003). Then, the deregulation of commercial banks in 1991 resulted in the establishment of 16 new banks each with capital above NT$10 billion, and they started to compete with existing banks for loans (Shih and Tsao 2004, 3). The keen competition led to banks raising the loan-to-value ratios and a significant increase in mortgage loans. The traditional form of home ownership, namely through self-build or inheritance, was largely replaced by a more market-based form. Over 70 per cent of urban homeowners in 1995 acquired their home through the housing market (Li 2002, 24). Also, in 1990, the Taiwanese government implemented a policy to subsidize housing mortgages as a complement to the monetary policy to lower the interest rates, and the fund for home loans with government subsidy increased from NT$40,000 million in 1990 to NT$204,400 million in 2001 (ibid., Figure 1). The number of households receiving housing loans from the government increased from 9,733 in 1993 to 23,353 in 1999 (Ramesh 2004, 128). The subsidy policy was replaced in 2000 by a NT$300 billion preferential housing loan programme which included the provision of housing loans with preferential interest rates to people between 20 and 40 years old who wanted to purchase their first home, together with a credit guarantee to get 20-year mortgages for up to 90 per cent of the total cost of buying a home (*Taiwan Journal*, 11 August 2000). The result was that more than 85 per cent of households in Taiwan have owned their dwellings since 2000 (DGBAS 2005a), a higher rate of homeownership than Japan, European countries and the United States. Even the share of owner-occupied households among low-income households was over 78 per cent in 1996 (Jao 2000, 81). In Taipei City, the rates for households owning a house reached 82.2 per cent in 2000 (Chen and Chang 2004, Table 1).

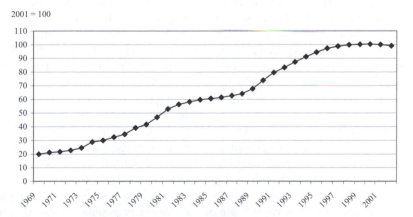

Figure 7.3 House rent indices in Taiwan Province, 1969–2002 (2001=100)
Source: DGBAS 2005c, Table 6.2.

The overall housing situation

The most prominent housing issue before the onset of the Asian financial crisis was expensive housing costs in Taiwan. At the peak of the boom in 1995, when the price was about four times what it was ten years previously as shown in Figure 7.1, a manufacturing worker had to spend 32 years of annual salary to buy an average sized pre-sale house (Yip and Chang 2003). Although housing prices have stabilized since 1997, housing affordability has not improved. In Taipei, with 2001 as the base year, the housing price fell from 100.5 in 1998 to 96.1 in 2004 (DBAS 2005). By contrast, the average housing price/disposable income ratio increased from 3.2 in 1990 to 5.6 in 2000 (Chen and Chang 2004, Table 1). The percentage of housing expenditure in the average family's total expenditure was 34.9 per cent in 2003 (DBAS 2003). On the other hand, rental expenses tend to be lower than ownership expenses. In Taipei, rent accounted for 19.3 per cent of disposable income in 2002 (DBAS 2003, 87). Compared with the owner occupied sector, the private rental market in Taiwan is very small. Rental houses are older, smaller and of lower quality, and most importantly, the high vacancy rate also keeps rents down (Figure 7.3).

The vacancy rate in the housing market stayed at a high level of about 13 per cent throughout the 1980s and 1990s (Peng and Chang 1995, 46). In contrast to the theoretical prediction that an oversupply of housing would suppress house prices, Taiwan experienced a surge in house price rises over a long period from the mid–1980s to the early 1990s (see Figure 7.1). In fact, the Taiwanese regard buying a pre-sale house as a forward or futures transaction (Chang and Ward 1993, 218). The higher the prices are, the more the people rush to buy pre-sale houses as they think the prices will continue to go up. Hua (2000, cited in Yip and Chang 2003) describes such economically irrational behaviour as 'an over-zealous consumption preference towards owner occupation'. But when the prices started to fall in 1996, people stopped buying pre-sale houses, and they would not buy the existing ones either since they were not the end users of these houses. As the homeownership rate exceeds 80 per cent, there are indeed not many people who want to buy a house for its 'use value'. Furthermore, the pursuit of a larger capital gain stimulated more speculative house building during the boom period, but when the construction started, it was not permitted to stop (according to government regulations, the builder must start within a year of obtaining the building permit upon penalty of forfeit of the bank loan, although there are cases where the builders have just taken the money and gone away), so adding more vacant units to the market means the prices go down. The overall vacancy rate in 1990 was already 13.3 per cent, and the added stock in the early 1990s pushed the vacancy rate close to 18 per cent in 2000 (DGBAS 2005b). In 2001, the number of unsold or unoccupied apartments dropped from 1.23 million in 2000 to 1.16 million or 16.5 per cent of the total (*Taiwan Journal*, 25 July 2003). Those households who are genuine homebuyers, most likely the first time buyers who account for a minor share of the Taiwanese population, mostly prefer to purchase the newly completed housing units instead of the long-standing vacant ones, thus the vacancy rate falls very slowly over time.

On the other hand, people who have vacant properties tend neither to release them on the market nor to let their units when the price is falling. Hua (2000, 131–32) finds that most of the vacant units are not on the market for sale or used strictly as second homes, but in the grey area between on-market and not-on-market status. They are used for storage, lent to relatives, rented if the tenants were personally known, or simply left empty. The relatively smaller capital gain through rent has indeed discouraged property owners from converting their second houses into private rental. Firstly, as rent has been kept at a low level because of the high vacancy rate, the rent received might not cover the maintenance and depreciation charges. Secondly, existing laws cannot fully protect the rights of landlords or renters. Furthermore, the low house tax rate (1.2 per cent of the value of the house) means a low holding cost. Unless the owners are in tight financial circumstances or the price is right, they often leave their units empty rather than rent to others: thus, Peng and Chang's (1995) finding that the vacancy rate decreases when the housing market is booming but increases when it goes into slump. In fact the Taiwanese housing market has reached the situation in which the high vacancy rate has no effect on the housing price movement.

In terms of housing standards, Taiwan has experienced a remarkable improvement over the last four decades. The squatter settlements of the 1950s and 1960s have been largely replaced by houses of higher quality, offering more space to their residents. The average size of a dwelling rose from 85.9 square metres in 1980 to 122.1 square metres in 2000 (DGBAS 2005a). In 2002, each person in Taipei enjoyed a floor area of 30.1 square metres (DBAS 2003), a standard that compared favourably with Tokyo and Hong Kong (Table 7.3). The 2000 Census reported that Taiwan had a total of 6,993,000 housing units of which 40 per cent are located in Taipei Municipality, Taipei County and Taoyuan County (all in the northern region of the island). As far as the type of housing is concerned, the majority of households in Taipei live in apartments – more than 80 per cent in 1995 compared with the national figure of 35 per cent of all Taiwanese households. Furthermore, about 40 per cent of dwelling units were aged less than ten years old, and about 80 per cent of them were constructed within the past 20 years, which in comparison with other areas in Taiwan means that Taipei has a relatively new housing stock (Chang and Lin 1999, 93). But, as in Japan, the rural land reform produced the same effect on the scale of residential development. The total cultivable land in Taiwan in 1955 amounted to 8,360 square kilometres and was distributed among 744,000 farm households, resulting in a small holding averaging 1.12 hectare per household (Hua 2000, 119). Rural land ownership has become more fragmented through the process of inheritance. In 1995, the average size of cultivated land was reduced to 0.83 hectare per household (ibid., footnote 4). Farmland released for urban development is therefore small in size. Furthermore, the less rigorous zoning regulations produce a mixed-use landscape in which many houses or apartment units are next to commercial or even industrial zones, thus creating noise pollution and heavy traffic jams in residential neighbourhoods.

Table 7.3 Comparison of housing conditions, Taipei, Taiwan, Tokyo, Japan and Hong Kong

	Taipei	Taiwan	Tokyo	Japan	Hong Kong
Living space					
Rooms per house	n.a.	4.6 ('00)[c]	3.5 ('98)[d]	4.8 ('98)[e]	n.a.
Floor space per person (m²)	30.1 ('02)[a]	31.6 ('00)[c]	15.5 ('98)[d]	18.2 ('98)[e]	13.3 ('98)[f]
Average flat size (m²)	102.4 ('02)[b]	122.1 ('00)[c]	61.9 ('98)[d]	92.4 ('98)[e]	45.0 ('98)[f]
Tenure (%)					
Homeownership	77.6 ('02)[a]	82.5 ('00)[c]	41.5 ('98)[d]	60.3 ('98)[e]	53.0 ('00)[g]
Public rental	n.a.	5.0 ('00)[c]	9.0 ('98)[d]	6.8 ('98)[e]	30.5 ('00)[g]
Private rental	n.a.	n.a.	41.6 ('98)[d]	27.3 ('98)[e]	14.6 ('00)[g]

Sources: a. DBAS 2003
    b. GIO 2004
    c. DGBAS 2005a
    d. Statistics Bureau 2000a
    e. Statistics Bureau 2000b
    f. Census and Statistics Department 1999
    g. HKHA 2000

Despite the lack of redistributive housing and welfare policies, income inequality in Taiwan has been moderate. Liang and Mai (2003) find that wage inequality between skilled and unskilled workers in Taiwan exhibited a declining trend in the mid–1980s, a phenomenon totally different from the United States' other trading partners, such as Chile and Mexico. Indeed, the key to achieving income equality lies outside the realm of the state. Rather, strong family support, the long period of economic growth, and increasing participation in the workforce by men, and by women before marriage, contributed to the relatively equal distribution of income, the impressive improvements in social well being and to the high home-ownership rate over the three decades of the 1960s to the 1980s. But starting from the early 1990s, social inequality, in terms of the income gap, has been worsening. The income gap between the top 20 per cent of households and the bottom 20 per cent rose from 4.58 in 1970, 4.97 in 1991, 5.51 in 1998, to 6.07 in 2003 (Hsieh and Hsing 2002, 522; Ku 2004, 315; DGBAS 2005b). The most radical jump happened in just one year, 2000–01, from 5.55 to 6.39. The widening income inequality was caused by the so-called 'digital divide' – the division between those workers in the high-tech industries whose salary rose dramatically and those in the traditional sectors whose salary was pushed down by the importation of foreign workers. In the owner-occupied sector, Hsieh (2004, 10) found that there was a growing income gap between rich and poor outright homeowners, because many of the latter were older and retired households with lower incomes primarily from pensions.

Effects of Economic Crises on the Housing Situation in Taiwan

Asia experienced a series of economic crises following the Asian financial crisis, the global economic recession and the 11 September terrorist attacks in the United States. While most Asian economies were severely affected by these crises, Taiwan has so far weathered the storms well.[5] The annual growth rate of GNP dropped from 7 per cent in the second half of 1997 to 4.6 per cent in 1998 and increased slightly to above 5 per cent in the following two years. Then, Taiwan suffered the worst economic performance in 2001. The growth rate contracted to –2.2 per cent, but it quickly bounced back to 3.9 per cent in 2002, 3.3 per cent in 2003 and by the end of 2004, it was estimated to be 5.9 per cent (DGBAS 2005b). Thus, the impact of the crises on Taiwan's residential market was relatively modest even though the average exposure of national economies to the real estate sector was large – in 1996, 35–45 per cent of private bank loans went to real estate; real estate debt, as a percentage of GNP, was 58 per cent (Quigley 2001, Table 1). Even though the debt to income

---

5   In fact, the bubble of the Taiwanese stock market in the late 1980s was so much more dramatic than the impact of the Asian financial crisis on Taiwan. The stock market bubble started to from in October 1986 when the stock price index was over 1,000. The index reached a peak of 12,682 on 10 February 1990 and then crashed to a low of 2,485 on 1 October in the same year. The stock price bust, in terms of extent and speed, exceeded the 1990 one in Japan and the 1997 ones in Thailand, Indonesia and Korea (Hua 2000, 121).

ratio of the household sector stood at 90.8 per cent and the outstanding household debt reached NT$6.6 billion at the end of 2002 (Shih and Tsao 2004, 1), the Taiwan household debt level was not excessive compared to those of Japan and other East Asian countries; the overall financial position of the household sector was largely sound.

There were many reasons why the Taiwanese housing market was quite robust. Firstly, there was less fluctuation in house price movements. The house price index for new units fell only 11.8 per cent between 1997 and 2003 (see Figure 7.1) as opposed to over 50 per cent in Japan and Hong Kong. Secondly, there was a high level of outright owners – about 72 per cent of all homeowners owned their property outright in 1992 (Li 2002, 26). Thirdly, the gross national savings rate was high; it was 26 per cent of GNP in 2003 (DGBAS 2005b). House buyers in Taiwan borrowed less and paid a higher percentage of down payment, on average around 46 per cent from 1972 to 1989 (Yip and Chang 2003); the average duration for homeowners to pay off their mortgages was about seven years (Lin and Lai 2003, 413). All these factors have minimized the devastating effects of economic recession on homeowners and contributed to the stability of the Taiwanese residential market.

Overall, the Taiwanese government has not done much to cope with the problems of high housing cost nor interfered in the land market in order to lower the land price, which constitutes 60–80 per cent of urban housing cost (Hua 2000, 130), as the Japanese and Hong Kong governments did. Rather, the major concern is the mounting high housing vacancy rate, which the government considered to be the major force in depressing housing prices. Since some of the empty flats are unsold units, builders and construction companies are unable to pay back loans. Already they have caused a high ratio of overdue loans in Taiwan's banking system. In 2002, the average non-performing loan ratio at local banks was 6.02 per cent (*Taiwan Journal*, 18 July 2003). In order to prevent further bankruptcy of certain builders and future troubles in the financial sector, various stimulation measures have been introduced, including the provision of low-interest loans and the imposition of lower interest rates by the CBC to help first time buyers (particularly young people aged 20 to 40 and low income families who are eligible for public rental housing) to absorb the vacant units. Also, to offset the adverse impact of economic crises on new homebuyers, in early 2002 the government made agreements with financial agencies to cover mortgage arrears for a period of six months on behalf of those unemployed households (estimated to be 190,000; Li 2002, 31) with mortgage repayment problems. Yet, the high homeownership rate has increasingly become a limiting factor to its further expansion and weakened the ability of the government in counteracting the pressure of the increased vacant stock. Figures 7.1 and 7.2 reveal that the growth of homeownership has decelerated despite the slow downward adjustment of house prices in the latter half of the 1990s. Recently, the government began considering subsidising renters instead of buyers to address the problem of the high vacancy rate (Ramesh 2004, 128).

The Challenges Ahead

Compared with spending on social security and welfare, government spending on public housing plays only a minimal role. Both the DPP and KMT never really had the intention to provide housing services to the public. They had also no clear housing policies that were designed especially to promote homeownership. Indeed, one would say that both parties have had a hands-off approach in letting the housing market follow its own course. Only the occurrence of a possible banking crisis or imminent local and national elections would force the parties to do something to attempt to solve the housing problems on hand. Since most Taiwanese citizens are already homeowners or landowners (at the end of 2003, 48.8 per cent of registered land in Taipei City was owned by the private sector (DBAS 2003)); the authorities in Taiwan have become very cautious about increasing the tax rates, as this would disturb people's treasured property values. Taiwanese homeowners also have no intention to push the government to increase its commitment in public housing provision as more public rental housing for the poor means a tax increase for the better-off. However, there are many difficult challenges that the Taiwanese state has to face and a necessity that it cannot avoid being involved in providing more housing as well as welfare services in the future.

The first challenge comes from the demographic and societal changes. In July 2004, there were about 2.12 million elderly in Taiwan, accounting for 9.4 per cent of the population, and by 2027, they will make up more than 20 per cent of the total population (*Taiwan Journal*, 5 November 2004). Because of the rise of nuclear families, the higher labour force participation of women, and the erosion of traditional family values by modernization and westernization, the original caring and supportive capacities of the family are waning. Most elderly people will live alone either voluntarily or involuntarily, as fewer and fewer younger people are willing to support their elderly family members. According to the survey on the living arrangements of the elderly, 14.5 per cent of elderly persons were living alone in 1992 (Hwang 1997, Table 1). Along with the rise of the single elderly is the growth of one-parent households. More traditional families are broken down as the divorce rate, measured by the proportion of population 15 years and older that was divorced, grew from 0.8 per cent in 1966 to 4 per cent in 1999 (Hsieh and Hsing 2002, 523). Given that most divorced women brought their children to live with their parents, the share of single parent families in all Taiwanese households increased slightly from 4 per cent in 1991 to 4.3 per cent in 2000 (Hsueh 2004, Table 4). However, judging from the experiences of both Asian and western countries, it can be expected that the percentage of single mothers living with their children independently will continue to increase. The government of Taiwan therefore needs to take this development more into account and prepare the housing and welfare systems for the future wave of challenges to accommodate the growing need of these non-traditional and often low-income families. At the same time, it is necessary to design policies to enable the family to realize its functions more fully, especially by relieving the pressures on Taiwanese women.

The second challenge comes from economic pressures. The developmental welfare model worked well as it produced high rates of economic growth into the 1990s, low rates of taxation, public expenditure and social provision, and considerable social stability even during the Asian financial crisis of the late 1990s. The success of the system was based on the exceptionally rapid economic growth in the last couple of decades and the proportion of the young population. However, the radical slump in the economic growth rate, just after the DPP government came to power in the year 2000, has further reduced its capacity to provide more welfare services; in particular democratization has raised public expectations of the state assuming more responsibilities and commitments to its citizens. Indeed, the deepening economic restructuring has caused massive unemployment. The unemployment rate rose from 1.4 per cent in 1981, to 2.9 per cent in 1999, jumped to the highest level of 5.2 per cent in 2002, and fell slightly to 5 per cent in 2003 (DGBAS 2005b). Unemployment is particularly serious for those who are 45–55 years old. This has made the issues of a) how to create job opportunities and b) the provision of decent unemployment benefits more critical, not to mention the expansion of homeownership to these vulnerable households. As mentioned earlier, the falling state revenues and the increased public debts at both central and local government levels exert tremendous pressures to squeeze public spending. Furthermore, the state capacity to deliver more welfare has been eroded by the constraint on the government's power to raise taxes. Currently, a neglect of welfare in favour of development is axiomatic of the policy of the Taiwanese state, given the budget constraints on any further expansion of housing and social welfare provisions.

Conclusions

In a strict sense, the development of the Taiwanese housing system follows the same path as the welfare system but with different coverage of the population. From the beginning, the welfare system was highly targeted on those who were regarded as important contributors to economic and political development; it has been expanded later to cover the entire population. Similarly, Taiwan first had a 'public housing policy' to address the housing difficulties of a minority of people who were not homeowners, but has later extended it to the great majority of the population who cannot buy houses in the market. Table 7.4 shows that political competition is the driving force behind welfare construction in Taiwan whereas the orientation of housing policies is dictated by the performance of the property market. Housing policy has gradually become part of economic policies to stabilize the banking system, replicating the same pattern of development as the housing system in Japan. But compared to Japan, the Taiwanese housing system features a much lesser degree of governmental involvement, and a stronger role for the market and the family in housing provision. Although the operations of both systems depend heavily on household savings, the Japanese government has been more active by setting up a Government-run public corporation (the Government Housing Loan Corporation) to channel the huge amount of household savings into the housing market (see Tang 2002). No such public institution is found in Taiwan; the flow of household savings is governed by the market. So, even though both systems are privately operated, the Japanese housing system is more regulated by the government than that of Taiwan.

Housing in Taiwan thus appears to be unique in the East Asian welfare models. Compared with other tiger regimes, state involvement is the most minimal. On the construction side, the state relies heavily on the private sector without giving special preference to encourage the construction sector to be more productive. The government in fact has placed much emphasis on facilitating public capital for the construction of big infrastructure projects, which are seen as more important for national economic development, rather than house building activities in the private and public sectors. On the consumption side, housing is regarded as a commodity of private consumption commensurate with the ability to pay, even in the allocation of public housing. Both the construction and consumption arenas are purely market dominated. Thus, the Taiwanese housing system does not fit in well with Doling's (1999) 'little tiger housing policy regime' in which the tiger states take a pro-active role in the provision of housing and are highly involved in organizing the factors of production [of housing] (page 247). What makes Taiwan different from other 'tigers' is that most of the land is privately owned. Land ownership is regarded as an important instrument for political and social stability given that the KMT implemented the land reform once it gained control of Taiwan in 1949. Thus land, together with the houses on it, is a politically sensitive issue and both DPP and KMT have been extremely cautious in imposing any strict legislation to regulate its use.

Nonetheless, one cannot refute the fact that the Taiwanese private unregulated housing system has achieved a high homeownership outcome and so far, it has sustained political and social stability in Taiwan even in times of recession. The success of this system has depended on the consistently high economic growth rates, a young population and a high rate of labour market participation. However, Taiwan is now struggling with an ageing population, declining economic growth, a higher unemployment rate and an emerging problem of long-term unemployment. While democratization has already created pressures for greater attention to social policy, and the economic crisis of the early 2000s has accelerated this trend, there is no public demand for the further expansion of the public housing programme to provide more housing services to the most vulnerable groups. So, even as the welfare system is expanding quickly according to the degree of democratization, housing policy directives remain unchanged. But the demographic and economic trends challenge the residual mode of housing provision. While the Taiwanese welfare model is increasingly approaching the European models in extending its social insurance systems, the Taiwanese government clearly needs to adopt a more reflective learning from Western experiences to expand the scope of its public housing programme to the deprived groups in society who are in the greatest need.

Table 7.4 Historical development of Taiwanese housing and welfare policies since 1945

Major housing policy	Economic event	Year	Political event	Major welfare policy
		1949	Establishment of ROC and KMT began military regime	
First government construction of housing for victims of typhoon		1953		Enactment of the Military Servicemen's Insurance Law
Establishment of 'Public Housing Committee of Executive Yuan'		1954		
Passage of statute for providing loans for public-housing construction		1957		
		1958		Establishment of labour insurance schemes
		1971	Expulsion of Taiwan from the UN	
	Oil crisis and slump in housing market	1973		
1st six-year public housing construction programme (1976–81)		1976		
		1979	Strategic alliance with US terminated	
		1980		Enactment of 'three laws of social welfare'
Four-year programme (1982–85) and relaxation of restrictions on commercial housing loans	Deep slump in property market	1982		
		1984		Promulgation of labour standard act
Postponement of four-year programme (1986–89) and permission to builders to secure commercial credit		1986	Establishment of DPP	
		1987	Termination of martial law	
	Property market revived	1989		
Launch of six-year programme (1992–97) including the policy to subsidize home mortgages		1990		
		1993		Provision of cash assistance to low-income families
		1994	DPP's candidate, Chen Shui-bian elected as Taipei's Mayor	
	Housing prices at peak	1995		Implementation of National Health Insurance programme
		1996	First presidential election	
	Unemployment rate rise	1998		Institution of unemployment benefit in labour insurance scheme
	Property market went into slump	March 2000	Chen Shui-bian became President and end of KMT rule of Taiwan	Provision of old-age allowance
Four-year freeze on public housing construction imposed	Increase of public debt	May 2000		Suspension on further social welfare reform

Chapter 8

From Tenants to Home-Owners: Change in the Old Welfare States

Richard Groves, Alan Murie and Christopher Watson

The previous chapters of this book have been concerned with emerging welfare state systems. The focus of these chapters has been on housing provision and it is argued that housing has been a keystone of welfare and economic development policies in all these countries. The systems of state intervention that have emerged merit being considered as welfare states. They fit within the broad notion of the state intervening to influence the distribution of income and opportunity, and the capacity of households to meet a socially acceptable minimum level of material welfare. These societies have not followed the traditional western welfare state model but this does not mean that it is appropriate to regard them as non-welfare state societies. Rather they are societies which have adopted, for a variety of reasons, different approaches to welfare. It has been argued that this is broadly because they had a different history from that associated with the development of the welfare state in the west. East Asian countries emerged from the Second World War with different political systems and different imperatives. They did not have the same organized demands from the labour movement for welfare reform; except for Japan they had not experienced the impact of the recession on an industrial economy between the wars because they did not have industrialized economies; and they did not have the pattern of representative democracy and strong labour and trade union representation that were so important in the establishment of welfare states in Europe.

This chapter aims to move the debate on by referring more fully to the older welfare states. It seeks to clarify the position of housing in the old post-Beveridge welfare state system in the United Kingdom, with brief reference to other parts of Europe, including the Netherlands and Sweden. The chapter revisits the discussion of the role of housing within the welfare state in the UK, drawing particularly on recent work by Peter Malpass (2005). From this, we argue that the older welfare state systems have been changing throughout the period of their existence. We are not concerned to chart the origins of the welfare state or to provide a comprehensive account of its development but rather to highlight the extent to which the classical welfare state established during and after the Second World War has been undergoing change in the period since.

Comparing the new welfare states with this classic welfare state means making a comparison with an idealization of a welfare state system rather than the reality.

It also means making a comparison with classic systems that no longer operate in practice. The changes that have taken place in the old welfare state systems and the changes which seem likely to take place over the next few years, place housing in a very different position than it was in the past. And a key feature of the new welfare states emerging in the older European systems is that they are seeking to rely much more on housing to deliver different aspects of welfare than they have in the past.

Housing in Welfare States

Malpass (2005) provides a valuable review of debates about the position of housing within the British Welfare State and includes new insights especially related to the wartime and immediate post-war periods. He addresses the extent to which the notion of housing as the wobbly pillar of the welfare state is an adequate picture and he also considers how far the association between the extent of decommodified (or state or not-for-profit) housing and the incorporation of housing within the welfare state is appropriate. This contribution provides an initial basis for discussion in this chapter.

Malpass distinguishes between broad and narrow definitions of the welfare state. The narrow approach tends to focus on a defined set of services delivered by public bodies. In the British context there is a conventional list relating to social security, education, health, housing and personal social services. In this kind of definition, what forms part of the welfare state relates to what the state provides; and the implication is that what is not provided through the state and its offspring is not part of the welfare state. A broader definition of the welfare state does not concentrate exclusively on the public services but also recognizes fiscal, occupational and other institutional forms of welfare provision. It refers to the different ways in which the state intervenes in the processes of economic reproduction and distribution to reallocate life chances. The emphasis in this is more upon the commitment of government to influencing the level of material welfare. It is the acceptance of responsibility by government rather than the way in which responsibility is carried out.

Welfare state systems, broadly defined, may then be characterized by differences in the degree to which the state accepts responsibility for a wide range of circumstances. Hence they allow for great variation in the way in which that responsibility is carried out. Welfare states can be thought of in terms of two dimensions: one measuring commitment, or the extent to which governments accept responsibility for well-being, and the other referring to the form or the way in which commitment is operationalized (Malpass 2005, 5). Malpass goes on to argue that it is reasonable to expect that governments accepting a high level of responsibility will opt for greater regulation and provision of public services, and if governments seek to limit their commitment they will shift the risk to individuals. We will return to this notion of commitment and form later in the discussion in this chapter.

Housing in the British Welfare State

Malpass's framework is important in understanding the position of housing in the British Welfare State. He argues that narrow approaches lead to a view that housing is a wobbly pillar of the welfare state because the public sector is so small compared with the market; and because there are significant user charges for public housing. He also argues that it has become a wobbly pillar because of the residualized character of the service but this is a point related to the present period rather than the characteristics of public sector housing at an earlier stage in the classical phase of the British Welfare State. Thus a debate which operates within a framework of a narrow definition of the welfare state presents housing in the UK as a wobbly pillar with one in three houses at the maximum in the public sector, compared with almost universal provision in education, health, national insurance and some areas of personal social services. Of course, a narrow definition also becomes one of the ways of defining countries which do not have public housing sectors as non-welfare states.

Leaving this aside, the debate about the British welfare state is that while it may have been the wobbly pillar, with relatively modest direct public sector housing provision compared with other services, there has still been scope to reduce the commitment to housing and this may be measured directly by the reductions in expenditure on public sector housing, the decline in the relative size of that sector, the privatization of public sector housing and the residualization of the sector. Once the central focus for debate is upon the public sector, then it is easy to measure whether the welfare state is becoming more or less significant in its role. The discussion within this framework of a narrow definition is not without its value. The well developed western welfare states have very different levels of state housing provision. The argument has been made that the British system, with one in three households living in state housing in 1980, suggests a high level of ambition to meet housing needs compared with its ambition in some other service areas and some other countries with well developed social security systems (Murie 1997). The quality of state housing and its expansion over the sixty years to 1980, is a measure of ambition which could be seen in contrast to a declining or ungenerous provision in other areas.

Malpass convincingly makes the case, however, for operating within a broader definition. We should not confuse the form of provision with the commitment. On this basis it does not matter whether there is a large public sector housing provision or not. The key issue is whether there is a commitment to achieve standards in relation to housing. This is linked with the argument in favour of referring to a modernization of housing policy or the restructuring of policy, rather than withdrawal or termination of policy. Thus the declining interest in providing public sector housing does not mean the end of housing policy, rather it means that government pursues its welfare objectives in relation to housing through different mechanisms and forms of provision, through encouragement of different types of not-for-profit housing, or of private sector housing. The fact that it may abandon public housing does not mean that it abandons objectives in relation to housing policy. It may mean that housing objectives are being pursued through other policies – those relating to economic policy, taxation, tax reliefs, benefits and planning. This argument becomes very close to the argument elsewhere in this book that we should not mistake the lack of public provision for the lack of commitment to some welfare targets. It would even be wrong to assume that low levels of public provision mean less ambitious targets, although that may sometimes be the case.

Within the framework of this broad definition it is then useful to discuss the development of housing in the British welfare state. This discussion, as has been said above, is concerned with the welfare state emerging under the influence of the Beveridge Report *Social Insurance and Allied Services* (Cmd. 6404) published in 1942 and the post-Beveridge period. The longer history of the development of the welfare state and of housing policy is available elsewhere (see for example Merrett 1979; English 1982). The conventional wisdom in accounts of the relationship between housing and this classical welfare state system, perhaps because they draw heavily upon the narrower definition of the welfare state, is that housing policy in Britain developed in the post war period very much as part of the Beveridge welfare state. This seems a non-problematic contention. For example Titmuss (1958) argued that the Second World War, because it involved the mass of the population, created an environment during the war and left a legacy after it which accepted the need for less inequality. It created an overall atmosphere which involved addressing the needs of the whole community and enlarging obligations to meet the needs of all citizens. The Beveridge Report itself referred to the need to engage with a series of interlinked problems and so the organization of social insurance was one part only of a comprehensive policy of social progress.

> Social insurance fully developed may provide income security ; it is an attack upon Want. But Want is one only of five giants on the road of reconstruction and in some ways the easiest to attack. The others are Disease, Ignorance, Squalor and Idleness (Cmd. 6404, para 8).

Equally it is apparent that pre-war experience had led many of those involved in policy towards an understanding of the need for planning. For example, Harold Macmillan, who was to become the first post-war Conservative Minister for Housing and subsequently Prime Minister during the period when the British welfare state underwent considerable changes, argued passionately in favour of orderly capitalism, rather than the economic and social disorder which would arise if there was no regulation (Macmillan 1934).

The general climate of debate was one which favoured public intervention in different forms in the provision of housing as well as other services. Malpass's argument however, is that it is difficult to identify more tangible and categorical plans in relation to housing. Radical new approaches were introduced following the Beveridge Report, in relation to social security, health and other services but government did not significantly reform the approach to housing. The debates within the civil service and government showed a reluctance to envisage a long term sustained intervention in housing provision. The increased public sector housing provision that emerged immediately after the war was part of a transitional and emergency programme which was expected to end once the emergency had been largely dealt with. It did not represent a wider acceptance of a different philosophy in relation to housing provision. Labour's housing policy in the 1940s and 1950s, for example, did not aspire either to provide for the middle classes or to make council housing affordable for the least well-off.

Whilst it remains the fact that housing was not integrated into the welfare state in the same form as some other services, this does not establish that it was not part of the welfare state and was not influenced by the thinking of the welfare state. There are other services which were provided essentially at a local level and which were marked by variations in provision from the outset. There was no aspiration to unification and nationalization across all services. While social security itself was universal in the true sense of the word and with uniformity of benefits, the principles of the National Health Service or education did not so clearly involve uniformity. The rhetoric of the Beveridge model hardly holds true beyond social insurance itself and even there the implementation of the social insurance policy did not mean an immediate adoption of universality. Universality was an aspiration, rather than an immediate reality. These issues are important for the present book because they establish that the classical welfare state in Britain, the Beveridge and post-Beveridge welfare state, incorporated a variety of forms of provision. In housing these different forms were always important.

Thus it can be argued that Malpass overstates his case. In the immediate post-war period the government introduced a radical new statutory planning and land-use framework for all new development activity, including house building. As soon as it was prudent to do so, a major slum clearance drive was introduced in the early 1950s coupled with an innovative private sector housing renewal programme. The government also proposed an ambitious new towns programme involving a major reorganization of responsibility. In order to implement its proposals, the government took the flagship programme of new public sector planned housing provision out of the control of local authorities and set up New Town Development Corporations to guide the new era of welfare state communities. Alongside these programmes there were two further policies which were critically important for housing provision and more universal than the provision of public housing, within the broader definition of the welfare state. These were private sector rent control and the provision of social insurance.

The private rented sector housed some 60 per cent of all households in 1945 and rent control served as a significant way of intervening to affect rent payments. Public sector housing was outside rent control, yet between rent control and the management of local authority housing, 70 per cent of the population were brought within a framework through which government could influence housing costs. In terms of wider definitions of the welfare state, this was the closest to a universalist approach to intervention to ensure that people were able to sustain their housing situation without disruptions to where they lived, even when their circumstances changed. Those it left out were already home-owners. Furthermore, if people did become unemployed or sick, entitlements to social insurance would reduce the risk of their being unable to maintain their rent payments.

From the outset the Labour Governments from 1945 to 1951, in implementing Beveridge and related proposals, made a series of compromises and pragmatic judgments including those in relation to benefit levels. In view of the economic and other pressures that held back their building programme it could be argued that a greater priority was given to housing than might have been anticipated. Equally if housing was intended to be a transitional programme, it proved not to be. Public housing continued to grow in numerical and in proportionate terms until 1981. Although there were undoubted shifts in emphasis and focus, this suggests that public housing provision remained a significant part of government intervention for a much longer period than envisaged. Alongside this continuing growth of public sector housing there was also a series of measures to support other forms of housing provision to affect the condition and quality of housing through slum clearance, improvement and repair, policies to deregulate private renting, to expand the level of provision by housing associations and to encourage the growth of home-ownership. The form of provision of housing within the British welfare state has passed through a process of evolution or modernization throughout the post-war period.

All this is perfectly consistent with the argument that the housing policy, planning and implementation process between 1942 and the early 1950s was not conducted within a coherent project called the welfare state. But Malpass argues that these circumstances represent differences between housing and the other key social policy areas in the early post-war years. He states:

> The key difference was that in the case of housing the government had to respond as quickly and effectively as possible to a most pressing social and political problem… In other policy areas there was not the same overwhelming urgency demanding immediate action, but there was in each case a clearly articulated commitment to progressive reform. (2005, 74)

While there is no reason to reject this view there is a danger that it becomes tinged by a rose coloured perception of other services. It is at least reasonable to question whether other services were not affected by exactly the same pressures: by the need to respond quickly and effectively in an environment where different crises were crowding in on government; by a need to make use of existing administrative and other arrangements rather than invent completely new ones. For example, in the central area of social insurance, not only did the Beveridge Report contain compromises in relation to rents, suggesting a level of benefit that would be too low for some regions and households within them, but Beveridge (1953, 309) himself admitted that he had to do a deal with Keynes under which Keynes, on behalf of the Treasury, agreed to support the scheme if the additional burden on the Treasury was limited to £100 million a year for the first five years. The consequence of this was that the actual level of benefits was set too close to the subsistence minimum. This consequence has affected social security in Britain ever since. Too many of those who qualify for national insurance benefits also qualify for means tested assistance benefits. Partly because of the treatment of rent, their needs are not fully covered by the social insurance benefit rates. If those benefits had been set higher there would be fewer people dependent on means testing.

Nor did government stick to its part of the social insurance contract. Through the 1940s and early 1950s, when lower unemployment rates meant that the contributions to the National Insurance Fund were higher than was needed, the Exchequer contribution was effectively not paid. This hardly fits with the view that in social insurance, governments retained a principled commitment to a high standard welfare state scheme. They were just as opportunistic as in their approach to housing. Indeed, the government's commitment to social insurance was possibly shorter lived than to housing provision and the reversion to a dependence on social assistance as the key determinant of incomes in older age was clear by the end of the 1950s. Had the Exchequer payments been fully made to the National Insurance Fund some more generous provision would have been possible. These circumstances also invite comparisons with the evolution of the Central Provident Fund in Singapore. Based on the UK National Insurance Fund this was used to underpin high levels of provision for housing, health, social security and education. The contrast demonstrates the absence in the UK of a sustained government commitment to the principles of a social insurance scheme.

By the 1960s the fiscal and occupational welfare state associated with pensions provision was arguably moving just as rapidly as in housing. The encouragement of private pension schemes dates from long before the Thatcher era and it would be perfectly reasonable to argue that in a period when government was still promoting direct state provision for housing it was developing an approach which it knew was insufficient to provide adequate incomes in retirement unless people also took out occupational pensions. Without this, they would inevitably become dependant upon National Assistance or Income Support as it later became.

Where does this take us in relation to the debates about the evolution of the old welfare states? Essentially the argument is that there was a commitment to addressing housing needs in the Beveridge welfare state but the form or the method through which this was to be achieved was never solely associated with the provision of public housing. There was a fragmented and mixed approach which envisaged the private sector playing a key role throughout. Over time housing policy, within the framework of the welfare state, has been 'modernized'. Rent control was modified and subsequently has been largely eliminated. The purpose, quality and nature of public housing provision and subsidized housing provision has been modified and has declined, and the role and size of the public sector has been affected by privatization. The forms of encouragement for home-ownership have changed but have become more central to the policy agenda.

As these different elements have matured, two important themes have emerged in relation to housing in Britain. Firstly the remaining public and not-for-profit housing sector has been increasingly associated with lower income households as part of a process described as residualization. Lower income households are represented in all tenures, but middle and higher income households have become less prominent within the council sector over time. It has become characterized by low income households and those with limited choice. Alongside this, property-ownership has been increasingly seen as a mechanism, not just for meeting housing needs but for protecting households against other contingencies, especially those associated with older age.

If households in the past tended to trade up in order to obtain better housing to live in, they now also trade up in order to increase the store of wealth afforded by home-ownership. In more recent years increasing numbers have also begun to become multiple owners through adoption of buy-to-let schemes. There is a general recognition that these two elements are increasingly associated with the limitations of both public and private pension schemes, and government has itself identified the advantages of increased investment in property as security in older age. It has encouraged access to and trading up in owner occupation through a variety of tax reliefs and has subsequently encouraged the buy-to-let market. By 2005 government had begun to talk about a property-owning welfare state.

The 'property-owning democracy' associated with the Prime Ministership of Anthony Eden in the 1950s was a vision of wider share ownership rather than ownership of housing. In the twenty-first century the strategy of the British government is much more clearly to encourage people to fend for themselves in older age through acquiring property and especially through buying and selling houses. This modernization of housing policy brings the old welfare states much more into line with the new welfare states of East Asia. It does not involve a dismantling of the old welfare states but the modernization of housing policy alongside the changing nature of other services; in this case, pensions in particular. In pensions policy, government consciously reduced its attempt to provide pensions in the 1980s. It encouraged private pensions systems, encouraged a transfer from the state earnings related pensions scheme and consciously chose not to upgrade benefit levels in line with wages. All of these were seen as part of a modernization programme in which the state encouraged people to make their own provision through their employers and through financial institutions by purchasing private pension policies. When private pension policies proved insecure, the next stage of modernization has been to encourage people to make use of the assets of home-ownership.

The modernized version of the old welfare state puts housing in a much more central position than it was before, but this is a position which is less to do with the provision of shelter alone and more to do with the provision of a wider base of security and independence. It involves a very significant shift away from the principles of uniformity and universality which are associated with social insurance provisions emerging from the Beveridge Report but not with direct housing provision. The provision that government now encourages people to make will not yield the same level of benefit to all households. The lottery of the market will continue to apply. For some people their own property or buy-to-let properties will provide them with very substantial assets and incomes in older age; for others, with much lower incomes, the state is less concerned with the type and uniformity of provision or its outcome, but is still committed to encouraging people to make provision for their own material welfare needs.

Housing and Asset Based Welfare

Housing policy in the UK in the twenty-first century is not built around decommodified social or public sector housing. Three decades of policy, from the IMF cuts of 1976 through to the five year policy plan of the Blair government in 2005, have envisaged a declining role for public sector investment and ownership. In the intervening period privatization and residualization have been important. But government has not withdrawn from housing or ceased to intervene. The promotion of home-ownership has become the dominating concern and has been pursued through different policies – from privatization of public housing under the Right to Buy, through deregulation and fiscal incentives; and through special schemes aimed at first time buyers and others (Mullins and Murie 2006). It has been suggested that the Labour Government rediscovered housing policy. A series of reports in the early 2000s[1] together presented a new and more comprehensive approach to housing than had existed for some years. But it was an approach more closely associated with the principles being advocated by international agencies such as the World Bank and International Monetary Fund rather than traditional Labour Party sources and it centred on home-ownership and improving the efficiency of markets rather than the enhanced provision of state housing. The state was not denying a role and responsibility in housing but the way that it intended to carry out this responsibility was largely market based.

During the 1990s and subsequently, government has increasingly begun to look at the possibilities of funding a variety of programmes, partly through the release of equity from home-ownership. As the costs of the welfare state have been seen to be disproportionate, so governments have looked to individuals to make provision for the purchase of services that were previously provided by the state. The growth of equity held in the form of home-ownership has attracted the attention of different parts of government, and indeed it is possible that too many parts of government have seen the opportunity to offload a difficult financing problem by calling into play the potential of equity release. If all of these schemes were to develop, there would be a situation in which home-ownership had grown not only to play a great role in the provision of shelter; and to become more important in inheritance and intergenerational transfers; but also to underpin the provision of other services. Home-ownership would be a source and store of wealth, but much as the situation in Singapore or China, the wealth held in the form of housing would be released especially in older age to meet the requirements of households in retirement.

---

1   The Communities Plan – *Sustainable Communities: Building for the Future*, ODPM 2003; the Barker Review – *Delivering stability: Securing our future housing needs*, ODPM/ HM Treasury 2004; The Home Ownership Task Force report – *A House of my own*, ODPM 2003; *Sustainable Communities: Homes for All*, ODPM 2005.

The accumulation of wealth through home-ownership, rather than being a by-product of the primary role of housing as shelter, or being an end in itself, was increasingly seen by government as a means to an end, and a device to assist in the financing of a range of services. In 1998 the government increased the limit for regulated lending under the Consumer Credit Act of 1974, and this made it possible to increase equity release type loans within the regulated lending system. Subsequent steps by government have shown a further willingness to encourage equity release.

The ownership of property involving an initial home and additional buy-to-let properties has been increasingly built into the thinking of government about the financing of personal and social services. In some areas, government policy has moved a long way. Whereas accounts of housing policy in the UK in the 1960s and 1970s highlighted the role of improvement and repair grants in supporting home-ownership, gentrification and the refurbishment of properties, the home improvement grant regime operated by local authorities has been changed fundamentally. By 2005, home improvement and repair grants had become very unusual and their value had declined significantly. They were subject to means tests and the emphasis in government policy had shifted towards expecting homeowners to borrow or release equity in order to finance improvements and repairs to property. In effect, there had been a withdrawal of grant support for this activity and a replacement by equity based private borrowing.

There is also a growing perception that state provision for older people in relation to long term care and pension provision was increasingly being replaced by private equity based investment. Home-owners moving into long term residential care in England are effectively expected to fund their long-term care out of the equity held in their home. How this is done is a matter for the elderly person and their family but only when the value of the asset has diminished substantially, is government willing to fund long-term care rather than draw upon this source.

In pension provision, the actions of government throughout the 1980s and 1990s significantly reduced the real and relative value of the state pension and any aspirations to link pensions to average earnings were effectively abandoned. The state retirement pension declined to a level where it was even closer to the means tested Income Support scheme. In this situation those who had no income in older age except for the state pension, would very often find themselves entitled to a higher income under means tested assistance programmes and this was confirmed with the introduction of the Pension Credit scheme. With such a low income in older age the attractiveness of equity release to provide a higher income was evident and government and other agencies increasingly recognized that this was a likely response by many home-owners.

Equity release has also been referred to in other contexts: to support work to improve energy efficiency in homes and to meet the costs associated with further and higher education provision. In a political environment where increasing taxation is difficult for any government to contemplate, even if they were to regard it as desirable economically, equity release becomes the funding of last resort for many schemes that, in the past, the state would have aspired to fund. The citizen, rather than being guaranteed a range of social benefits as a right of citizenship, is being reminded that they could afford to purchase these services through the market by drawing upon the wealth that they have accumulated in home-ownership.

Asset ownership and increased home-ownership are critical to the longer term agenda for the Labour government. This is apparent also in two new asset based welfare policies – the Saving Gateway and the Child Trust Fund. Both were designed to provide opportunities for saving and asset ownership, especially to lower income households. Announcing these two policies, the Treasury in 2001 described asset based welfare as part of the new approach to welfare policy and as the fourth pillar of welfare, with new policies designed to give the benefits of saving and asset holding to everyone.

A paper produced by the Chartered Institute of Housing and the Institute of Public Policy Research (Hill et al. 2002) considered the development of equity stakes for the benefit of social housing tenants. It was a response to the developing debate on asset based welfare, especially within Government and Labour Party circles and was concerned with how to give access to capital to poorer individuals and communities. The paper suggested four basic approaches: tenant asset accounts, through which tenants accrue a share in the equity of the property related to number of years of tenancy; shared ownership, where tenants purchase tranches of equity in the dwelling they live in; a link to the collective equity in the stock of the landlord, rather than in relation to their own home; and a link to the collective equity of an area, through a Community Trust. Although these proposals were not evidently taken up by Government, they formed part of the backdrop to the wider adoption of shared ownership and Homebuy proposals by Government in 2005. They can also be seen as part of the discussion about an asset based welfare state, which received increasing attention in the lead up to the General Election in that year. In particular, the former Labour Minister Alan Milburn in 2003 had expressed the view that the most substantial inequalities were not simply between income groups, but between those who own shares, pensions and housing, and those who rely solely on wages or benefits. Milburn argued that owning assets helps create a buffer for people in times of crisis and encourages people to take more responsibility for themselves. The same theme was apparent in the Labour Party manifesto in 2005. This referred to ways in which tenants can be helped to gain an equity stake in the value of their home. The new policy agenda of the Labour government after 2002 had an even clearer focus on home ownership.

The Communities Plan (ODPM 2003) has been seen as typifying a revival of government interest in housing. The Deputy Prime Minister, John Prescott, in the Foreword to the Plan stated

> We are determined to put an end to poor housing and bad landlords, to deliver more affordable housing, especially for key workers and young families, and to develop new sustainable communities...

The Communities Plan also highlighted concerns over the operation of the planning system and its responsiveness to the different problems in different parts of England. The Treasury-promoted review of the planning system signalled further changes. In April 2003 Kate Barker was asked by the Chancellor of the Exchequer and Deputy Prime Minister to conduct a review of housing supply in the UK. The Barker Review Final Report, *Delivering Stability: Securing our Future Housing Needs* (2004), considered the weak responsiveness of the new build housing market in the face of rising house prices and the Treasury's concern that this feature of the UK housing market had several undesirable economic consequences:

- rising house prices driving up the 'affordability threshold' as incomes fail to keep pace in many areas, leading to:
- high demands for public subsidy towards new affordable homes, and
- the inability of high price areas to attract workers on ordinary salaries, and
- the leakage of equity into consumer spending leading to difficulties in controlling the money supply and hence implications for the setting of interest rates and inflation.

These consequences were seen by the Review adversely to affect economic growth and to prevent the clear convergence of the UK economy with the economies in the Euro-zone, hindering the achievement of a major macroeconomic and European policy objective.

The Barker Review had 36 recommendations including changes to the planning system and incentives for local authorities to speed up delivery. The review was concerned to achieve long-term stability of the housing market and this required a substantial increase in house building – mainly but not wholly for sale. Alongside this, in March 2003, the Government had asked Baroness Dean, then Chair of the Housing Corporation, to lead a home-ownership task force to look at practical ideas to support home-ownership; helping tenants and others on modest incomes to buy a home, whilst minimizing the loss to social housing (Dean 2003). The Government accepted the majority of the Task Force's recommendations in May 2004. These included measures to streamline the existing products and provide more advice and information to individuals about sustainable home-ownership. The new focus on affordability in these plans continued the process of seeking to deliver housing policy through the market and the planning system rather than direct public sector provision.

Early in 2005 and in the lead up to the General Election anticipated in that year, the Government issued a Five Year Plan (ODPM 2005) setting out the next phase in the delivery of the Sustainable Communities Plan. This paper continued with the themes identified in the Communities Plan in 2003 but included a greater focus on first time buyers and the availability of a new Homebuy scheme to enable housing association and council tenants the chance to buy a share of their home. The paper reaffirmed government support for the approach set out by the Barker Review, the Home-Ownership Task Force and the Egan Review (ODPM 2004), which had identified skills shortages related to the regeneration agenda. It also confirmed the government's commitment to an increased supply of public as well as private sector housing.

The focus of policies was on increasing home-ownership over time. A new scheme to help first time buyers involved using public land for new homes in order to keep costs down; in effect the costs of land would not be fully included in the initial costs of house purchase. The new package for social tenants was entitled 'Choice to Own' (an interesting development from 'Right to Buy'). This emphasized giving social tenants a choice about how to move into home-ownership rather than the 'Right to Buy' being the only route in. Public money could be used more effectively to give people alternatives in home-ownership other than the Right to Buy: 'Choice to Own' included an extension to the Homebuy scheme to give tenants in the social rented sector the right to buy a share in their home and in turn to buy the property outright.

The policy stance was unambiguous. Paragraph 4.1 stated: 'The Government supports home-ownership. People's homes have become more and more important to their sense of security and well-being' (ODPM 2005).

What was emerging was a policy more closely associated with those we have observed in the East Asian economies, but tailored to the complexities of the British housing market. This involved a much more comprehensive series of interventions to enable different groups to access home-ownership and to create different routes into the tenure through different types of loan and by buying different proportions of the property so that the widest possible proportion of households would be able to make use of one scheme or another. It is in principle, like the privatization policies outlined in China, a comprehensively managed approach to the expansion of home-ownership from a mass to a universal tenure. The remaining role of social housing is explicitly that of a safety net for households who choose not to own, or who are unable to use any of the routes into home-ownership.

In addition to the Right to Buy, the right to acquire and the extension of Homebuy to tenants in the social rented sector, the government said it would explore options to offer tenants wanting to move out of higher demand areas, interest-free loans linked to the value of the property they buy. They also committed themselves to continuing to work to ensure that people had the information needed to manage home-ownership; with new regulatory arrangements for mortgages to ensure that people are given a 'key facts' illustration to explain the costs of the mortgage, referring to details of monthly repayments and the effect of interest rate increases on payments. They were committed to working with lending and insurance industries to promote more flexible repayment arrangements and to increase the availability of mortgage payment protection products. The planned introduction of Home Information Packs from January 2007 was designed to raise awareness of repair and maintenance responsibilities, and to help buyers make informed choices about purchasing properties. It was also argued that it would make buying and selling a home quicker, more reliable and more transparent, and provide owners with key information about the energy efficiency of their homes to help them manage their household budgets more effectively (ODPM 2005, para 4.22).

The Chancellor of the Exchequer, in his pre-Budget statement in December 2005, withdrew previously announced plans to allow new self-investment personal pensions (SIPPs) to be invested in residential property. The pre-budget speech stated that SIPPs and all forms of self-direct pensions, would be prohibited from obtaining tax advantages and investing in residential property and certain other assets. From 6 April 2006 this would ensure that tax relief was given only to those whose purpose in making the contribution was to provide themselves with a secure retirement income. This action took away one of the more explicit new ways in which government was encouraging the development of an asset based welfare system. However existing trends in the market were already moving in that direction and even without the additional tax relief it seems probable there will be a continuing investment by some older and established owner occupiers in the purchase of second homes and buy-to-let properties as an investment, in anticipation of older age and of retirement. The driver is the security and performance of investment in property, compared with the alternative products available for pension investment. The underlying trend towards asset-based welfare lies in the general promotion of and support for the performance of owner-occupied markets, rather than any special taxation treatments. Indeed, since the removal of mortgage interest tax relief, beginning in 1993, the attractiveness of investment in housing has increased. It is its relative performance compared with other investments, rather than its explicit taxation treatment, that has made the investment attractive.

By 2006 home-ownership was no longer competing with state housing in a two pronged housing strategy, nor was it the favoured method in a confused policy agenda. It was the dominant element in a new, comprehensive approach to housing. But the implications of the new approach went further. The Treasury, the Department of Work and Pensions and government as a whole increasingly referred to 'The Asset State' and to property-ownership as at the heart of the welfare state. The increased wealth stored in home-ownership (and ownership of more than one home) provided a resource that could be used in older age and could offset the erosion of the state pension scheme and the failure of private pensions. Government had begun to see home-ownership not just as a popular form of housing tenure but as a pillar on which other policies could be built. Concern about inequalities in wealth focused on the households which would not have resources they could fall back on – because they were not home-owners. Consequently the government sought to further expand home-ownership through shared ownership and Homebuy schemes and actively considered ways of providing equity stakes for tenants. Home-ownership began to have a key role in the development of the welfare state – and through this housing was moving from wobbly pillar to potential cornerstone of the new welfare state.

Wider European Perspectives

The situation in other European welfare states is not the same as in Britain. Esping-Andersen's categorization puts the narrowly defined welfare state in the Netherlands, Scandinavia, Germany or France in a different category than the liberal welfare state in Britain. However, it has been argued that there is not a good correlation between this narrow categorization and a wider definition that would include housing, education or health services where payments in kind rather than through benefit are involved. This wider categorization puts Britain in a more generous category with a more redistributive agenda than is implied by the categorization based on social security (see Chapter 1).

Leaving this issue aside it is striking that in those European welfare states that did have large not-for-profit sectors, social housing has tended to go along the same route as Britain. They have seen a tendency for residualization of the social and public rented sector and the encouragement of owner occupation as an element of privatization. The movement of more affluent households towards owner occupation has been a common feature. Although it is generally argued that Britain has been in the forefront of this direction of change, what was at one time seen as a British phenomenon is now evidently a more general European one. Again the processes of change are different. In Germany for example the post-war subsidy system provided subsidy to landlords on the basis that they guaranteed to provide subsidized rented housing for a fixed time period, usually twenty-five years. Once this period expired, housing associations were no longer obliged to continue to provide social rented housing, and could move towards letting on a purely commercial basis. The subsidized housing schemes began to fall in the 1980s and some but not all landlords have opted for a more conventional private landlord model. As a result the size of the social rented sector has declined and it has become more clearly targeted on lower income groups (Novy, 1991; Haussermann, 1994). The stratification within the housing system in Germany may also be argued to be more clear cut than in Britain as there is less low income owner occupation than in the British situation.

In both the Netherlands and Sweden the forms of social or public housing have been different than in the UK. In the Netherlands, municipal housing providers began to be replaced with the transfer of stock to housing associations at a very early stage and that process has been completed since. In more recent years the share of the social rented sector within the housing market has also begun to decline and there is evidence of residualization. Some limited privatization has also taken place partly to fund renewal and regeneration. The pattern is much slower, but the direction of change is the same as in Britain (van Kempen and Priemus 2002; Aalbers 2004; English 1982).

A similar pattern can be seen in Sweden where again the form of public housing was different, with considerable funding for co-operatives and a resistance to privatization. However, in more recent years some privatization has taken place and the trend is towards a residualization of the public rented sector. This residualization itself is a result of the encouragement of owner occupation and the preferences expressed by middle and higher income groups but the clearer stratification is also a cause of the movement away from that sector by the same middle and higher income groups. Other examples of privatization and a trend towards a sharper segregation and residualization of social housing are evident in France and in Italy. Social and public rented housing which was at one stage seen to be a feature of a redistributive welfare state has become characteristic of a more unequal society. Large post-war housing estates are increasingly associated with poorer sections of the community, foreign workers and those who are dependent upon welfare benefits. There is less social mix and the reputation of public housing has changed.

Conclusions

If we shift attention away from decommodified housing provision and the level of public housing provision, the account of the old welfare states becomes very different. It is not an account of withdrawal from provision; rather it is an account of the development of a more coherent pattern of provision with a residual or reserve state provision and the encouragement of market provision to meet a variety of material needs. The modernization of the old welfare state has involved the development of a less fragmented housing provision system with clearer signals for different income groups and social classes about the types of provision of which they should take advantage. It is a more clearly stratified system which seeks to be comprehensive but not through the universal provision of a public service. It does not seek to be uniform but is comprehensive in providing for households with different needs and capacities. It encourages people to see the inequalities associated with the market as part of taking responsibility for planning and meeting household needs. It shifts the risk and the responsibility to the individual in a period when individuals do not resist that. It takes advantage of the general view developed in a rising housing market that home-ownership provides opportunities for increasing wealth and storing wealth in a secure place. It represents a significant shift in the approach to welfare provision.

In this it may be argued that there is a coincidence between global pressures, the policy environment advocated by international agencies and the increased individualization of welfare. Because the increasingly competitive East Asian welfare states do not rely on high levels of taxation and benefit, then any attempt to compete in relation to labour costs means that the old welfare states need to reduce their social wage. Increased means testing and the reduction of generous benefits is highly consistent with the responses to global pressures as well as the demands associated with increased individualization and privatization. While global pressure may be an additional influence it does not account for the overall direction of change over a lengthy period.

What we are seeing is the reconstruction of the welfare state in the context of changes in the global economy: the newly emerging welfare state is more stratified and the associations between residence and income or social class are more clear cut. Ethnic dimensions are also more evident. The argument that the welfare state confirms people's status rather than changes it, has become more justifiable across Europe. The pressure on budgets has led to a general reduction in the generosity of welfare benefits and the attraction of investing in owner occupation has become stronger for both government and middle and higher income groups. The pattern identified in Britain is being reproduced elsewhere in Europe and the new model welfare states in these countries put individual property-ownership in a more central position, much more comparable with that of East Asia.

Chapter 9

The Property Owning Welfare State

Richard Groves, Alan Murie and Christopher Watson

The discussion in this book has built on an existing literature that typified welfare states regimes in different ways. The seminal contribution by Esping-Andersen developed three welfare state regime types which have been widely used, sometimes uncritically, in the literature. This typology has tended to underpin more recent typologies of housing policy and systems of housing provision. Consequently there has been a considerable coincidence between types of welfare state and types of housing policy as represented in the literature. The earlier chapters have challenged this in two respects:

- First and most fundamentally, the approach is ethnocentric. Although it is not Anglocentric it is built principally on an analysis of European and North American economies and does not adequately embrace the traditions associated with other, and especially developing, economies;
- Second it has been argued that the typification of welfare states does not engage adequately with the different nature of housing provision and the extent of decommodified housing provision in different countries. The first chapter presented data which show the difficulty in predicting the type of housing provision system from the nature of the welfare state. This is not a fundamental criticism of the approach to typification but it suggests caution when extrapolating from the typology presented by Esping-Andersen and used so widely by others.

Against this background and partly to complement the debates in the existing literature, this book has focused on housing and particularly on housing provision in six East Asian countries. It has done this to address the two issues identified above and to provide a constructive addition to the existing literature. The material presented has involved separate accounts of different countries rather than comparative research. It has enabled us to develop a fuller picture of the housing dimension which is critical to what has been termed an economic development or 'productivist' model in which social policy is clearly subordinated to economic policy – the fourth world of welfare capitalism associated in particular with East Asian economies. The contention is that East Asian welfare states have broad features that set them apart from the three types of welfare capitalism identified elsewhere. These distinguishing features do not deny that there are differences within the East Asian systems, nor that there have been different patterns of change within this group in recent years. Nevertheless they establish that in considering welfare state systems and in particular in considering the case of housing within them, we need to take a broader perspective and to acknowledge at least four types of welfare state system.

East Asian Welfare States

The country-by-country chapters in this book show that the distinguishing features of East Asian welfare systems are associated particularly with their origins. In this respect, the argument is similar to that of Esping-Andersen who pointed to the importance of political coalitions and to the political sphere for explanation of why welfare states developed, and why they developed in the ways they did. They are not the inevitable product of a particular stage in economic or in urban development nor are they the inevitable consequence of types of political system. Rather they reflect the interests, alliances and political coalitions that were effective at key points in time.

In the East Asian welfare states, the development of welfare provision was associated with threats to the existing political system and to national stability; and with nation building as a fundamental part of post-war reconstruction. In particular, at the end of the Second World War, the threat of communism was influential in determining the political economies of East Asian countries. While this has been most marked in Taiwan and Korea, and with the obvious exception of the People's Republic of China, it was also highly significant in each of the other countries. Taiwan, for example, fearing invasion from China, remained under martial law until 1987. The Korean War of 1950–53 was fought over the ideological differences between the communist forces in the north and those opposed to communism in the south. At the same time, the post-war presence of the Americans in South Korea and Japan and of the British colonial governments in Hong Kong and Singapore was also important in establishing and continuing to support non-communist regimes in these countries. As a consequence, all these governments emerged from the devastating experience of war and embarked on the process of nation building during the 1950s and 1960s by seeking to ensure economic stability in a 'top down' way. In East Asia (with the exception of China), the external threat has generally been stronger than any internal threat and the process of building a welfare state has been very different from that in some of the Western European economies where the importance of civil society, of electorally based demands and of organized labour and political parties have been crucial.

These distinctive origins are associated with two other common characteristics: first, the single-minded focus on economic performance and second, the focus on the mainstream population, which was seen as crucial to achieving economic performance. It may be argued that these elements are evident within traditional welfare states as well. The corporatist welfare regimes and the systems associated with Eastern and Central Europe often involved rewarding key sections of the labour force rather than focusing on the poorest sections of the population; and there have been elements in all welfare state systems which are concerned to address economic growth and performance. The use of government expenditure as an economic regulator and the manipulation of welfare spending to achieve economic goals is nothing new. The evidence presented in this book, however, is that the emphasis given by the East Asian welfare states to economic performance and to the mainstream population has been crucial to their economic development. The clearest examples of this are in the priorities of the post-war governments of Japan, Taiwan and Korea but most of the other countries illustrate similar tendencies. It means that their welfare systems have developed with little attention to redistribution, concepts of citizenship rights, comprehensiveness of provision, or concern for the poorest sections of the community. In many cases, this wider welfare agenda has seemed to be an unaffordable luxury, as in Taiwan or, until recently, in Korea. In Japan during the 1970s, it was argued that welfare states focusing on redistribution and providing benefits for the poor encouraged economic inefficiency, undermined the work ethic and were 'inferior' models.

It follows from this discussion that the distinguishing features of the East Asian welfare states can be referred to most simply in the sense of what they are *not*:

- they have not set out to provide a safety net for meeting the needs of the whole population;
- they are not based on concepts of citizenship rights, nor on a process of democratic negotiation and bargaining;
- they have developed in the absence of a well established civil society, and of institutions for representation, participation and engagement between citizens and government.

They are also less 'bottom up' and are less concerned with addressing the problems of previous decades than was the case in the traditional welfare states. Thus it can be argued that the European welfare states emerging at the end of the Second World War were often focused upon avoiding a re-emergence of the problems of the inter-war period, such as prolonged economic recession and mass unemployment, which contributed to the outbreak of the Second World War. The East Asian welfare systems, in contrast, are more forward looking and focused on national and economic stability and growth.

In setting out the distinctive features of East Asian welfare states, it has been suggested that Confucianism is a significant connecting thread (for example, Jones 1990). Yet the chapters in this book do not see Confucianism as a key element in the East Asian approach to welfare provision. Confucianism is a background feature and often a convenient justification for particular types of action but it is not a determining feature. Confucianism is not the sole source of ideas and governments can draw different elements from the Confucian tradition – about respect, loyalty and trust; and about hierarchy, inequality and deference. Both of these aspects are apparent within the systems that have developed. But, as the country chapters have shown, it is global processes that have become increasingly significant determinants of what has been happening. If the East Asian welfare states in their earlier phase were characterized by considerable autonomy and the ability to develop distinctive national policy approaches, the period since the Asian financial crisis of 1997 has been one in which global pressures increasingly have been evident and have constrained or moderated the distinctive national elements between countries. It has also been argued that popular political demands have been more influential in this later phase. In relation to the arguments put forward by Jones, the suggestion is not to deny the historic importance of Confucianism but to see it as a background rather than a determining feature; and to focus more upon global and popular political pressures as increasingly important determinants of the nature and direction of the modern East Asian welfare states.

In view of the connecting threads and particularly the importance of the economy in determining the East Asian approach to housing and welfare, it is appropriate to refer to these countries as economy-driven welfare states. The term highlights the significant common thread yet allows for the important differences that clearly exist between countries and systems in the region.

Variation

The argument that economy-driven welfare states are distinct from the old welfare states, does not deny that there is great variation between the countries discussed in this book. In broad terms they share a distinctive type of welfare system, but just as the liberal or corporate or redistributive welfare states identified by Esping-Andersen and others are different in more than just fine detail, so there are differences here. The most important are:

1. *Differences of scale* The book looks at two city-states, Singapore and Hong Kong, now one of two systems within China. In population, in area and in the nature of economic organization and development, these city-states are very different from the other countries referred to. These include China, with the largest population in the world, and its great variety of circumstances from the booming coastal belt and major inland cities such as Beijing, to other parts which have seen very little of the positive impacts of economic growth and the liberalization of the economy. Japan has the second largest economy in the world but with very different historical and institutional structures to those of China. Korea and Taiwan are both distinctive countries, with their own political histories and faced by particular political threats in the early 21st century.

2. *Ideological and political reference points* The ideological influences in these countries are very different. They range from those associated with communism to those that are actively anti-communist. But there are also major ideological and political differences between the non-communist governments. These differences may be highlighted, for example, by the efforts of the People's

Action Party in Singapore to achieve 'a stakeholder society'; the concentration of the post-war Japanese government on the 'social mainstream'; and the mix of public and private sector roles encouraged by the former British colonial administration of Hong Kong. There are countries, such as China, which are multicultural and those which are monocultural, such as Japan and Korea. These ideological, political and religious differences and the influence of each on the others means that each country has evolved its own distinct form of representative government, ranging from the single party system in China to the modern representative democracy in Korea.

3. *Triggers for policy action* The development of the economy-driven welfare state has not followed from some achieved level of economic development. Often it has developed, in a similar way to that suggested by Esping-Andersen, in response to an immediate crisis, such as the 1953 Shep Kip Mei fire in Hong Kong, or the changed political status of Taiwan in 1979. Developments in housing policy have invariably been responses to growing housing crises. In Singapore it was a particular conjuncture of events, ethnic tension and the incidence of floods and fires together with housing shortages and poor conditions, that precipitated action in 1959 by the incoming national government. In Taiwan, rapid industrialization during the 1960s and 1970s led to major rural–urban migration and acute housing shortages in Taipei and other cities. The government responded with a six year public housing programme in 1976. The relative underdevelopment of housing policy and welfare state systems in Japan and Korea may possibly be attributed to the absence of this kind of trigger event, although both countries experienced acute housing shortages at the end of their respective hostilities in the 1940s and 1950s. The Japanese government initiated the 'three pillars of housing policy' in the early 1950s but it was another decade before the Korean government in 1962 established the Korea National Housing Corporation as a self-financing agency to construct public housing. In China, housing policy reforms were introduced more gradually during the late 1970s and formed part of Deng Xiao Ping's wider programme of economic reform in the early 1980s, but these too were in response to widespread problems in urban housing conditions and growing difficulties with the provision of housing through government work units. In each of these countries, therefore, the development of housing policy was a response to crisis and in some circumstances there was a key event which triggered activity and led governments to embark on a much more interventionist approach to housing and welfare provision. In each case, however, external influences have also played a part.

4. *Formative external influences* The most visible formative influences on housing policy development were those of previous colonial governments. Not surprisingly, of all these East Asian countries, Hong Kong, a British colony until 1997, exhibits the strongest western influences on its housing policies and institutions. For about 25 years from its inception during the mid 1950s, the housing programme in Hong Kong provided subsidized accommodation

for rent according to prescribed allocation mechanisms and waiting lists which closely resembled those of post-war public sector provision in Britain, in all but the nature of the stock itself. Ironically, however, policies to encourage subsidized home-ownership were only introduced after the 1984 UK-China Agreement on the future of Hong Kong. Whilst the post-colonial Hong Kong Special Administrative Region (SAR) Government in 1997 introduced radical plans for an enhanced programme of privatization of the state managed public sector stock, this was more an acknowledgement of the relative success of the Singaporean model than an adoption of the UK privatization policies of the Thatcher governments of the 1980s. In Singapore, some of the institutional arrangements, including the establishment of the Central Provident Fund (CPF), grew out of arrangements put in place by the former colonial government, but the real impetus to housing policy development, such as the linking of the CPF and the Housing and Development Board (HDB) in 1968 (see Chapter 2), arose from policy-decisions by the newly formed, independent People's Action Party government. The current Singapore model of state managed private ownership, is a hybrid unique to that country.

The development of the welfare state systems in Japan and Korea was influenced initially by the presence of the Americans following the Second World War in Japan, and the Korean War in Korea. But, as Hirayama points out in Chapter 5, the Japanese government never intended to adopt western-style welfare approaches to the provision of public housing and this form of state-subsidized social programme has never been adopted by Japan. The Korean government in the early 1960s was perhaps somewhat influenced by the British model of public housing but could not afford to sustain a public rental housing programme. Instead, the Korea National Housing Corporation was established as a self-funding agency and introduced its own form of short-term rental provision, requiring early sales into private ownership to recoup its initial investment and thus, to sustain the new build programme. One of the main aims of the policy reform process in China was to reduce the burden of provision falling solely on the government by diversifying the costs to include 'owners' as well as the government and the work units. Among the influences on the Chinese government at this time of transformation was the wave of privatization taking place internationally during the 1980s as well as the success of the Singapore model in encouraging personal savings as a means towards ownership. The pattern emerging from these formative influences tends to suggests that whilst these countries have been aware of western style housing and social welfare programmes they have tended to seek their own solutions to their housing problems, rapidly moulding and subsuming any western influences into their own way of formulating policy in response to their own housing challenges.

5. *Distinctive institutional and governance arrangements* Each of the countries exhibits a distinctive approach in terms of institutional development and governance arrangements. A selection of examples serves to illustrate the

point. The recent history of housing policy in China has seen dramatic changes: first, a socialist transformation of the housing system during the post-war period gave local government and work units the key responsibility for housing provision; then, over the last quarter of a century, local housing reform bureaux have overseen a unique privatization process which has not only transferred ownership but has also seen major institutional changes through the introduction of large-scale development companies, managing agents and local revolving loan funds. Although the institutional and governance arrangements for housing are now beginning to resemble those of other East Asian economies, the recent history of the process and continuing centralized control means that the Chinese system remains a unique form of housing welfare provision.

Other countries, such as Korea and Japan, exhibit uniqueness in respect of some of the issues referred to by Jones and others, concerning the nature of working relationships between government and business. The relationships include in many cases the construction industry and government; the operation of ruling elites; the nature of relationships between civil servants and businesses and a particular type of corporate governance. The *chaebol* system in Korea illustrates this point. *Chaebol* are large conglomerate firms that traditionally have had strong ties with the government of Korea. Modelled on the former *zaibatsu* system of Japan and under the financial and political influence of the Korean government, the *chaebol* have played a major part in the development of the Korean economy from the 1960s onwards.

Contrasting relationships between the governments of Hong Kong and Singapore and their development industries have also strongly influenced their respective post-war housing programmes. Because of land scarcity, the ownership and control of land and the role of the development industry have always been highly significant in the economies of both countries. Most of the land is government-owned in both cases, but the two city-states have approached the governance of the development industries in different ways. In Singapore, land release to the private sector is carefully controlled and private property developers are closely regulated by the state. Most house-building activity has been undertaken by state controlled enterprises and it is only in recent years that the government has been willing to liberalize controls on the development industry. Hence, the government has been able to exercise control over speculative activity in the housing market and to re-cycle the surpluses of the state–controlled enterprises in the public interest. In Hong Kong, the house-building and development industry is essentially privately-owned. It forms an important political lobby and in recent years especially it has successfully influenced both the colonial and the SAR governments to support market conditions, including land release, to sustain a mixed economy in the provision of housing but in circumstances where the private sector has a hegemonic role.

6. *Time frames and global influences* The triggers for policy action referred to above occured at different times and there are two main dimensions to this. The

first relates to timing within the framework of economic, political and national development in each of the countries and reflects the willingness or capability of governments to implement housing and social welfare programmes. The second relates to timing in terms of the international or global context, in response to key global economic and political changes. These differences in timing are critical. Whereas Hong Kong and Singapore developed highly interventionist housing policies in the 1950s and 1960s, China did not embark on the privatization and commercialization policies, which transformed its cities, until the late 1990s. China is at a relatively early stage in a process of reform, following major privatization of housing provision, whereas in other cases, systems have matured and institutional and financial arrangements have been developed and refined. The changes that are occurring in Hong Kong and Korea illustrate countries in a mature or second phase of policy development very different from the first phase evident in Taiwan or China.

The development with greatest influence on housing and welfare policies in East Asian countries in recent years, however, has been the effect of global changes and most notably, the impact of the Asian financial crisis. The financial downturn has affected all the economies in the region, and in some instances the impact on public housing policies has been dramatic. The Japanese economy went into decline in the early 1990s, predating the Asian financial crisis in 1997 and precipitating an unprecedented and long-term recession. In response to this, the government has pursued increasingly radical housing policies since the mid 1990s, which have sought to reduce the state sector, de-regulate the private sector and increasingly emphasize market solutions to housing requirements. The impact on housing policy in Hong Kong has been equally severe. The financial crisis forced the SAR government to scrap its ambitious plans for an expansion of home-ownership, to withdraw from the public provision of home-ownership flats and to adopt a policy of retrenchment in public sector house-building. The problem for the Hong Kong government, however, is more far-reaching in that the public sector house-building programme has been funded largely through home-ownership sales and without this income there is serious doubt over the future capacity of the government to sustain its programme. In Korea, house prices and *chonsei* rents fell significantly as a result of the financial crisis and the public house-building programme slumped to about half of the output of previous years. The crisis coincided with the election of a new government which not only introduced a wide range of policy measures to support the private sector, but also managed to sustain a modestly increased programme of low-cost, public sector rental housing targeted towards low-income households. This twin-pronged approach has been continued by the present government, which is currently pursuing a programme of underpinning the private sector with anti-speculation measures and the introduction of a secondary mortgage market, whilst at the same time supporting a programme to build one million permanent public rental dwellings over the decade to 2012.

   • Although also affected to various degrees by the Asian financial crisis, the remaining three countries appear to have weathered the storm without fundamental policy changes, but each for a different reason. Whilst the crisis wiped out millions of S$ in house prices and share values in Singapore, the strength of the economy and the robustness of its housing and economic institutions were sufficient to enable the government to ride out the worst effects. Nonetheless, various reforms have been implemented, including restructuring the Housing and Development Board (HDB) and encouraging the commercial banks to enter the mortgage market. In Taiwan, the 'laissez-faire' nature of government housing policy together with a high rate of existing private ownership, high savings rates and modest borrowing requirements, all tended to minimize the effects of the crisis on the market as compared with other East Asian countries. Although there were fears of the impact of the crisis in China it seems that the size of the expanding economy and the momentum of the process of housing reform, both tended to insulate the housing market from more serious consequences.

7. *The direction of travel* Because of all the elements referred to above, and in particular because of the impact of globalization and of growing internal political pressures, the direction of travel within these economy-driven welfare systems is different. In Hong Kong and Singapore, actions have been taken which will maintain the role of the state as a direct provider or manager of housing whereas in China the process of dismantling state management and control is continuing. In Japan, the very small state sector is likely to remain but not to grow in size and to have a more marginalized role; whereas in Korea a much more significant role is envisaged for the state in housing provision, especially in creating a much larger, albeit still modest level of public sector housing provision. To some extent the different directions of travel reflect differences in the nature of past interventions and they fit with a model of path dependency. With the exception of China, there are no signs, however, of a convergence of housing provision systems within the East Asian economy-driven welfare states.

Comparing Directions of Travel

The analysis of the six East Asian countries suggests it is more important to understand their directions of travel than to revisit a debate about types of welfare state. Although it is important and valuable to have some broad typology of welfare state systems, too much of the focus of debate has been on this kind of typology rather than developing an understanding of change and directions of travel. A criticism of Esping-Andersen's representation of welfare state regimes rests upon the extent to which they are robust for a particular phase rather than in addressing change over time.

One counter to this is the emphasis on path dependency and there is no doubt that the origins and past route of travel significantly determine the legacy with which different welfare systems work – the legacy in terms of organizational, financial, institutional and political systems. Even allowing for this, the notion of path dependency does not deny that the future direction of travel could involve divergence or convergence. Countries with common starting points can begin to diverge for various reasons. It may be that, in the housing context, the potential for a 'big bang' change is much greater than in other areas of welfare. It is more possible to change the ownership and financial regime associated with housing than it is to make changes in a social security system; and housing provision systems are less dependent on inputs from professionals such as doctors or teachers, which would continue to have a determining influence on service delivery, irrespective of the formal organizational and financial arrangements.

Focusing on the direction of travel, rather than the debate about types of welfare state, the chapters of this book emphasize the importance of recognising change over time. Most of the countries referred to have moved from an early phase of economic and welfare state development to a mature stage in which development has become much slower. The outcomes from the earlier phase have begun to shape later policy development but politicization and democratization also have begun to have an impact with growing public demands for significant service improvements as seen, for example, in present-day Korea. At the same time, changing external threats and the different impact of economic and political shocks are evident, as is the capacity of different systems to absorb these shocks.

It is these kinds of debates that explain why Hong Kong has abandoned its promotion of home-ownership through the Home Ownership Scheme (HOS) and has reverted to a more traditional public sector provision system. Change in the Hong Kong economy and property market had made the previous policy less attractive. In contrast the Singapore government has been able to maintain its basic approach to housing provision in spite of the very considerable impact of economic change. The strength and maturity of financial arrangements have enabled the Singapore government to continue its policies with much more modest policy changes than are apparent elsewhere.

In the situation following the series of economic crises affecting East Asia a number of divergent approaches can be identified: Singapore is holding to the model, but with a small enhancement of privatization; Hong Kong is reverting to the old public sector model; in Japan there is a retrenchment to a more market-led model, whilst maintaining a small public sector provision without expansion; Taiwan is continuing with its market model; and China is rolling out the market model, with minimal moderation, although it does appear to be learning from the others and there is evidence that it is seeking to avoid the 'bubble' economy effect – the risk that the boom in property prices will be followed by a slump that will impact on the rest of the economy. Korea is the greatest exception: faced with new challenges, it is adopting a new dual interventionist role, maintaining the promotion of finance for home-ownership but envisaging a growth in public sector housing for rental and for subsequent ownership.

There are three most obvious groupings: first, the state managed or controlled approach associated with the two 'city states' as we have called them, Hong Kong and Singapore; second, a relatively unmoderated private sector model with a growing private landlord class – this is evident in Japan, Taiwan and China; and third, a more innovative dual approach that has emerged in Korea. Whilst the Singapore and Hong Kong governments are maintaining the economy-driven approach, they are seeking also to moderate inequalities. In Korea there is an active programme to maintain the approach, but with growing intervention, characterized by a longer-term perspective than was the case with previous interventions. In China, the commercialization and liberalization of the housing market continues to be seen as a key element of the economy-driven approach in its early phase, whereas in Japan and Taiwan it remains significant but at a later stage in the economic process and with a less rapid pattern of economic growth.

These observations lead to a relatively simple conclusion that within the East Asian welfare state systems there is greater similarity in the formative phase, allowing for different time frames. But after the initial transformation the welfare state systems are moderated by different patterns of economic change, demographic change, the growth of civil society with rising expectations of government, political change, globalization, external shocks and new inequalities arising in response to all of these changes. This does not deny the broad brush distinguishing features of welfare states referred to above, but it does suggest that, to understand direction of travel, reference is needed to a wider range of factors. Some of these are still fundamentally political ones and there is no implication that individual country responses to the same pressures will be the same.

Visions of Home-ownership

A central theme of this book has been the extent to which home-ownership and the promotion of home-ownership for the mainstream of society has been a common feature of the welfare systems emerging across East Asia and has become a more prominent feature elsewhere. Against this background can be identified some key characteristics and implications arising from the promotion of home-ownership.

First, however, it is important to recognize the success of the East Asian welfare systems in reducing the most visible shortages. The decline in overcrowding and sharing of accommodation, or the amelioration of the worst housing conditions, for example, are comparable with the achievements in European countries. While many of the latter countries achieved such a change over a longer period of time and through the development of direct 'state' or 'not-for-profit' housing provision, the major advances in this respect in East Asia have been achieved without such direct state provision – except in Hong Kong and Singapore. Even in these latter cases, the promotion of market housing has also been a major contributor comparable with the European models.

The promotion of home-ownership has had a positive impact on shortages but has generated a pattern of emerging inequality, some of which, it could be argued, was intended but some of which has been unintended. The promotion of a market based system implies encouraging people to invest more of their incomes and savings in housing. Inequalities in housing will reflect inequalities elsewhere especially if the operation of the property market facilitates speculation. There are some important additional inequalities emerging, particularly related to multiple property ownership. There are also important implications arising from a system which is dependent upon individual home-ownership, when a market downturn occurs; and one of the most important issues raised by the home-ownership systems in East Asia relates to the problems they are experiencing in a period of market downturn. The impacts felt in Japan, Hong Kong, Taiwan and to a lesser extent, Singapore and Korea raise an additional kind of inequality, especially when the downturn in the market continues over a long period of time. There are very significant cohort effects in the experience of home-ownership. Some people invested in property at the right time and have become wealthy as a result. Others invested at the wrong time and are impoverished. There are winners and losers in this situation and inequalities are associated with time and place to a much greater extent than was associated with the traditional welfare state systems in Europe. In this sense the welfare state model in East Asia has been one that generates inequality rather than limits it and the movement of other welfare state systems towards such a model is likely to have the same effects.

Three important sources of inequality are built into East Asian welfare states:

- First there are differences that are generational, or cohort-based. The generation that entered home-ownership under the most favourable conditions when prices were lowest has often experienced an enormous increase in the value of their property. Even when a market downturn occurs, it does not wipe out the gains they have made. Later generations do not buy under such favourable circumstances and are more likely to have experienced a downturn which damages or destroys advantage for them. In the traditional welfare systems, the major beneficiaries were not the generation who first voted for and financed welfare provision but rather were the next generation who benefited from improved provision in education, housing, health and social security. The improvements in these services were achieved some years after the initial establishment of the welfare state. In East Asia, the position is different. The greatest beneficiaries in welfare state terms have been the earlier generation, although the later generation may have benefited more from the buoyancy of the economy and of the types of employment and employment regimes involved.
- Second, who wins and who loses is influenced by external factors affecting both East Asian and older welfare states, not least the continuous debates on what governments can afford to spend to support welfare regimes.

- Third, the extent to which the East Asian welfare states have rewarded key occupational groups, (e.g. government employees, employees of larger and more successful businesses), is reflected in the institutionalization of occupational status within the welfare state and property system.

This leads to the two other dimensions of inequality associated with East Asian welfare states:

- The first relates to place: to hot and cold spots, to negative equity and to the uneven value of housing assets. In the case of Japan, for example, there are significant inequalities between households in the same property class, depending on where and when they bought. In some cases property values have fallen and some households have significant negative equity. In other cases property values have increased. This volatility and unevenness in the development of the housing sector is mirrored throughout the world. The more a welfare state system rests upon property ownership, the more it will be a system that is associated with, or generates rather than moderates inequalities.
- The second major dimension of inequality is between three groups that can be regarded as different property classes:

  a Householders who have not entered the home-ownership system. They are excluded from the advantages that can result from the increase in asset values. They are also protected against the disadvantages of a downward turn in the market, negative equity and the other contingencies associated with ownership.
  b Owner-occupiers, or the owners of single properties that they do not live in. They have the advantages associated with rising property values and share in the benefits of the rising market; however they can be exposed to problems if there is a downturn in the market, and the benefits of home-ownership are not guaranteed or certain in every case.
  c Finally, and largely missing from the debate about housing privatization internationally, is the evidence of an emerging group of multiple property owners – a new property owning class, who do not simply own the property they live in but have purchased other properties as well. In many cases, these are people who were in advantageous occupational positions, advantageous generational positions and in the right place in terms of the property and economic cycle. This privileged group of households has been able to benefit from the development of the property market to the extent that they have become a new landlord class. This does not mean they are not exposed to risks, but it is striking that there has been some growth in a more conventional private rented sector in economies that did not previously have one. The *chonsei* system in Korea has survived at a high level, but there is also a growing monthly rental market. The private

rented sector has grown in Japan and Hong Kong, and there is evidence that it is growing also in China and Taiwan.

Legacies

Where then does this pattern of development leave the East Asian welfare states? They have high levels of home-ownership but also in some cases high levels of private renting. Only in Hong Kong is there a large public sector housing legacy and a legacy of managed housing – although in Singapore, there is a much larger state controlled sector. There are new generational and inherited wealth inequalities and a new private landlord class. One of the implications of this is that there are new divisions of interest, and new patterns of dependency and stratification emerging in these countries. Political demands around the housing question now relate to differences in position in relation to the property market: differences between renters and owners; differences between owners in different positions in relation to the value of their property and the nature of their investment; and differences related to the numbers of properties owned. These legacies are likely to have some influence on the pattern of development of housing policy and welfare systems. Will countries with a newly established property owning class be considerably constrained in the ways they respond to future crises by the political demands of property owners? It may be argued that the Hong Kong case illustrates the power of property-related interests to alter the direction of policy. Perhaps in the future, economies and welfare systems will be much more shaped by the interests of a new propertied class than they were in the past.

Conclusion

The discussion in this book has focused on the East Asian welfare states but the argument has been that the insights gained from them are relevant in a wider international context, where other countries are increasing the role of home-ownership and are seeing property ownership as a more significant part of welfare provision. Reference was made, for example, to the recent tendency of the UK government to identify the advantages of asset ownership or property ownership and to see the potential of equity release from housing as a way of managing the contingencies of older age, poor health and dependency. Equity release from housing is increasingly seen as a means of supplementing the state pension scheme which was originally envisaged as providing income in retirement, when the foundations of the welfare state were laid down. As the traditional welfare states adjust to include a greater emphasis on property ownership, they are exposed to the same kinds of issues that have been identified for the East Asian welfare states.

By 2006 the cross-party political agenda for housing in the UK is not to see housing as a sideshow or wobbly pillar alongside a generous, redistributive welfare system. Housing has become, rather, the keystone for a more individualistic economic and social policy agenda. Citizens' welfare rights are less prominent. It is citizens taking responsibility for their own welfare and investment in home-ownership that provides the mechanism for welfare at different stages of life. Home-ownership increasingly is seen as the key to life chances and command over resources.

The traditional welfare states are adopting approaches to housing and welfare that are more associated with those of East Asia. Both see housing as a key economic driver and a key component in a property-owning welfare strategy.

In conclusion, the evidence presented in this book demonstrates the significance of a fourth model of welfare provision based much more firmly around a set of principles associated with nation-building and economic growth. This East Asian model is a significant alternative to the more traditional European model and places greater emphasis on property ownership and home-ownership. Individual property ownership encouraged through privatization and home-ownership policies has begun also to be attached to traditional welfare models, especially in Europe. This stage in the development of the welfare state in East Asia is beginning to see an adjustment in the way these states work. They are no longer in an early or formative phase where the description of their objectives or distinguishing features is all that can be offered. They are now at a stage where some of the outcomes from this kind of system can be seen. The outcomes are both positive and negative; they are about successful economic development, and about successful improvement in urban living conditions and housing. However, the outcomes also are associated with growing inequality. The East Asian welfare states in their mature or later stages have acquired new distinctive characteristics associated with property ownership and inequalities in relation to the property market.

Just as the traditional welfare states have subsequently been criticized because of their failure to eliminate inequality and because the social division of welfare has often benefited middle class and higher income groups rather than being consistently redistributive, so the East Asian welfare states can be criticized in the same way.

The older welfare regimes have come under increasing challenge because of their failure to achieve what was hoped for them and because of issues of fiscal crisis. The East Asian welfare states are likely to come under challenge because of the evidence about social inequalities and the potential costs associated with these inequalities, especially if there is an increasing development of civil society and its associated institutions. With the growth of a private landlord class it would be reasonable to expect new debates about the future direction of welfare state provision. There may be capacity through the market to provide housing for lower income groups; and the demands for a public housing sector may not develop in these economies in the way that has been assumed by some.

There are also issues about the management and regulation of private sector housing and about the regeneration and renewal of cities. It is likely to become more important that the market based home-ownership system should develop mechanisms for continuous improvement; and that social inequalities will grow and become a source of instability unless there is the growth of a new set of policies to manage the legacy of inequality.

It is unlikely that the East Asian welfare states will develop the same types of arrangements for public housing or other services that were apparent in the old welfare states; but probably they will develop some new responses to patterns of inequality and some of these elements will have similarities to those in the older welfare states. To this extent we may see some convergence as the older welfare states move towards a property owning model and the economy-driven welfare states address the new patterns of inequality generated by the emphasis on individual home-ownership.

The new property owning welfare states in East Asia and Europe have housing and home-ownership at their core. All the modernised liberal, corporate or redistributive welfare regime types have embraced home-ownership and housing is more central to each of them than in the past. Governments increasingly encourage individual investment and asset accumulation, partly to meet the need for shelter in a way that is preferable to direct state provision or more highly subsidised systems; and partly because home-ownership also gives individuals and families a store of wealth that can be drawn upon to meet future needs as they arise – rather than relying on state provision. This store of wealth can be drawn on also to fund non-housing welfare needs, especially in older age.

The property owning welfare state involves more minimalist provision through the state than the traditional redistributive or corporate approaches but seeks to adopt a different mechanism for individual welfare provision than the older Poor Law or liberal systems. Individual asset ownership, largely associated with the ownership of housing, has enabled the state to reorganise and modernise its role in a way that is more in tune with global economic pressures and economic orthodoxies about the role of the state; and about taxation and welfare benefits. In this sense the new welfare states emerging in East Asia and Europe will still reflect different legacies, political systems and policy histories, but they will all include a significant role for housing and for home-ownership. They will be built on the uneven contours of the property market and marked by inequalities and accidents of time and place. rather than reflecting a more planned, egalitarian and redistributive approach.

Bibliography

Aalbers, M.B. (2004), 'Promoting Home ownership in a Social-Rented City: Policies, Practices and Pitfalls', *Housing Studies* 19:3, 483–95.

Allen, J., Barlow, J., Leal, J., Maloutas, T. and Padovani, L. (2004), *Housing and Welfare in Southern Europe* (Oxford: Blackwell).

Almanac of China's Economy, 1981 to 1990, compiled by the Editors Committee of the Almanac of China's Economy (Beijing: Economic Management Publishing House).

Asher, M. (2002), 'Social Security Institutions in Southeast Asia after the Crisis', in M. Beeson (ed.), *Reconfiguring East Asia: Regional Institutions and Organizations after the Crisis* (London: Routledge-Curzon, 83–98).

Asher, M. (2004), 'Retirement Financing in Singapore' (Mimeo).

Aspalter, C. (2002), *Democratization and Welfare State Development in Taiwan* (Hampshire: Ashgate).

Barker, K. (2004), *The Barker Review – 'Delivering Stability: Securing Our Future Housing Needs'* (London: ODPM/HM Treasury).

Barlow, J. and Duncan, S. (1994) *Success and Failure in Housing Provision: European Systems Compared* (Oxford: Pergamon Press).

Beijing Economic Daily, 1 June 1999.

Beijing Municipal Housing System Reform Office, Land and Property Management Bureau, Finance Bureau, Personal Bureau, Supervision Bureau, Older Cadres' Bureau and Housing Fund Management Centre (2003), Circular on the Disciplines of Issuing Staff Housing Subsidies in Administrative Bodies and Public Institutions in Beijing. Internal document, Housing Reform Office, No. 078.

Beijing Municipal Construction Commission (1997), *Beijing Real Estate 1996* (Beijing: Air Aviation Industry Press).

Beveridge, W. (1953), *Power and Influence* (London: George Allen & Unwin).

Bhaskaran, M. (2003), *Re-inventing the Asian Model: The Case of Singapore* (Singapore: Eastern Universities Press for the Institute of Policy Studies).

Bian, Y. and Logan, J. (1996), 'Market Transition and the Persistence of Power: The Changing Stratification System in Urban China', *American Sociological Review* 61:5, 739–58.

Boelhouwer, P. and van der Heijden, H. (1992), *Housing Systems in Europe, Part 1: A Comparative Study of Housing Policy* (Delft: Delft University Press).

Castells, M. (1977), *The Urban Question: A Marxist Approach* (London: Edward Arnold).

Castells, M. et al. (1988), *Economic Development and Housing Policy in the Asian Pacific Rim: A Comparative Study of Hong Kong, Singapore and Shenzhen Special*

Economic Zone, Monograph 37, (Berkeley, Institute of Urban and Regional Development, University of California).

Castells, M., Goh, L., and Kwok, R.Y.-W. (1990), *The Shek Kip Mei Syndrome: Economic Development and Public Housing in Hong Kong and Singapore* (London: Pion).

Census and Statistics Department (1999), *Hong Kong Annual Digest of Statistics 1999* (Hong Kong Government Printer).

Census and Statistics Department (2005) http://www.info.gov.hk/censtatd/eng/ hkstat/fas/labour/ghs/labour1_index.html.

Central Provident Fund, Singapore, *Annual Reports*, various years.

Chan, H.-S. and Lin, H.-F. (2003), 'Taiwan: An Emerging New Welfare State (1990–2002)', *National Policy Forum, July*, (http://www.npf.org.tw/monthly/ 0303/theme-205.htm).

Chang, C.-O. and Lin, C.-Y. (1999), 'Taipei', in Berry, J. and McGreal, S. (eds), *Cities in the Pacific Rim: Planning Systems and Property Markets* (London and New York: E & FN Spon, 89–106).

Chang, C.-O. and Ward, C.W.R. (1993), 'Forward Pricing and the Housing Market: The Pre-Sales Housing System in Taiwan', *Journal of Property Research* 10, 217–27.

Chen, A.M. (1996), 'China's Urban Housing Reform: Price-Rent Ratio and Market Equilibrium', *Urban Studies* 33:7, 1077–92.

Chen, H.-H.N. (2002), 'Taiwan', in Agus, M.R., Doling, J. and Lee, D.S. (eds), *Housing Policy Systems in South and East Asia* (New York: Palgrave Macmillan, 84-103).

Chen, S.-M. and Chang, C.-O. (2004), *'Changing Studies on Households' Employment Structures and Commuting Decisions – The Evidence Based on the 1990's and 2000's Data in Taipei, Taiwan'*, paper presented in the 9th Asian Real Estate Society (AsRES) International Conference, 9–12 August, Delhi, India.

Cheung, J. (2000), 'Fresh Action Unneeded', *South China Morning Post*, 27 June 2000.

Chiu, R. (1996), 'Housing Affordability in Shenzhen Special Economic Zone: A Forerunner of China's Housing Reform', *Housing Studies* 11.4, 561–80.

Chiu, R. (2001), 'Commodification of Housing with Chinese Characteristics', *Policy Studies Review* Spring 2001 18:1, 75–95.

Chua, B.H. (1997), *Political Legitimacy and Housing: Stakeholding in Singapore* (London: Routledge).

Chung, J. (1995), 'Economic Development and Housing Policy' in Lee G.Y. and Kim, H.S. (eds), *Cities and Nation: Planning Issues and Policies of Korea* (Anyang-shi: Korea Institute for Human Settlements, 327).

Cmd 6404 (1942), *Social Insurance and Allied Services* (London: HMSO).

Committee on Singapore's Competitiveness (1998), *Committee on Singapore's Competitiveness Report* (Singapore: Ministry of Trade and Industry).

Croissant, A. (2004), 'Changing Welfare Regimes in East and Southeast Asia: Crisis, Change and Challenge', *Social Policy and Administration* 38:5, 504–24.

Crosby, A.R. (1986), 'Redevelopment in the Public Sector', *Planning and Development* 2:1, 21, cited in Lau, K.Y. and Suen, S.K. (1989), *Redevlopment of Public Housing Estates in Kwai Tsing District, Hong Kong: A Study Report* (Hong Kong: Kwai Tsing District Board, 3).

Cullingworth, J.B. (1972), *Problems of an Urban Society Volume 2 The Social Content of Planning* (London: George Allen & Unwin).

Cumings, B. (1987), 'The Origins and Development of the Northeast Asia Political Economy: Industrial Sectors, Product Cycles and Political Consequences', in Deyo, F.C. (ed.), *The Political Economy of the New Asian Industrialism*, (Ithaca and London: Cornell University Press, 44–83).

Dean, Baroness (2003), *Report of the Home ownership Task Force 'A House of My Own'* (London: ODPM).

Department of Budget, Accounting and Statistics (DBAS), Taipei City Government (2003), *The Statistics Summary of Taipei City*, (http://www.dbas.taipei.gov.tw/ News_week/CE_Tree_Eng.asp).

Department of Budget, Accounting and Statistics (DBAS), Taipei City Government (2005), *Indices of Consumer Price in Taipei – Major Groups*, (http://www.dbas. taipei.gov.tw).

Department of Statistics, Singapore, *Census of Population Reports, Singapore*, various years.

Department of Statistics, Singapore (2001), Singapore Population.

Department of Statistics, Singapore, *Yearbook of Statistics: Singapore*, various years.

Directorate-General of Budget, Accounting and Statistics Yuan (DGBAS) (2005a), *2000 Population and Housing Census*, (http://www.dgbas.gov.tw/census~n/ six/ lue5/cen8904e.rtf).

Directorate-General of Budget, Accounting and Statistics Yuan (DGBAS) (2005b), *Key Economic and Social Indicators*, updated on 25 January, (http://www. dgbasey.gov.tw/dgbas03/english/key/kesi.xls).

Directorate-General of Budget, Accounting and Statistics Yuan (DGBAS) (2005c), *House Rent Price Indices*, updated on February, (http://eng.stat.gov.tw/ct. asp?xI tem=7474&ctNode=1559).

Doling, J. (1997), *Comparative Housing Policy: Government and Housing in Advanced Capitalist Countries* (London: Macmillan).

Doling, J. (1999), 'Housing Policies and the Little Tigers. How do they compare with other Industrialized Countries?' *Housing Studies* 14:2, 229–250.

Doling, J. (2002), 'The South and East Asian Housing Policy Model' in Agus, M.R., Doling, J. and Lee, D.S. (eds), *Housing Policy Systems in South and East Asia* (Basingstoke: Palgrave Macmillan, 178–88).

Donnison, D. (1967), *The Government of Housing* (Harmondsworth: Penguin).

Economic Review Committee: Sub-Committee on Policies Related to Taxation, the CPF System, Wages and Land (2002), *Refocusing the CPF System for Enhanced Security in Retirement and Economic Flexibility*.

English, J. (ed.) (1982), *The Future of Council Housing* (London: Croom Helm).

Esping-Andersen, G. (1990), *The Three Worlds of Welfare Capitalism* (Cambridge: Polity Press).

Forrest, R. and Murie, A. (1995), 'From Privatization to Commodification: Tenure Conversion and New Zones of Transition in the City'. *International Journal of Urban and Regional Researches* 19:3, 407–22.

Forrest, R., Kennett, P. and Izuhara, M. (2003), 'Home-ownership and Economic Change in Japan', *Housing Studies* 18:3, 277–93.

Forrest, R. and Lee, J. (2004), 'Cohort Effects, Differential Accumulation and Hong Kong's Volatile Housing Market', *Urban Studies* 41:11, 2,181–96.

General Office of the State Council (1991), *On Comprehensive Reform of Urban Housing System*, Document No. 73.

Goodman, R. and Peng, I. (1996), 'The East Asian Welfare States: Peripatetic Learning, Adaptive Change, and Nation-Building', in Esping-Andersen, G. (ed.), *Welfare States in Transition: National Adaptations in Global Economies*, (London: Sage, 192–224).

Gough, I. (2001), 'Globalization and Regional Welfare Regimes: The East Asian Case', *Global Social Policy* 1:2, 163–89.

Government Information Office (GIO) (2004), *Taiwan Yearbook 2004*, (http://www. gio.gov.tw/taiwan-website/5-gp/yearbook).

Guangzhou Municipal People's Government (2000), 'Circular on Implementation of Housing Cash Distribution', Internal Document, Guangzhou Municipal People's Government, No. [2000] 18 in Guangzhou Municipal Housing System Reform Office (2000) Selected Documents on Housing Reform in Guangzhou and Questions and Answers.

Hang Seng Bank (1998), *Hang Seng Economic Monthly* (Hong Kong: Hang Seng Bank Limited, May).

Harada, S. (1985), 'Sengo jutaku housei no seiritsu katei [The Establishment Process of Housing Laws in Post-War Japan]' in Institute of Social Science, Tokyo University (ed.), *Fukushi Kokka vol. 6: Nihon no Syakai to Fukushi [The Welfare State vol.6: Japanese Society and Welfare]* (Tokyo: Tokyo University Press, 317–96).

Harada, S. (2001), 'Toshi keikaku seido no kaisei to nihon toshi hou no yukue [Changes in Urban Planning Laws and their Future]' in Harada, S. (ed.) *Nihon no Toshi Hou vol. 2 [Japanese Urban Laws, vol.2]* (Tokyo: Tokyo University Press, 477–502).

Hausserman, H. (1994), 'Social Housing in Germany' in Danermark, B. and Elander, I. (eds), *Social Rented Housing in Europe: Policy, Tenure and Design* (Delft: Delft University Press).

Hayakawa, K. (1979), *Jutaku Binbou Monogatari [Housing Poverty in Japan]*, (Tokyo: Iwanami Shoten).

Hayakawa, K. (2002), 'Japan', in Agus, M.A., Doling, J. and Lee, D.S. (eds.), *Housing Policy Systems in South and East Asia* (Basingstoke: Palgrave Macmillan, 20–37).

Hayakawa, K. and Ohmoto, K. (1988), 'Toshi jutaku mondai shi gaisetsu [History of the Urban Housing Question]', in Tokyo shisei chosa kai [The Tokyo Institute for Municipal Research] (ed.), *Toshi Mondai no Kiseki to Tenbo [History and Perspectives of Urban Questions]* (Tokyo: Gyosei, 233–76).

Hayakawa, K. and Wada, Y. (1968), 'Jutaku mondai no kiso ninshiki [Basic Reflections on the Housing Question]' in Hayakawa, K., Wada, Y. and Nishikawa, K. (eds.), *Jutaku Mondai Nyumon [Introduction to the Housing Question]* (Tokyo: Yuhikaku, 8–31).

Hill, S., Lupton, M., Moody, G. and Regan, S. (2002), *A Stake Worth Having* (London: Chartered Institute of Housing and Institute of Public Policy Research).

Hirayama, Y. (2000), 'Collapse and Reconstruction: Housing Recovery Policy in Kobe after the Hanshin Great Earthquake', *Housing Studies* 15:1, 111–28.

Hirayama, Y. (2003a), 'Home ownership in an Unstable World: The Case of Japan', in Forrest, R. and Lee, J. (eds.), *Housing and Social Change: East-West Perspectives* (London: Routledge, 140–61).

Hirayama, Y. (2003b), 'Housing Policy and Social Inequality in Japan' in Izuhara, M. (ed.), *Comparing Social Policies: Exploring New Perspectives in Britain and Japan* (Bristol: Policy Press, 151–71).

Hirayama, Y. (2004) *Differentiation of Housing Experiences in Post-War Japan.* Paper presented at the Asia-Pacific Network for Housing Research Conference, Hong Kong, 5–6 February.

Hirayama, Y. (2005), 'Running Hot and Cold in the Urban Home-ownership Market: The Experience of Japan's Major Cities', *Journal of Housing and the Built Environment* 20:1.

Hirayama, Y. and Hayakawa, K. (1995), 'Home-ownership and Family Wealth in Japan' in Forrest, R. and Murie, A. (eds.), *Housing and Family Wealth: Comparative International Perspectives* (London: Routledge, 215–30).

Holliday, I. (2000), 'Productivist Welfare Capitalism: Social Policy in East Asia', *Political Studies* 48, 706–23.

Hong Kong Census and Statistics Department, *Hong Kong Annual Digest of Statistics various editions.*

Hong Kong Census and Statistics Department, *Hong Kong Social and Economic Trends 1997 ed.*

Hong Kong Economic Journal, 19 June 2000.

Hong Kong Government Housing Department (1999), *Housing Authority Quarterly Statistical Report (June 1999)* (Hong Kong: Housing Department).

Hong Kong Government Housing Department (2004), *Housing Authority Quarterly Statistical Report* (March 2004) (Hong Kong: Housing Department).

Hong Kong Government Rating and Valuation Department (various years, 1983 2004) *Hong Kong Property Review* (Hong Kong: Government Printer).

Hong Kong Government Rating and Valuation Department http://www.info. gov. hk/rvd/property/index.htm.

Hong Kong Housing Authority (1993), *Report of the Ad Hoc Committee to Review the Housing Subsidy Policy* (Hong Kong: HKHA).

Hong Kong Housing Authority (1995), *Safeguarding Rational Allocation of Public Housing Resources: Consultation Document* (Hong Kong: HKHA).

Hong Kong Housing Authority *1995/96 Annual Report* (Hong Kong: HKHA).

Hong Kong Housing Authority (2000), *Housing in Figures* (Hong Kong: HKHA).

Hong Kong Housing Authority (2000), *Public Housing Development Programme March 2000* (Hong Kong: HKHA).

Hong Kong Housing Authority (2001), *Memorandum for the Home-ownership Committee: Tenant Purchase Scheme Phase 5, Paper No.: HOC 96/01.*

Hong Kong Housing Authority (2003), *Housing Authority Quarterly Statistical Report March 2003.*

Hong Kong Housing Authority (2004), *Housing Authority Performance Indicators March 2004.*

Hong Kong Housing Authority (2004), *Housing Authority Quarterly Statistical Report March 2004.*

Hong Kong Housing Authority (2005), *Press Release 14 January* (Hong Kong: HKHA).

Hong Kong Housing Society (2000) Website (http://www.hkhs.com/) accessed on various dates.

Hort, S.E.O. and Kuhnle, S. (2000), 'The Coming of East and South-East Asian Welfare States', *Journal of European Social Policy* 10:2, 162–84.

Housing and Development Board, Singapore, Annual Report, various years.

Housing and Development Board, Singapore. Info web site at www.hdb.gov.sg.

Housing Reform Steering Group of the State Council (1994), 'The Decision on Deepening Urban Housing Reform', in Housing Reform Steering Group of the State Council (ed.) *Urban Housing System Reform* (Beijing: Reform Press).

Howlett, B. (ed.) (1998), *Hong Kong: A New Era – A Review of 1997* (Hong Kong: Information Services Department).

Hsieh, B.-M. (2004), *The Distribution of Household Income and Housing Consumption between Tenure in Taiwan*, paper presented at the 9th AsRES International Conference, 9–12 August, New Delhi, India.

Hsieh, W.-J. and Hsing, Y. (2002), 'Economic Growth and Social Indicators: The Case of Taiwan', *International Journal of Social Economics* 29:7, 518-26.

Hsueh, C.-T. (2004), 'Examining the Feminization of Poverty in Taiwan: A Case of the 1990s', *Journal of Population Studies* 29, 95–121 (in Chinese).

Hsueh, L.-M. and Chen, H.-L. (1999), 'An Analysis of Home-ownership Rate Changes in Taiwan in the 1980s', *Asian Economic Journal* 13:4, 367–88.

Hua, C.-I. (2000), 'The Sticky Land Price in Taiwan: Its Causes, Effects, and Future', in Mera, K. and Renaud, B. (eds), *Asia's Financial Crisis and the Role of Real Estate* (New York and London: M.E. Sharpe, 115–37).

Hwang, Y.-R. (1997), 'Housing for the Elderly in Taiwan', *Ageing International*, Winter/Spring, 133–47.

Igarashi, Y. and Ogawa, A. (2003), *Toshi Saisei wo Tou [Denouncing 'Urban Regeneration']* (Tokyo: Iwanami Shoten).

Izuhara, M. (2000), *Family Change and Housing in Post-War Japanese Society: The Experiences of Older Women* (Aldershot: Ashgate).

Jao, C.-C. (2000), 'The Impact of Tax Revenue and Social Welfare Expenditure on Income Distribution in Taiwan', *Journal of the Asia Pacific Economy* 5:1/2, 73–90.

Japan Federation of Employers' Associations (1984), *Wagakuni Kigyo no Jutaku Taisaku no Susei [Trends in Employee Housing Benefits in Japan]* (Tokyo: Japan Federation of Employers' Associations).

Japan Institute of Life Insurance (2003), *Kigyo no Fukuri Kosei ni Kansuru Chosa [Research on Employee Benefits]* (Tokyo: Japan Institute of Life Insurance).

Japan Statistical Association (2001), *Tokei de Miru Nihon [Japan in Statistics]* (Tokyo: Japan Statistical Association).

Johnson, C. (1982), *MITI and the Japanese Miracle* (Stanford, California: Stanford University Press).

Johnson, C. (1987), 'Political Institutions and Economic Performance: The Government-Business Relationship in Japan, South Korea, and Taiwan', in Deyo, F.C. (ed.), *The Political Economy of the New Asian Industrialism* (Ithaca and London: Cornell University Press, 136-64).

Jones, C. (1990), 'Hong Kong, Singapore, South Korea and Taiwan: Oikonomic Welfare States', *Government and Opposition* 25:4, 446–62.

Jones, C. (1993), 'The Pacific Challenge: Confucian Welfare States', in Jones, C. (ed.), *New Perspectives on the Welfare State in Europe* (London and New York: Routledge, 198–217).

Kemeny J. (1981), *The Myth of Home-ownership: Public versus Private Choices in Housing Tenure* (London: Routledge).

Kemeny, J. (1995), *From Public Housing to the Social Market: Rental Policy Strategies in Comparative Perspective* (London: Routledge).

Kemp, P. (1997), *A Comparative Study Of Housing Allowances* (London: HMSO).

Kempen, R. van and Priemus, H. (2002), 'Revolution in Social Housing in the Netherlands: Possible Effects of New Housing Policies', *Urban Studies*, 39:2, 237-253.

Kim, S.-J. (1992), 'A Model of Rental Housing Choices in the Korean Market', *Housing Studies* 29:8, 1,247–64.

Kim. K.-Y. and Kim, K.-W. (2002), 'The Role of Housing Finance in Providing Adequate Housing for all Koreans' *KNHC 40th Anniversary Celebrations International Housing Symposium, Housing Welfare, Policy, and Financing* 22 October.

Kim, K.-W. (2001), *Land Market and Land Policy Issues: A Critical Review* (Seoul: Seogang Kyungjenonzip).

Koh, C., (2002), 'Public Housing Policy in Korea'. *KNHC 40th Anniversary Celebrations International Housing Symposium, Housing Welfare, Policy, and Financing* 22 October.

Korea Housing Bank, (each year) *Monthly Housing Financial Review* (Seoul: KHB).

Korea National Housing Corporation (1992), *Jukong 30 Nyunsa [The History of KNHC]* (Seoul: KHNC).

Korea National Housing Corporation (2004), *Jukong Handbook [Information on Housing Construction]* (Seoul: KHNC).

Krause, L., Koh, A.T., and Lee, T.Y. (1987), *The Singapore Economy Reconsidered* (Singapore: Institute of Southeast Asian Studies).

Krugman, P. (1994), 'The Myth of Asia's Miracle', *Foreign Affairs* 73, 62–78.

Ku, Y.-W. (2004), 'Is There a Way Out? Global Competition and Social Reform in Taiwan', *Social Policy and Society* 3:3, 311–20.

Kwon, H.-J. (1997), 'Beyond European Welfare Regimes: Comparative Perspectives on East Asian Welfare Systems', *Journal of Social Policy* 26, 467–84.

La Grange, A. and Yung, B. (2001), 'Aging in a Tiger Welfare Regime: The Single Elderly in Hong Kong', *Journal of Cross-Cultural Gerontology* 16, 257–81.

Lau, K.Y. (1993), 'Urban Housing Reform in China, Amidst Property Boom Year' in Cheng, J. and Brosseau, M. (eds), *China Review 1993* (Hong Kong: The Chinese University Press, 24.1–24.35).

Lau, K.Y. (1995), 'Issues in Housing Policy in Guangzhou: A Study on Housing Provision for Households with Housing Difficulties', in Cheng, J. and MacPherson, M. (eds), *Development in South China* (London: Longman).

Lau, K.Y. (2002), *A Critique of 'the Housing Policy for Hong Kong's Future' Shown in the 2002 Housing Policy Statement*, Paper presented at 'The Housing Policy for Hong Kong's Future' Symposium, co-organized by Hong Kong Policy Research Institute and Department of Public and Social Administration, City University of Hong Kong, 9 December 2002 (in Chinese).

Lea, M.J. and Renaud, B. (1995), 'Contractual Savings for Housing: How Suitable are they for Transitional Economies?' World Bank Policy Research Working Paper 1516.

Leaf, M. (1997), 'Urban Social Impacts of China's Economic Reforms', *Cities* 14:2, v–vii.

Lee, H.L. (1999), *Economic Management in Singapore: Scenarios, Strategies and Tactics*, speech given at the Economics Society of Singapore Annual Dinner, 12 February 1999. (Monetary Authority of Singapore web site at www.mas.gov.sg).

Lee, J. (2000), 'From Welfare Housing to Home-ownership: The Dilemma of China's Housing Reform', *Housing Studies* 15:1, 61–7.

Lee, K.Y. (2000), *From Third World to First: The Singapore Story 1965–2000* (Singapore Press Holdings).

Lee, P. and Murie, A. (1979), *Poverty, Housing Tenure and Social Exclusion* (Joseph Rowntree Foundation).

Legislative Council Secretariat (2004), *Information Note: Financial Position of the Housing Authority from 1997/98–2003/04, December.*

Legislative Council Secretariat http://www.legco.gov.hk/yr04-05/english/sec/library/0405in14e.pdf

Leung M.Y. (1999), *From Shelter to Home: 45 Years of Public Housing Development in Hong Kong* (Hong Kong: Hong Kong Housing Authority).

Li, S.M. (2000a), 'Housing Consumption in Urban China: A Comparative Study of Beijing and Guangzhou', *Environment and Planning A* 32, 1,115–34.

Li, S.M. (2000b), 'The Housing Market and Tenure Decisions in Chinese Cities: A Multivariate Analysis of the Case of Guangzhou', *Housing Studies* 15:2, 213–36.

Li, W.D.H. (1998), *Housing in Taiwan: Agency and Structure?* (Aldershot: Ashgate).

Li, W.D.H. (2002), 'The growth of mass home-ownership in Taiwan', *Journal of Housing and the Built Environment* 17, 21–32.

Liang, W.J. and Mai, C.-C. (2003), 'Capital Flows, Vertical Multinationals, Wage Inequality, and Welfare', *Review of Development Economics* 7:4, 599–608.

Lim, K.L. (2001), 'Implications of Singapore's CPF Scheme on Consumption Choices and Retirement', *Pacific Economic Review* 6, 361–82.

Lim, Seo-hwan (2002), *Jutaekjungchakbansiki [The History of Korean Housing Policy]* (KNHC).

Lim, Chong-Yah (2004), *Southeast Asia: The Long Road Ahead* (New Jersey; London: World Scientific).

Lin, C.-C. and Lai, Y.-F. (2003), 'Housing Prices, Mortgage Payments and Savings Behavior in Taiwan: A Time Series Analysis', *Asian Economic Journal* 17:4, 407–25.

Liu, C.J. (Deputy Governor of Zabei District, Shanghai) (2001), 'Ensuring the Successful Experiment of Social Housing Provision' in *Housing Reform and Real Estate Work Circular, No 24-26, 2001*, Housing and Real Estate Industry Department, Ministry of Construction (unpublished internal circular, 25–33).

Liu, Paul K.C. and Tung, A.-C. (2003), 'Urban Development in Taiwan: Retrospect and Prospect', *Journal of Population Studies* 26, 1–25 (in Chinese).

Liu, Z.F. (2003), *Promote Healthy and Sustained Development of Housing and Real Estate – Speech at the 2003 Annual Housing and Property Conference. Wuhan, 13 January 2003.*

Logan, J., Bian, F. and Bian, Y. (1998), 'Tradition and Change in the Urban Chinese Families: The Case of Living Arrangements', *Social Forces* 76:3, 851–82.

Low, L. and Aw, T.C. (1997), *Housing a Healthy, Educated and Wealthy Nation through the CPF* (Singapore: Times Academic Press for The Institute of Policy Studies).

Machimura, T. (2003), 'Narrating a "Global City" for "New Tokyoites". Economic Crisis and Urban "Boosterism" in Tokyo' in: Dobson, H. and Hook, G.D. (eds.), *Japan and Britain in the Contemporary World: Responses to Common Issues* (London: Routledge Curzon, 196–212).

MacMillan, H. (1934), *Reconstruction: A Plea for a National Policy* (London: Macmillan).

Malpass, P. (2005), *Housing and the Welfare State: The Development of Housing Policy in Britain* (Basingstoke: Palgrave Macmillan).

McCarthy, D., Mitchell, O.S. and Piggott, J. (2002), 'Asset Rich and Cash Poor: Retirement Provision and Housing Policy in Singapore', *Journal of Pension Economics and. Finance* 1, 197–222.

McGuire, C.C. (1981), *International Housing Policies: A Comparative Analysis* (Lexington MA: Lexington Books).

Merrett, Stephen (1979), *A Theory of the Capitalist Land Market* Town Planning Discussion Paper; no.33 (London: University College London).

Merrett, S. (1979), *State Housing in Britain* (London: Routledge & Kegan Paul).

Miles, D. (1994), *Housing, Financial Markets and the Wider Economy* (New York: John Wiley).

Miller, T. (1997), *Becoming Stakeholders of Hong Kong: Home-ownership. Speech by the Director of Housing at the monthly luncheon meeting of the Hong Kong Institute of Real Estate Administration,* 19 February 1997.

Miller, T. (2000), *Public Housing in Hong Kong: 45 Years of Achievement – Challenge to Come*, Paper presented at International Conference on Housing, Singapore: Housing and Development Board, April 2000.

Mills, E. and Song, B. (1979), *Urbanization and Urban Problems of Korea: 1945-1975* (Cambridge: Harvard University Press).

Ministry of City Services (1957a), 'Report about the First National Housing Conference to the Fifth Office in the State Council', in Housing and Property Management Department of Xian (ed) (1960), *Collection of Documents on Housing and Property Management in Xian*, Vol.1, 32–44.

Ministry of City Services, (1957b) 'On Strengthening City Housing and Property Management' in Housing and Property Management Department of Xian (ed) (1960) *Collection of Documents on Housing and Property Management in Xian*, Vol.1, 24–32.

Ministry of Construction and Transportation (2004), *Jutaekeobmupyonram [Information on Public Housing]* (Seoul: MOCT).

Ministry of the Interior (MOI) (2004), *Construction and Planning Administration*, (http://www.moi.gov.tw/english/Construction.asp).

Ministry of Land, Infrastructure and Transport (2003), *Tochi Hakusyo [Government White Paper on Land]*, (Tokyo: National Printing Bureau).

Ministry of Trade and Industry, Singapore, Economic Survey of Singapore, various years.

Ministry of Urban and Rural Construction and Environmental Protection, (1982) 'Suggestions on Further Implementation of Private Housing Policies', (Document No 445, 1982) in Tang, S.H and Xie, W.D. (eds) (1992), *China Real Estate Guide (zhongguo fangdichan wushi quanshu)* (Beijing: Modern Time Press).

Miyake, J. (1985), 'Jutaku shijo ron [On the Housing Market]' in Shin Kenchikugaku Taikei Henshu Iinkai [Committee on Architectural New Theories] (ed.), *Shin Kenchikugaku Taikei Vol.14: Haujingu [New Theories of Architecture Vol.14: Housing]* (Tokyo: Shokoku Sha, 73–153).

Monetary Authority of Singapore, *Annual Report*, various years.

Monetary Authority of Singapore (2001), *Quarterly Bulletin 3:1, March*.

Mullins, D. and Murie, A. (2006), *Housing Policy in the UK* (Basingstoke: Palgrave).

Murakami, Y. (1992) *Han Koten no Seiji Keizai Gaku [Anti-Classical Political Economics]* (Tokyo: Chuou Koron Sinsha).

Muramatsu, M. and Okuno, M. (eds.) (2002) *Heisei Bubble no Kenkyu [Study of the Heisei Bubble]* (Tokyo: Toyo Keizai Shinpou Sya).

Murie, A. (1997), 'The Social Rented Sector, Housing and the Welfare State in the UK', *Housing Studies*, 12:4, 437–62.

Murie, A. and Nevin, B. (1979), *Beyond a Halfway Housing Policy: Local Strategies and Regeneration* (London: Institute for Public Policy Research).

National Statistical Office (1970-2000), *Population and Housing Census* (Daejeon: NSO).

Novy, K. (1991), 'Housing Policy in West Germany: Winners and Losers in the Deregulation Battle', in Novy, K. and Norton, A. (eds), *Low Income Housing in Britain and Germany* (London: Anglo-German Foundation).

ODPM (2003), *The Communities Plan – 'Sustainable Communities: Building for the Future'* (London: ODPM).

ODPM (2004), *Skills for Sustainable Communies* (London: ODPM).

ODPM (2005), *Sustainable Communities: Homes for All* (London: ODPM).

Ofstedal, M.B., Reidy, E. and Knodel, J. (2004), 'Gender Differences in Economic Support and Well-Being of Older Asians', *Journal of Cross-Cultural Gerontology* 19, 165–201.

Ohmoto, K. (1985), 'Fukushi kokka to wagakuni jutaku seisaku no tenkai [The Welfare State and Housing Policy in Japan]', in Institute of Social Science, Tokyo University (ed.), *Fukushi Kokka Vol. 6: Nihon no Syakai to Fukushi [The Welfare State Vol.6: Japanese Society and Welfare]* (Tokyo: Tokyo University Press, 397–455).

Ohmoto, K. (1991), *Shogen: Nihon no Jutaku Seisaku [Testimony: Housing Policy in Japan]* (Tokyo: Nihon Hyoron Sha).

Ohmoto, K. (1996), 'Kyoju seisaku no gendai shi [Modern History of Housing Policy]' in Ohmoto, K. and Kaino, M. (eds.), *Gendai Kyoju: Rekishi to Shiso [Housing Policy: History and Ideology]* (Tokyo: Tokyo University Press, 89–120).

Oizumi, E. (1994), 'Property Finance in Japan: Expansion and Collapse of the Bubble Economy', *Environment and Planning A* 26:2, 199–213.

Oizumi, E. (2002a), 'Housing Provision and Marketization in 1980s and 1990s Japan: A New Stage of the Affordability Problem?' in Dymski, G.A. and Isenberg, A. (eds.), *Seeking Shelter on the Pacific Rim: Financial Globalization, Social Change, and the Housing Market* (Armonk, New York: M.E. Sharpe, 169–86).

Oizumi, E. (2002b), *Restructuring of Japan's Housing Finance Policy: Should the Government Housing Loan Corporation (GHLC) be Abolished?* Paper presented at the European Network for Housing Research 2002 Conference, Vienna, 1–5 July.

Ong, S.E. and Sing, T.F. (2002), 'Price Discovery Between Private and Public Housing Markets', *Urban Studies* 39, 57–67.

Ooi, G.L. (1990), Town Councils in Singapore: Self Determination for Public Housing Estates (Singapore: Times Academic Press).

Ooi, G.L., Siddique, S. and Soh, K.C. (1993), *The Management of Ethnic Relations in Public Housing Estates*, (Singapore: Times Academic Press).

Peng, C.-W. and Chang, C.-O. (1995), 'An Analysis of the Housing Vacancy Rate Phenomenon and Reasons in Taiwan,' *Journal of Housing Studies* 3, 45–71 (in Chinese).

People's Daily, Overseas Edition, 2 February 1995.

Phang, S.Y. (1992), *Housing Markets and Urban Transportation: Economic Theory, Econometrics and Policy Analysis for Singapore* (Singapore: McGraw Hill).

Phang, S.Y. (1996), 'Economic Development and the Distribution of Land Rents in Singapore: A Georgist Implementation', *American Journal of Economics and Sociology* 55, 489–501.

Phang, S.Y. (2000), 'How Singapore Regulates Urban Transportation and Land Use' in Yusuf, S., Wu, W. and Evenett, S. (eds.), *Gendai Kyoju: Rekishi to Shiso [Housing Policy: History and Ideology]* (Tokyo: Tokyo University Press, 89–120).

Phang, S.Y. (2001), 'Housing Policy, Wealth Formation and the Singapore Economy', *Housing Studies* 16, 443–59.

Phang, S.Y. (2003), 'The Social Compact in Singapore: The Changing Role of Housing' in Yap, M.T. (ed.), *Singapore Perspectives 2003* (Singapore: Eastern Universities Press for The Institute of Policy Studies, 111–24).

Phang, S.Y. (2004), 'House Prices and Aggregate Consumption: Do they Move Together? Evidence from Singapore', *Journal of Housing Economics* 13, 101–19.

Phang, S.Y. and Wong, W.K. (1997), 'Government Policies and Private Housing Prices in Singapore', *Urban Studies* 34, 1,819–29.

Priemus, H. and Boelhouwer, P. (1999), 'Social Housing Finance in Europe: Trends and Opportunities', *Urban Studies* 36:4, 640.

Pugh, C. (1985), 'Housing and Development in Singapore', *Contemporary Southeast Asia* 6, 275–307.

Quigley, J.M. (2001), 'Real Estate and the Asian crisis', *Journal of Housing Economics* 10, 129–61.

Ramesh, M. (2003), *'One-and-a-half Cheers for Provident Funds in Malaysia and Singapore'*, paper prepared for the UNRISD project on 'Social Policy in a Development Context'.

Ramesh, M. (2004), *Social Policy in East and Southeast Asia: Education, Health, Housing, and Income Maintenance* (London and New York: Routledge-Curzon).

Real Estate Information Network for East Japan (2003), *Shisan Deflation no Jokyo to sono Eikyo ni tsuite [Asset Deflation and its Impacts]* (Tokyo: Real Estate Information Network for East Japan).

Renaud, B. (1993), 'Confronting a Distorted Housing Market: Can Korean Policies Break with the Past?' in Krause, L.B. and Park F.-K. (eds), *Social Issues in Korea: Korean and American Perspectives* (Seoul: Korea Development Institute).

Renaud, B. (2004), *Performance and Change: East Asian Housing Policies After Fifty Years*, paper presented at the International Housing Conference on 'Housing in the 21st Century: Challenges and Commitments'. Hong Kong, 2–4 February.

Research Institute of Employee Benefits (2003), *Fukuri Kosei Taishoku Kyufu ni kansuru Sogo Chosa [Comprehensive Research on Employee Benefits]* (Tokyo: Research Institute of Employee Benefits).

Ronald, R. (2004), 'Home-ownership, Ideology and Diversity: Re-evaluating Concepts of Housing Ideology in the Case of Japan', *Housing, Theory and Society* 21:2, 49–64.

Saito, A. and Thornley, A. (2003), 'Shifts in Tokyo's World City Status and the Urban Planning Response', *Urban Studies* 40:4, 665–85.

Sandilands, R.J. (1992), 'Savings, Investment and Housing in Singapore's Growth 1965–90', *Savings and Development* 2:16, 119–43.

Sato, T. (2000), *Fubyodo Syakai Nihon [Inequality in Japanese Society]* (Tokyo: Chuo Koron Shinsya).

Secretary for Housing, Planning and Lands (2002), *Statement on Housing Policy*, 13 November.

Shanghai Property and Land Resource Management Bureau (2001), 'Shanghai Municipal Social Housing Implementation Suggestions' in Housing and Real Estate Industry Department, Ministry of Construction (unpublished internal circular).

Sherraden, M. (1997), 'Provident Funds and Social Protection. The Case of Singapore' in Midgely, J. and Sherraden, M. (eds), *Alternatives to Social Security* (Connecticut: Alborne House).

Shih, Y.C. and Tsao, C.-M. (2004), 'Household Debt in Taiwan – Trend and Policy Responses', *Central Bank of China Quarterly Journal* 26:3, 1–12.

Son, J.-Y., Won, Y-H. and Moon, C-G. (2001), *Housing*, mimeo.

State Council (1988), *Implementation Plan for a Gradual Housing System Reform in Cities and Towns, Document No. 11*.

State Council (1998), *The Notice on Further Reform of Urban Housing System and Speeding up Housing Development, Document No. 23*, 3 July.

State Housing and Property Management Bureau (1967), 'Letter to Guangxi Industrial and Commercial Management Bureau on Private Housing Rent and Landlord Shares', in Housing and Property Management Department of Xian (ed) (1984), *Collection of Documents on Housing and Property Management in Xian* (Vol.2, 618).

State Statistics Bureau (1998), *China Statistical Yearbook 1998* (Beijing: China Statistical Publishing House).

State Statistics Bureau (2003), *China Statistical Yearbook 2003* (Beijing: China Statistics Press).

Statistics Bureau, Management and Coordination Agency (2000a), *1998 Housing and Land Survey of Japan, Volume 5: Results for Prefectures, Part 13, Tokyo-to* (Tokyo: Japan Statistical Association).

Statistics Bureau, Management and Coordination Agency (2000b), *1998 Housing and Land Survey of Japan, Volume 1: Results for Japan* (Tokyo: Japan Statistical Association).

Tachibanaki, T. (1998), *Nihon no Keizai Kakusa [Economic Inequality in Japan]* (Tokyo: Iwanami Shoten).

Tanaka, T. (2002), *Gendai Nihon Keizai [The Contemporary Economy in Japan]* (Tokyo: Nihon Hyoron Sha).

Tang, P.Y.C. (2002), *A Comparative Analysis of Housing Systems in Tokyo and Hong Kong*, unpublished Ph.D. dissertation, Centre for Urban and Regional Studies, University of Birmingham.

Tang, P.Y.C. (2003), *Why does Japan Have No Housing Policy?* paper prepared for the 1st APNHR conference 'Housing and Sustainable Urban Development', University of Malaya, 1–4 July.

The Government of the Hong Kong Special Administrative Region (1997), *Better Housing for All*, (Hong Kong Government Printer, 8 October 1997).

The Straits Times. Singapore. Various dates.

The World Bank (2004), *World Development Report 2004* (New York: Oxford University Press).

Titmuss, R.M. (1958), War and Social Policy in *Essays on the Welfare State* (London: Unwin).

Turner, B., Hegedus, J. and Tosics, I. (eds) (1992), *The Reform of Housing in Eastern Europe and the Soviet Union* (London and New York: Routledge).

United Nations Economic Commission for Europe (1966), *Major Long-term Problems of Government Housing and Related Policies* (New York: United Nations).

Urban Redevelopment Authority, Singapore. Real Estate Information System.

Wang, Y.P. (1992), 'Private Sector Housing in Urban China Since 1949: The Case of Xian', *Housing Studies* 7:2, 119–37.

Wang, Y.P. (1995), 'Public Sector Housing in Urban China 1949–1988: The Case of Xian', *Housing Studies* 10:1, 57–82.

Wang, Y.P. (2000), 'Housing Reform and its Impacts on the Urban Poor in China', *Housing Studies* 15:6, 845–64.

Wang, Y.P. (2001), 'Urban Housing Reform and Finance in China: A Case Study of Beijing', *Urban Affairs Review* 36:5, 620–45.

Wang, Y.P. (2003), 'Progress and Problems of Urban Housing Reform' in Finer, C.J. (ed.), *Social Policy Reform in China: Views from Home and Abroad* (Aldershot: Ashgate, 176–90).

Wang, Y.P. (2004), *Urban Poverty, Housing and Social Change in China* (Oxon: Routledge).

Wang, Y.P. and Murie, A. (1996), 'The Process of Commercialisation of Urban Housing in China', *Urban Studies* 33:6, 971–89.

Wang, Y.P. and Murie, A. (1999a), *Housing Policy and Practice in China* (Basingstoke: Macmillan).

Wang, Y.P. and Murie, A. (1999b) 'Commercial Housing Development in Urban China', *Urban Studies* 36:9, 1,475–94.

Wang, Y.P. and Murie, A. (2000), 'Social and Spatial Implications of Housing Reform in China', *International Journal of Urban and Regional Research* 24:2, 397–417.

Weiss, L. (2000), 'Developmental States in Transition: Adapting, Dismantling, Innovating, not "Normalizing"', *The Pacific Review* 13:1, 21–55.

Wen, H.P. and Ming, P., *Daily News*, (2000). *Report of Interview with the Chief Executive of the Hong Kong Special Administrative Region, 30 June.*

Werczberger, E. (1997), 'Home-ownership and Rent Control in Switzerland' *Housing Studies* 12:3, 337–53.

White, G. and Goodman, R. (1998), 'Welfare Orientalism and the Search for an East Asian Welfare Model' in Goodman, R., White, G. and Kwon, H. (eds), *The East Asian Welfare Model: Welfare Orientalism and the State* (London and New York: Routledge, 3–24).

Wong, A. and Yeh, S. (eds.) (1985), *Housing a Nation: 25 Years of Public Housing in Singapore* (Singapore: Housing and Development Board).

Wong, K.P. and Wong, S. (1975), 'An Economic Analysis of HDB Construction Activity' in Yeh, S. (ed.), *Public Housing in Singapore* (Singapore: Singapore University Press, Chapter 4).

Wu, F. (1996), 'Changes in the Structure of Public Housing Provision in Urban China', *Urban Studies* 33:9, 1,601–27.

Wu, F. (2001), 'Housing Provision Under Globalisation: A Case Study of Shanghai', *Environment and Planning A* 33, 1,741–64.

Xie, J.J. (2003), *Striking for New Territory of Housing and Real Estate Work*, Unpublished Report to the National Housing and Real Estate Conference, Wuhan, 13 January.

Yamada, Y. (2000), 'Nihon no jutaku shijo, seisaku to jutaku mondai [The Housing Market, Public Policy and Housing Problems]' in Adachi, M., Oizumi, E., Hashimoto, T. and Yamada, Y. (eds.), *Jutaku Mondai to Shijo, Seisaku [Housing Problems, the Market and Policy]* (Tokyo: Nihon Keizai Hyoron Sha, 25–56).

Yamada, Y. (2001), 'Toshi tochi mondai no keizai kozo [The Economic Structure of Urban Land Questions]' in Harada, S. (ed.), *Nihon no Toshi Hou vol.1 [Japanese Urban Laws, vol.1]* (Tokyo: Tokyo University Press).

Yang, Z.H. (2003), *How to Work Out the Social Housing Difficulties in Beijing.* http://www.realestate.cei.gov.cn//gg00/j030509a.htm

Yap, M.T. (2002), 'Employment Insurance: A Safety Net for the Unemployed' in Institute of Policy Studies, Report Prepared for the Remaking Singapore Committee.

Yergin, D. and Stanislaw, J. (2002), *The Commanding Heights: The Battle for the World Economy* (New York: Simon & Schuster).

Ying, M.Y. (Deputy Governor of Changning District, Shanghai) (2001), 'Experiments and Creation, Seriously Carrying out Social Housing Pilot Test Work' in Housing and Real Estate Industry Department, Ministry of Construction (unpublished internal circular).

Yip, N.M. and Chang, C.-O. (2003), 'Housing in Taiwan: State Intervention in a Market Driven Housing System', *Journal of Comparative Asian Development* 2:1, 93–113.

Young, A. (1992), 'A Tale of Two Cities: Factor Accumulation and Technical Change in Hong Kong and Singapore' in Blanchard, O.J. and Fischer, S. (eds.), *NBER Macroeconomics Annual 1992* (Cambridge: MIT Press, 13–54).

Young, A. (1995), 'The Tyranny of Numbers: Confronting the Statistical Realities of the East Asian Growth Experience', *Quarterly Journal of Economics* 110:3, 641–80.

Zhang, Y.L. (Vice Minister of City Services) (1957), 'Speech on Urban Housing and Property Management at the Second National Conferences of City Housing Directors', in Housing and Property Management Department of Xian (ed) (1960), *Collection of Documents on Housing and Property Management in Xian*, (Vol.1, 44–62).

Zhou, M. and Logan, J.R. (1996), 'Market Transition and the Commodification of Housing in Urban China', *International Journal of Urban and Regional Research* 20:3, 400–21.

Index